GEOGRAPHICAL COMPANION TO THE BIBLE

Other Books by Denis Baly

THE GEOGRAPHY OF THE BIBLE

CHOSEN PEOPLES

MULTITUDES IN THE VALLEY

BESIEGED CITY

PALESTINE AND THE BIBLE

ACADEMIC ILLUSION

GEOGRAPHICAL COMPANION

TO THE

BIBLE

by

DENIS BALY

McGRAW-HILL BOOK COMPANY, INC.
New York Toronto London
1963

Library of Congress Catalog Card No. 63–14214
03598

Printed in Great Britain

GENERAL CONTENTS

All the biblical quotations are taken from the Revised Standard Version of the Bible, copyrighted 1946 and 1952, except those at the head of each essay and under the photographs. These are taken from the Authorized, or King James, Version.

INTRODUCTION

ONE of the major problems for the Bible reader of today, whether he be a theological student or an ordinary layman anxious to understand the Scriptures, is that of pinning the biblical events down in time and space. Centuries of meditation and preaching have lifted them from the solid earth into the heavens, and have encrusted them with such a marvellous patina of sanctity that it is no longer possible to discern within the mysteries the earthy, and often brutal, happenings of ancient history. This would hardly matter if the Christian Gospel were a matter of complete other-worldliness or concerned solely with "moral and spiritual values". But it is neither of these things. Fundamental to the argument is the claim that our salvation took place in history, and that God became Man at a definite time and in a definite place. To neglect either the history or the place is, therefore, to run serious risk of failing to understand the argument, and no longer to feel the impact of the hammer-blows in which it is presented.

More than twenty years of teaching the Bible to students, many of whom come to it for the first time in class, have convinced me of the truth of this. They read it in a kind of bewildered vacuum, as if the people of whom it speaks were no more than insubstantial ghosts, and the country they inhabit a mere cloud cuckoo land. Even when they come to know it well, it remains only too often a "dead" book, presenting academic arguments to be learned for examinations and then forgotten, for they cannot picture that world which it takes for granted, or convince themselves that human beings ever lived and moved in it.

This book, therefore, is an attempt to satisfy this want and to supply solidity and substance to what for many is still a world of shadows. Palestine is a real country, and despite the Sunday School pictures, and the writings of best-selling journalists, a terribly unsentimental one. It can be gorgeously arrayed in brilliant springtime colours, or dusty and barren and brutal; it can never be dull. Its too often bloody history is the story of our salvation, and my purpose will be achieved if, for some readers at least, the shadow takes on reality.

The whole book is directed to this end, and therefore some things have had to be left out. It has not proved possible, for reasons of clarity on the maps, to show every single site that is mentioned in the Bible, though they are all listed in the gazetteer at the back, and some indication of their position given. However, this is not important, for those that have been left out are places which are mentioned only in lists of tribal territory, etc. Moreover, they can be found in any good biblical atlas. What the book does attempt to do is to show facets of the geography of Palestine which are not easily to be learned elsewhere. The maps have all been drawn with this end in view, and their justification is perhaps this: they are the kind of maps which I find I have continually to draw on the board in class, in order to explain this or that point in the biblical history or argument. This encourages me, therefore, to hope that they may be useful to others engaged in the same study. Whether they are or not the reader alone can say.

I cannot close this introduction without recording my gratitude to the Dean and Faculty of General Theological Seminary in New York, and my deep sense of the honour they paid me in asking me to deliver the Winslow Lectures there in November 1961. About half the written material in this book first saw the light of day in the form of those lectures. It has all, however, been revised and very greatly expanded for the purposes of this book, for which also the maps have been specially drawn.

Finally, my thanks are due to Donald and Judy Menzi for their assistance with the typing of the manuscript, and the cheerful manner in which they enabled me to meet the deadline.

DENIS BALY

Kenyon College, 1963

I

LAND OF THE BIBLE

MAPS AND DIAGRAMS

I

THE NORTH COUNTRY

Behold, these that go toward the north country have quieted my spirit in the north country.
(*Zech.* 6 : 8)

THE PERSON who attempts to combine geography and biblical scholarship is faced at the very beginning with a question which permits no easy answer: how large an area is he to cover in his survey? The ordinary biblical atlas concentrates its attention upon a tiny rectangle whose length, from north to south, is merely the distance from the source of the Jordan to the southern end of the Dead Sea, and whose breadth extends from the Mediterranean in the west to Rabboth Ammon in the east—an area, that is to say, of no more than 160 by 90 miles. There may be, it is true, a more general map showing the whole Middle Eastern world, another extending to the borders of what is now Turkey to illustrate the wanderings of the Patriarchs, a third of Egypt and Sinai as a background to the Exodus, and perhaps a fourth of Mesopotamia, but this is likely to be all.

The advantages of such a limitation are many and obvious. The tiny rectangle just described comprises all the territory from Dan to Beersheba, the traditional limits of the "Holy Land" (1 Sam. 3 : 20; 2 Sam. 3 : 10; 17 : 11; 24 : 2, 15; 1 Kings 4 : 25; 2 Chron. 30 : 5), within which the great majority of the biblical events occurred. It is upon this area that much of our study must be directed, and for most of the maps in a biblical atlas to be devoted to it means that we can therefore examine it in greater detail. This is certainly desirable, because the land of Palestine, though small, is exceedingly complex, and holds within its narrow confines a fascinating geographical variety, which requires most careful study if the effects upon the Israelite way of life are properly to be understood.

Yet, to examine Palestine in this way is to place serious obstacles in the path of biblical understanding. The geographer, just as much as the biblical scholar, is concerned with a way of life, with a *totality of experience*, which expresses itself in what may properly be described as "cultures", wherein man's activity is seen as a whole, each part being integrated with another. To this end "geography is concerned to provide accurate, orderly and rational description and interpretation of the variable character of the earth surface";[1] it is "that discipline that seeks to describe and interpret the variable character from place to place of the earth as the world of man".[2] For the biblical student the expression, and interpretation, of this way of life, this totality of experience, is set forth in that surprising library of writings which we know as the Bible. To this end, therefore, the mind of the student must be allowed to range as far as he will, and a concentration upon detail, however necessary and desirable a part of his study this may be, may actually hinder his comprehension of the whole.

The totality of the experience, however, belongs not only to space but to time; that is to say, it is dynamic rather than static. The student we have been supposing, who is concerned with both geography and the Bible, needs to keep steadily before his mind that in neither study is he concerned with something merely stationary, or with that which is steadily but mechanically evolving. Rather is it a living thing, whose component parts continually interact upon one another, producing by this unbroken interplay of forces a pattern of great delicacy and complexity, but one which can continue to exist only because it is changing. In Old Testament studies it used to be thought that we were concerned with the steady and predictable development of religion from an animistic simplicity to the complex spirituality of the period after the Exile. However, this strongly evolutionary pattern is now being replaced by concepts that are at once more flexible and more fluid. Increasingly is it realized "that while the documents can be approximately dated, the material in them can be ranked in no neat chronological progression. One cannot assume that earlier documents are to be preferred over later ones, or that to date a document pronounces a verdict on the age and historical value of its contents. . . . Even when the material has been given written form, oral tradition does not necessarily leave off, but may continue to function side by side . . . shaping, sifting and augmenting the material."[3]

The continual re-examination, and reinterpretation, of the historical experience which this process reflects is paralleled by the geographical material. The Israelites entered a country whose landscape had already been much modified by the activity of man, who had cut down trees, planted crops, and built cities with strong stone walls, for perhaps as much as seven thousand years before the Exodus,[4] and had lived and hunted there for tens of thousands of years before that. This activity of man had itself, of course, been largely shaped by the pressure of the geographical factors, which directed his steps into those places where he could most easily live. So the Israelites were heirs to a changed and changing environment which helped to determine their own way of life, and yet was itself continually to be remodelled, at any rate in part, by the multifarious handiwork of the farmer and the *bedu*, the warrior and the merchant, the builder, the administrator and the king. Not to see the matter in these terms is to misunderstand the whole subject.

Therefore, the geographer is not *primarily* concerned with the exact identification of biblical sites, though to be sure much of this identification has to be done before he can even begin. Such identification falls rather within the province of the archaeologist, at whose feet the geographer must sit, for it usually turns upon questions of a technical archaeological character. Instead, the geographer's job is that of interpretation, of piecing together the material he has gained from the geologist, the climatologist, the archaeologist, and the experts in a variety of fields, and of essaying then a total picture of the effect of all this upon, and its interrelation with, the whole activity of man.

This is a large order, and it is not to be fulfilled if ever one allows oneself to become *imprisoned* even within those frontiers and boundaries which must be drawn if the study in hand is to remain coherent and manageable. There is a continual need of a synoptic vision, and this is reinforced by the nature of the biblical argument itself, as it interprets to men what is before "the eyes of the Lord, which range through the whole earth" (Zech. 4 : 10). Leaving aside for a moment the first eleven chapters of Genesis, which draw so much of their imagery from the land of Shinar (e.g. Gen. 2 : 4–6; 7 : 11; 11 : 2), the history begins at Haran (Map III) in the piedmont steppes at the foot of the Anatolian ranges, and throughout the Book of Genesis continually returns thither, as Abraham sends Eliezer "to my country and my kindred to take a wife for my son Isaac" (Gen. 24 : 4), or Isaac in his own turn commands his son, "You shall not marry one of the Canaanite women. Arise, go to Paddan-aram to the house of Bethuel your mother's father" (Gen. 28 : 1–2). Equally important to the story is Egypt. It is as necessary for Abraham to be known to have been driven there by famine, if he is to be seen as the father of Israel (Gen. 12 : 10), as it is for St. Matthew to establish that Jesus was called from Egypt (Matt. 2 : 15), if it is to be clear that in Him all Israel has its fruition, and is enabled at last to "fulfil all righteousness" (Matt. 3 : 15).

So much attention has been given to Palestine as the "Promised Land" that the perpetual *foreignness* of Israel in Canaan needs now to be emphasized. Basic to the prophetic understanding is the argument that the Israelites do not really belong to the land where they now live, and therefore they must not adopt its manners and customs. "A wandering Aramean was my father" (Deut. 26 : 5) and "We were Pharaoh's slaves in Egypt" (Deut. 6 : 21)—such is the meaning of "the testimonies and the statutes and the ordinances" (Deut. 6 : 20). The wanderings of the Jews are the very foundation of the biblical assertions, and the basis of the prophetic confidence. "Look to the rock from which you were hewn," insisted Isaiah of Babylon, "and to the quarry from which you were digged. Look to Abraham your father and to Sarah who bore you; for when he was but one I called him, and I blessed him and made him many" (Is. 51 : 1–2). If Abraham had not been known to be "a stranger and a sojourner", reduced to "bowing down before the people of the land" when he bought so much as his burying ground (Gen. 23 : 1–20), the argument would have been of none effect. So likewise of none effect was the argument of the people to Jesus that they had "never been in bondage to any one" (John 8 : 33), for the unshakeable fact of their bondage and their deliverance was the ground of their whole existence. (Cf. Phil. 3 : 20; Heb. 11 : 9; 13 : 14, for the New Testament development of this theme.)

This, however, is but one aspect of the manner in which the world beyond Dan and Beersheba was of importance to the Israelites. It impinged continually upon their consciousness, not only as their ancient homeland but as an ever-present source of fear and profit. They lived not only by agriculture but by trade, with the great Trunk Road from Assyria to Egypt running directly across the Northern Kingdom and past the foot of the Judaean hills. Of Zebulun and Issachar it was said, "They suck the affluence of the seas and the hidden treasures of the sand" (Deut. 33 : 19). Solomon "had a fleet of ships of Tarshish at sea with the fleet of Hiram", and they brought back to him "gold, silver, ivory, apes, and peacocks" (1 Kings 10 : 22). He imported horses from Anatolia and sent them to Egypt, whence also he bought chariots to export to the Hittites and to Syria (1 Kings 10 : 28–29). Solomon's control of the great trade routes did not survive the division of the kingdom at his death, but whenever his successors were strong they emulated his achievements, building (though not always effectively) "ships of Tarshish to go to Ophir for gold" (1 Kings 22 : 48), and claiming authority over "Damascus and Hamath, which had belonged to Judah" (2 Kings 14 : 28).

They were normally unable to maintain their control over the surrounding country, and even the mighty Ahab had to fight for Ramoth Gilead on the very borders of Israel (1 Kings 22 : 3), and in the glorious days of Jeroboam II the people rejoiced when they had taken Lo-debar and Karnaim for themselves, though these places were but a short distance across the Jordan (Amos 6 : 13). Constantly the precious territory had to be defended, the frontiers refortified, and a hardwon glacis if possible established, in order to provide some security for those who longed to see their "children's children and peace upon Israel" (Ps. 128 : 6). So Uzziah "went out and made war against the Philistines", and "God helped him . . . against the Arabs that dwelt in Gurbaal, and against the Meunites [people who encamped almost on his doorstep!]; the Ammonites [just across the Jordan] paid tribute to Uzziah, and his fame spread even to the border of Egypt" (2 Chron. 26 : 6–8). In times of strength these defences were pushed as far abroad as possible, for according to Assyrian records Ahab in 853 fought as far north as Qarqar, beyond Hamath on the Orontes, but in times of weakness the enemy could penetrate to the very gates of Jerusalem itself (1 Kings 14 : 25 ff.).

It is necessary thus to place the little kingdoms of Israel and Judah in their setting, lest we misinterpret their environment and no longer call to mind what they could never forget: the exciting, menacing world outside their borders. To study the land of Palestine in detail, with only an occasional side glance at the lands beyond, is to misunderstand the thinking of those living in fear that "out of the north evil shall break forth upon all the inhabitants of the land" (Jer. 1 : 14); men who trembled when, just to the east of the Dead Sea, "Ar is laid waste in a night, Moab is undone" (Is. 15 : 1), and who "set out to go down to Egypt . . . to take refuge in the protection of Pharaoh" (Is. 30 : 2).

It is therefore fitting to examine first the larger stage, and only when we have a clear picture of it in our minds to turn our eyes to that smaller part of it which we call Palestine. The largest vista of which we need at first to take account is that great sickle of cultivable land known as the *Fertile Crescent* (Fig. 1). Here, in the region between the Mediterranean and the Indian Ocean, the two vast impenetrable belts which form the girdle of the Old World meet and cross. On the one hand are the lofty mountain chains which extend from the Atlantic seaboard into China, a well-nigh unbroken line of snow-capped peaks running from the Pyrenees through the Alps and Carpathians, southwards into Greece, and curving round again into Anatolia and the rugged Armenian mass. Thence they stretch on either side of Persia, by way of the Zagros and the Elburz, to meet again in the Pamirs and once again divide, pressing ever eastwards through the Karakorams and Himalayas into Burma. Another line continues by way of the Kun Lun between Tibet and the Tarim basin into the Nan Shan and then the Tsinling of central China, and yet a third line of mountains in the north extends from the Tien Shan, past the Altai and Yablonoi, to the dim and mountainous recesses of the Arc of Verkhoyansk. Especially in Asia do they form towering obstacles to movement, though not always impassable. The high plateaus which they enclose, particularly in Anatolia and Persia to the west, were the home of fierce mountain peoples, and even at times the centres of great empires.

The other great obstacle is the desert, an enormous expanse of almost waterless country which begins on the Atlantic shores of Africa and then stretches right across the continent into, and beyond, the plateau of Arabia. Here it lies to the south of the mountain belt, but in Persia it crosses it, extending thereafter along the northern side, through Turkestan, the Hungry Steppe, the Tarim basin, and the Gobi desert of southern Mongolia.

The further extensions of these two formidable barriers do not here concern us, but near where they cross they are interrupted. First, the River Nile, which rises far to the south, penetrates northwards to the Mediterranean, laying a green and fertile carpet through the tawny Saharan waste. Then, further east, the Tigris and Euphrates, which rise

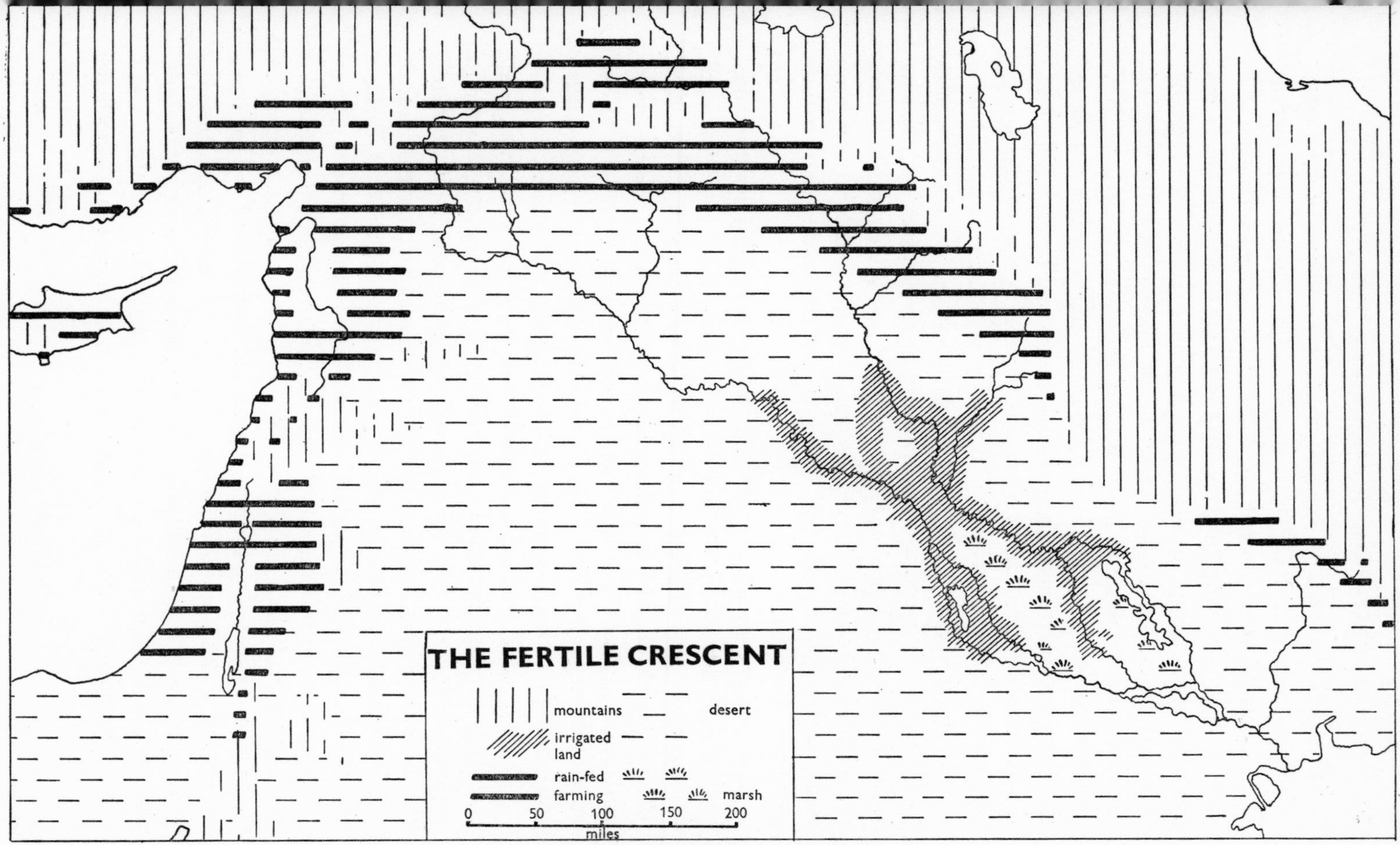

Fig. 1. The Fertile Crescent

This is the name often given to the crescent-shaped area of cultivable land extending from the Persian Gulf in the east to southern Palestine in the west, and lying between the Mediterranean Sea, the high mountains and plateaus of Anatolia and Persia, and the Arabian desert. On the west coast and in the northern piedmont region there is sufficient rain for agriculture, while in Mesopotamia the water for cultivation is supplied by the twin rivers of the Tigris and Euphrates.

in the Anatolian ranges, cut south-eastwards past the foot of the Zagros mountains to the Persian Gulf, making as they do so another interruption in the desert. Moreover, where the Euphrates leaves the mountains it is no more than forty miles from the Mediterranean coast, stretching some 400 miles or more from the edge of the Anatolian shores to the coasts of Sinai and Africa. This long extent of the Mediterranean shore, running more or less from north to south, is often known as the Levant Coast, and receives rain in winter from the cyclonic storms which pass along the Mediterranean trough. These rains do not extend far inland, for here the Mediterranean climate is almost at odds with that of the desert, especially in the south, where the unreliable moisture dies away almost entirely and the desert comes close against the shore. Yet, the cultivable land is sufficiently broad to form a kind of bridge between the rich silt lands of the Nile and those of the Euphrates. As probably every book on the subject has pointed out, it is this character of a bridge between the two great imperial powers which has largely determined the history of the tiny Levantine states.

It is another commonplace of the geography books that this coastland is divided longitudinally into four strips, or north-south zones, varying in height and in width but everywhere present: the Coast Plain, the Western Highlands, the Rift Valley, and the Eastern Plateau. The existence of these ever-present structural lines has reinforced the bridge-like character of the region and has further guided the feet of marching armies and peaceful merchants in a northward or southward direction.

This is certainly true, but it would be false to imagine that the picture is really as simple as this. Instead, there is a much more complex structural pattern which is also reflected in the history of the area. To understand this pattern one must first grasp that the dominant structural form in the whole of this Levantine region is that known to geologists as "block formation". That is to say the main physical features (mountains, plains, valleys, and so on) are the result of the fracturing of the ancient crystalline block of Arabia, which underlies the whole area, the broken parts then being pushed either up to form mountains and plateaus, or down to form valleys and plains. The strains and stresses which produced this fracturing, and consequently these blocks and rifts, extended over a long period, but there was a strong tendency for the fractures to develop mainly in two directions: either from north to south or from north-east to south-west.

Other fractures, however, developed at right angles to these, and so we find that the whole Levantine region is divided, not only longitudinally into the four north-south zones already mentioned, but also latitudinally by great dividing fractures striking inland from the coast, and by other lines running from north-west to south-east. The consequence is a pattern rather like this, in which any one of the four directional tendencies may help to determine the lie of the land:

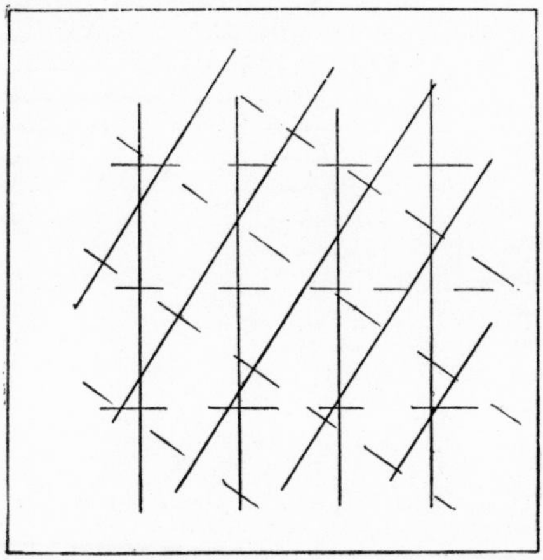

Fig. 2. The Structural Pattern of Palestine

If one looks at the Levant coastlands with this pattern in mind (see Figs. 4 and 5) at least three of these east–west dividing lines can be seen, splitting the whole area into four sub-regions in which either the north–south tendency, or the north-east–south-west one, is apparently dominant. These four sub-regions are (i) Northern Syria in which the mountains are mainly north–south; (ii) The Lebanon–Anti-Lebanon region which is dominated by the north-east–south-west tendency. It is divided from northern Syria by the Tripoli gap; (iii, iv) The Palestinian area, which is the one with which we are most concerned, is further complicated by a marked difference between the northern and southern sections, the dividing line being roughly parallel with the northern end of the Dead Sea. We need, therefore, to distinguish *five* physical regions, as follows:

A. *Northern Syria*, lying north of the Tripoli gap.
B. *Lebanon–Anti-Lebanon*, between Tripoli and Tyre.

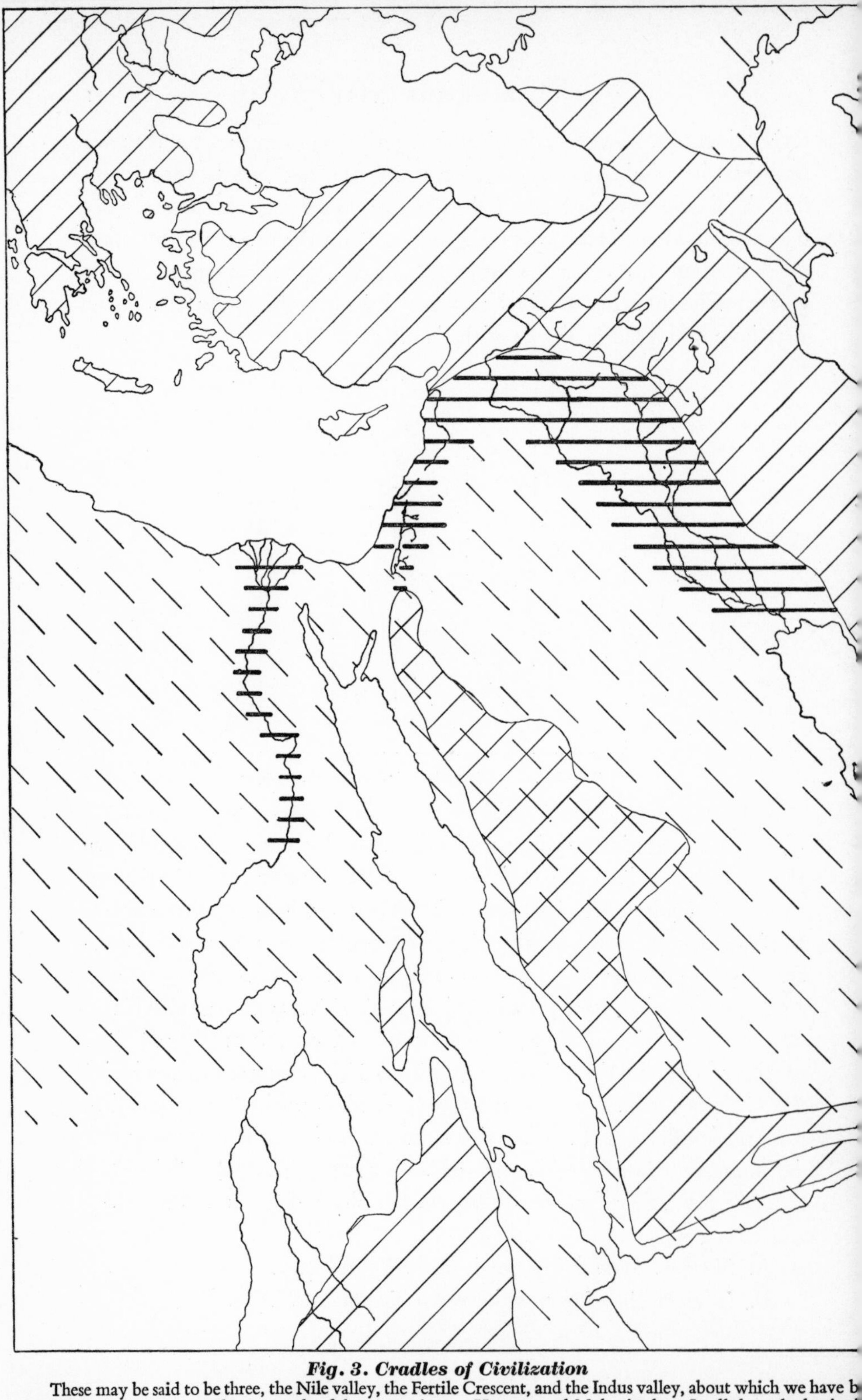

Fig. 3. Cradles of Civilization

These may be said to be three, the Nile valley, the Fertile Crescent, and the Indus valley, about which we have b learning much more recently as a result of the excavations at Harappa and Mohenjo-daro. In all three the beginni of civilization seem to be associated with an alluvial plain in which settled agriculture depends on irrigation, ei natural or artificial. Even the Palestinian region is not really an exception to this, for the oldest known town, tha

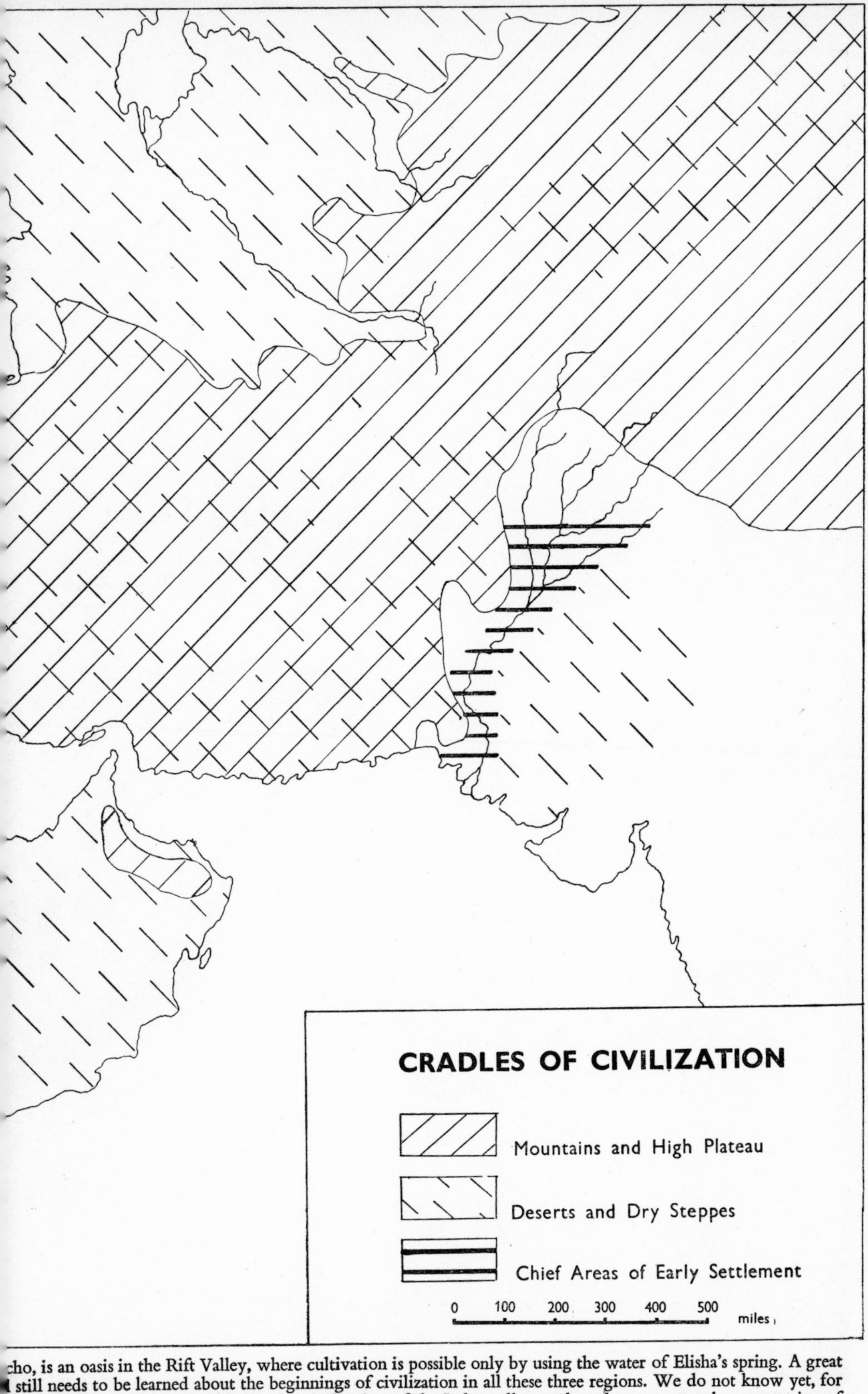

cho, is an oasis in the Rift Valley, where cultivation is possible only by using the water of Elisha's spring. A great l still needs to be learned about the beginnings of civilization in all these three regions. We do not know yet, for ance, how far back we should take the civilization of the Indus valley, and we have as yet only a smattering of owledge about the culture of southern Arabia, though it cannot go as far back as that of the three regions marked this map.

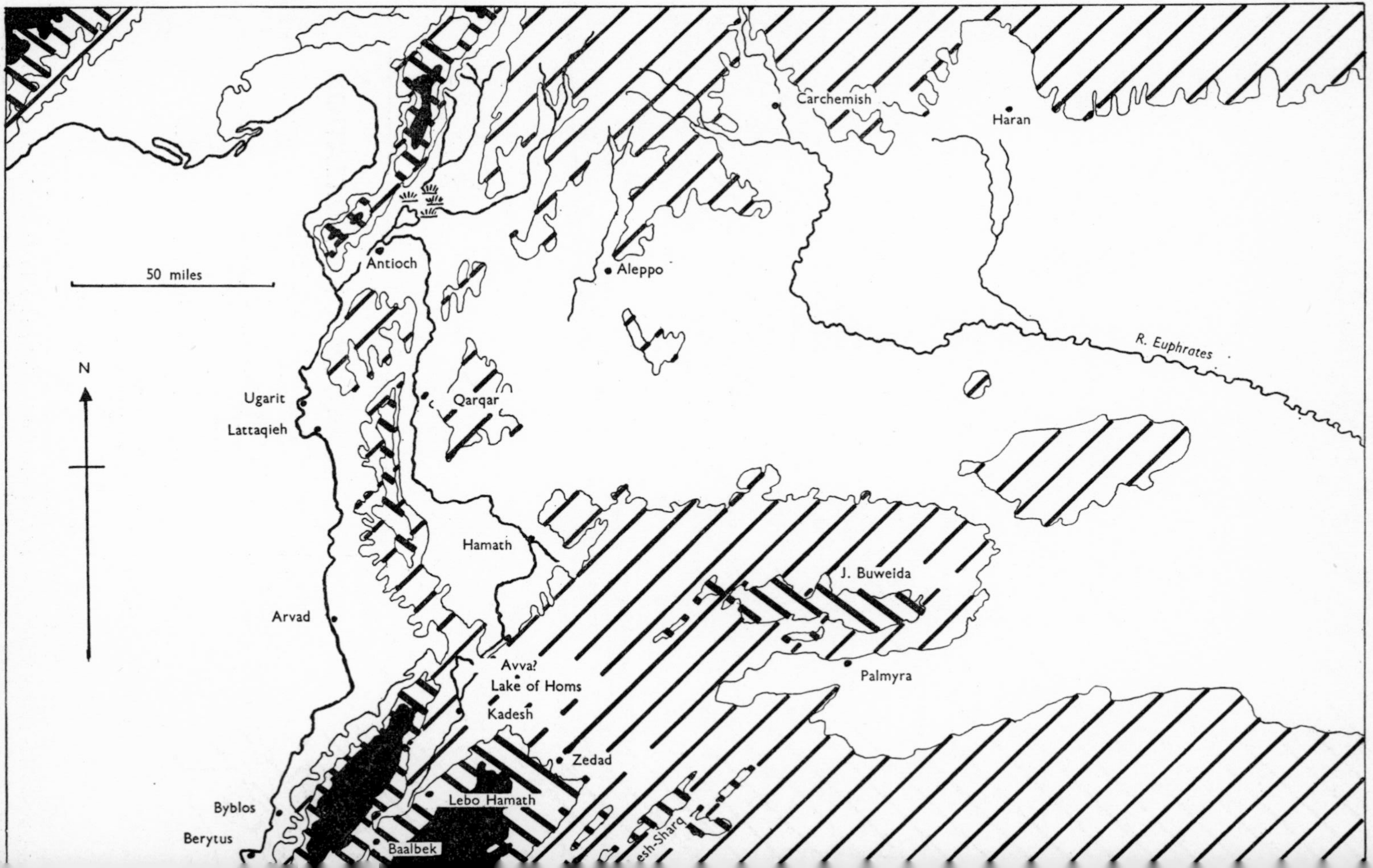
Carchemish
Haran
Antioch
50 miles
Aleppo
R. Euphrates
N
Ugarit
Qarqar
Lattaqieh
Hamath
J. Buweida
Arvad
Avva?
Lake of Homs
Palmyra
Kadesh
Zedad
Byblos
Lebo Hamath
Berytus
Baalbek
esh-Sharq

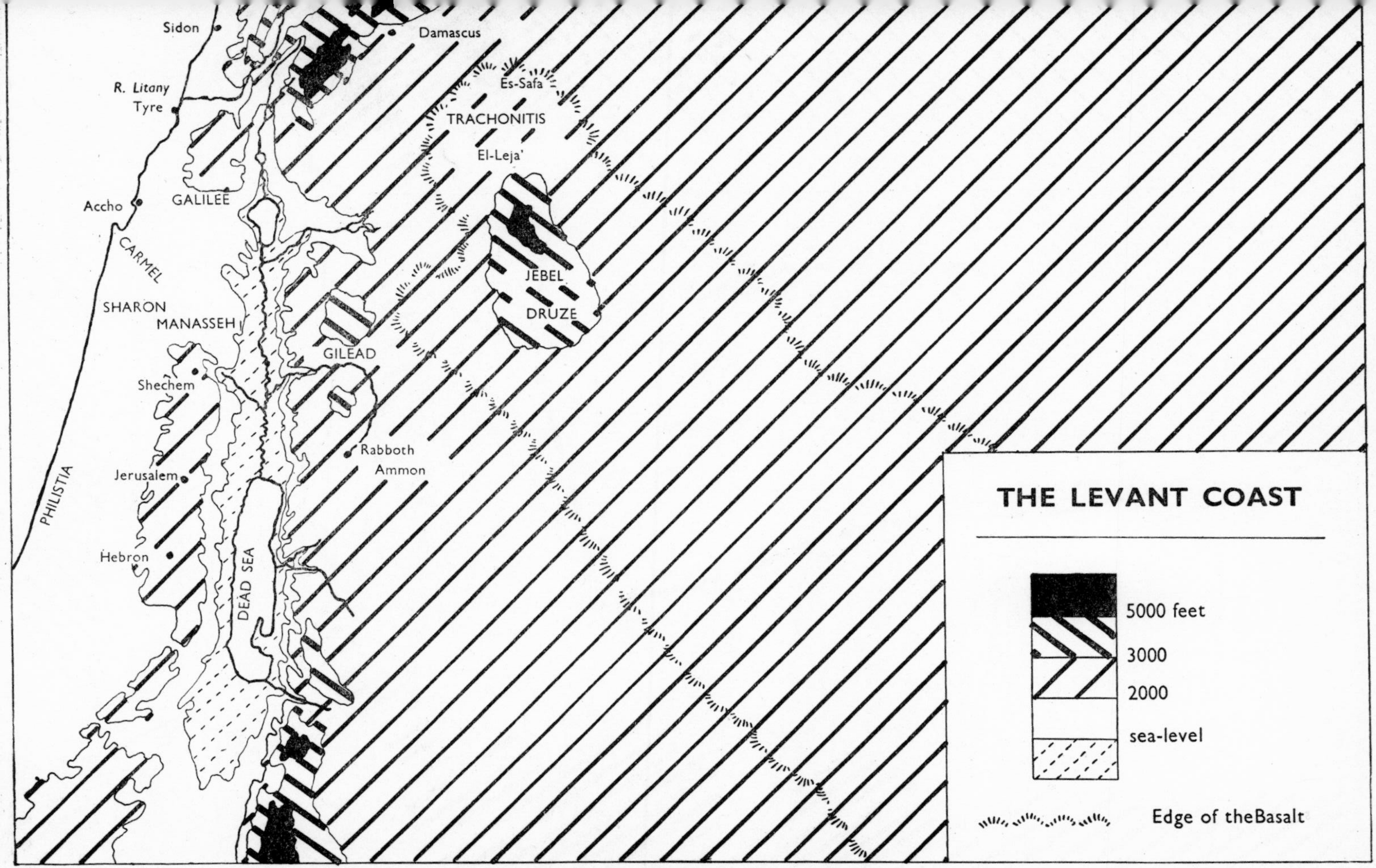
THE LEVANT COAST
5000 feet
3000
2000
sea-level
Edge of theBasalt
Sidon
Damascus
R. Litany
Tyre
Es-Safa
TRACHONITIS
El-Leja'
Accho
GALILEE
CARMEL
JEBEL
DRUZE
SHARON
MANASSEH
GILEAD
Shechem
Rabboth
Ammon
Jerusalem
PHILISTIA
Hebron
DEAD SEA

Fig. 4. The Levant Coast

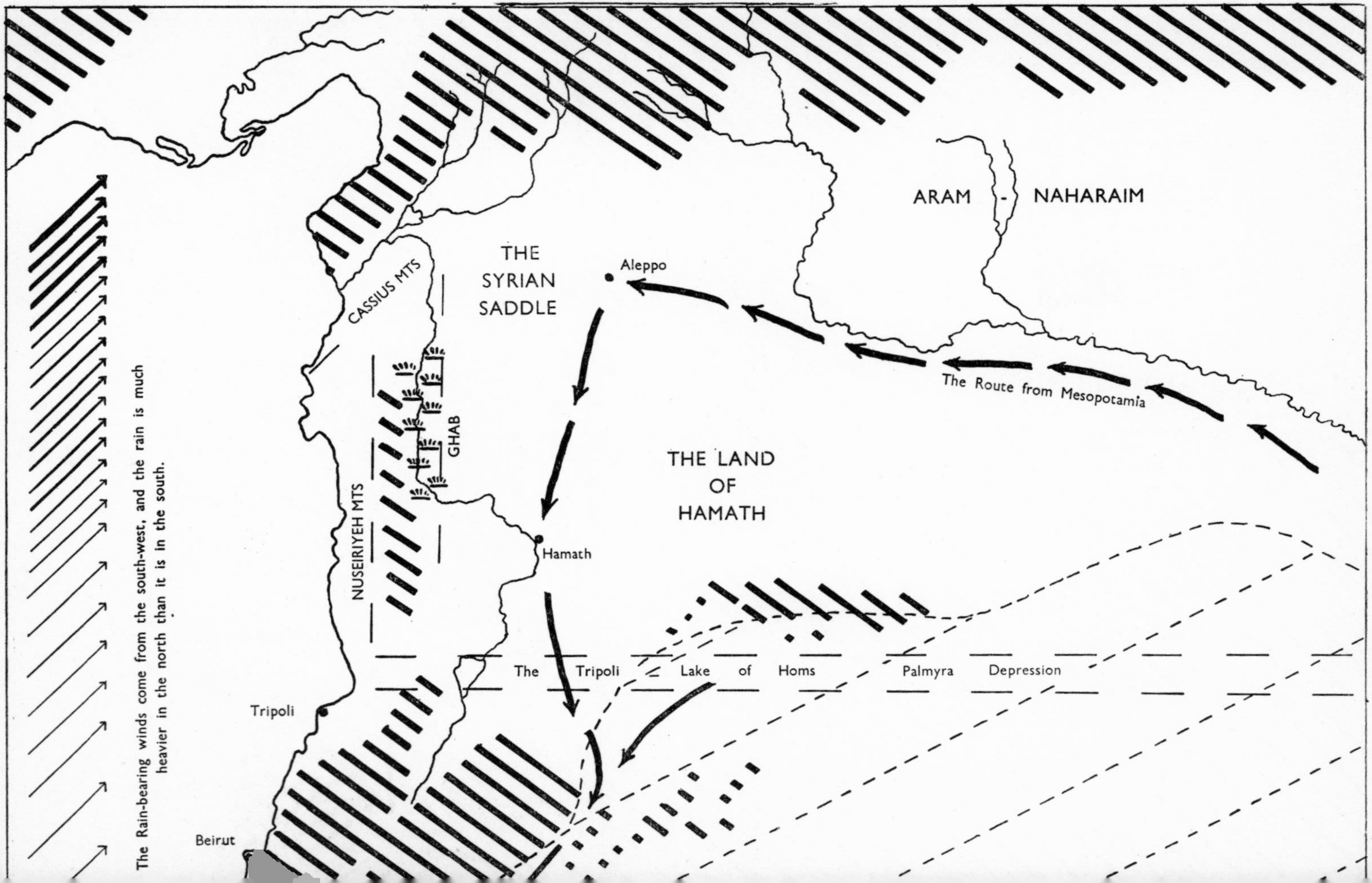
ARAM - NAHARAIM
THE SYRIAN SADDLE
Aleppo
The Route from Mesopotamia
CASSIUS MTS
GHAB
NUSEIRIYEH MTS
THE LAND OF HAMATH
Hamath
The Tripoli - Lake of Homs Palmyra Depression
Tripoli
Beirut
The Rain-bearing winds come from the south-west, and the rain is much
heavier in the north than it is in the south.

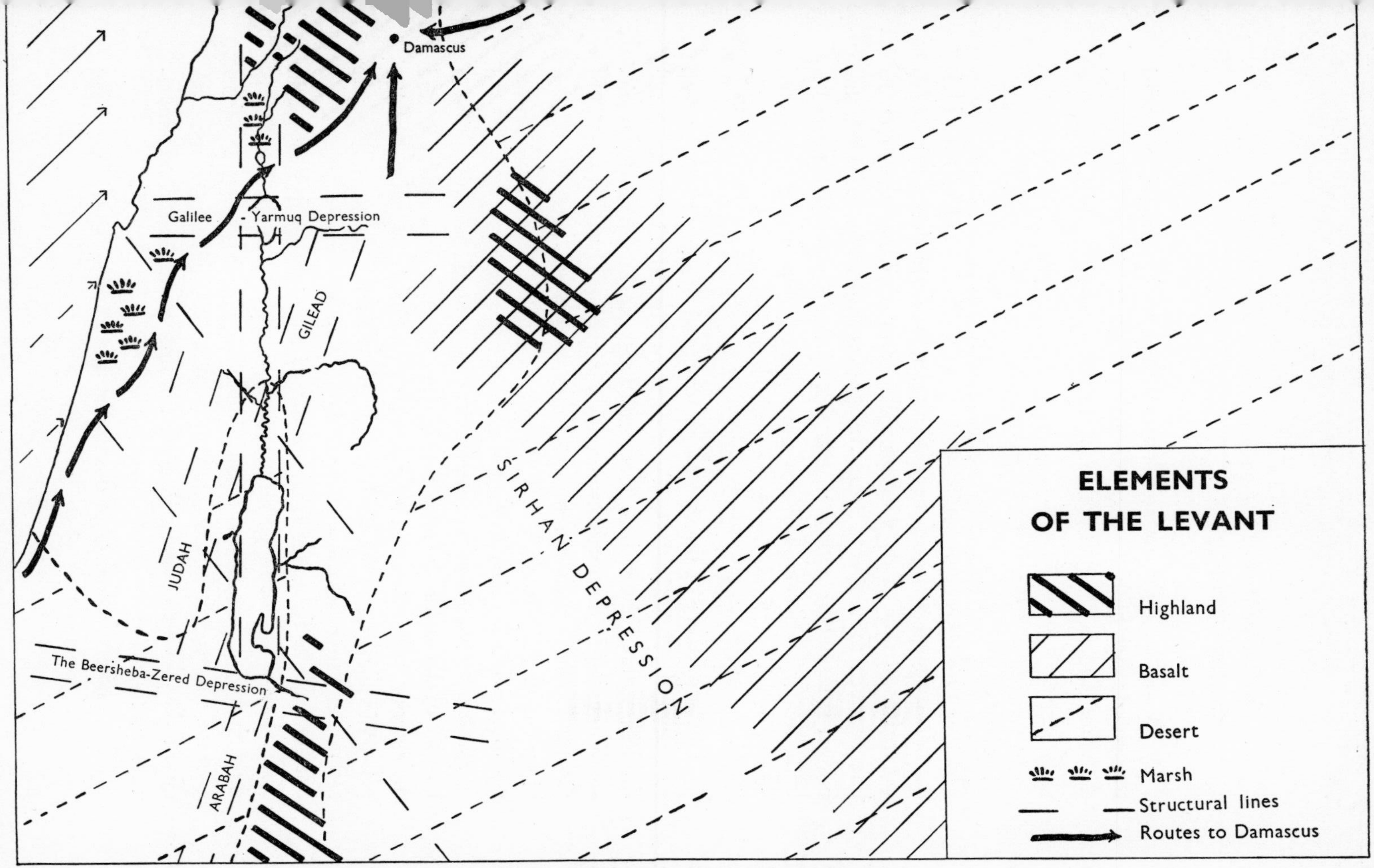

Fig. 5. Main Elements of the Levant

C. *The Israelite Zone*, between Dan and the Dead Sea.

D. *The Judaeo–Moabite Zone*, roughly level with the Dead Sea.

E. *The Negeb–Edomite Zone*.

It should be borne in mind that although the general structural tendency in each of these zones appears to be either N–S or NW–SE, yet the other tendency is always present, and the present lie of the land is a combination of both of them.

A. NORTHERN SYRIA

This is a broad region, sometimes known as the "Syrian saddle", in which the rich irrigated valley of the Euphrates approaches close to the well-watered coastlands of the Mediterranean, thus providing the necessary link between the imperial centres of Mesopotamia and the Levantine bridge. It should be noticed that in this northern region the rainfall is both greater in amount and also more assured than it is to the south, being carried here far to the interior, which is consequently good steppe-land rather than desert.

The importance of the two major structural directions may be well seen along the coast. In the southern part, the Nuseiriyeh mountains and the Rift Valley behind them (here called the Ghab) follow the north-south line, but in the northern part this is interrupted by the Amanus and Cassius ranges, which run from north-east to south-west, the Cassius range running out to sea in Ras Shamra, or Ugarit. This crossing of the two major fault lines has resulted in a complicated drainage. In the region of Antioch the waters of the interior rift valleys break through to the sea by way of the lower Orontes, but the drainage is far from adequate and the interior valleys remain to this day exccedingly marshy. Another NE–SW valley lies on the southern side of the Cassius range, ending near the modern town of Lattaqieh, but the tiny stream which drains it has not cut back as far as the Ghab, as did its sister stream further north. The valley is important, however, as providing one of the few breaks through to the coast. At its coastal end stood Ugarit, the home of the Ugaritic tablets, which have thrown so much valuable light upon the life of the Levant coastal region in the middle of the second millennium B.C.

The southern boundary of this region is marked by a very important depression striking inland almost due eastwards from what is now the port of Tripoli. Its course may be traced by way of the Rift Valley which divides the Nuseiriyeh mountains from the Lebanon ranges, the Lake of Homs, the low-lying area south of Jebel Buweida which contained the famous oasis of Palmyra (Plates X and XI), and finally that section of the Euphrates valley which lies due east of Mari (Fig. 24). It is clear that this depression was of considerable historical importance, as providing an important east–west line of communication and also, in some sense, a frontier. This was because it cuts across the line of hills which form the continuation of the Anti-Lebanon, swinging eastward through the Jebel Buweida–Jebel Bishri range towards the Euphrates south of Deir ez-Zor. In Jebel Buweida these hills run almost due east and west, the north-easterly direction being resumed in Jebel Bishri, and the depression to the south contains not only the important oasis of Palmyra, with a wide area of lake and marshes, but also a series of wells which make possible a fairly easy caravan route to Mari on the Euphrates. Where this east–west depression crosses the hills the great north–south Trunk Road swings round the basalt dam from near Homs on the Orontes to Qaryatein, about half-way between Damascus and Palmyra. West of Homs it is possible to continue by the Tripoli Homs gap to the sea.

The Jebel Buweida–Jebel Bishri range marks the southernmost extension of the good steppeland, and therefore forms an important climatic barrier, the region to the south of it being desert. The line from Palmyra to the sea seems to have acted as something of a political frontier between the region dominated by the town of Hamath (2 Sam. 8 : 9) and that which lay under the authority of Damascus, and there is some evidence that the more expansive political spirits in Israel regarded the line from Palmyra to the sea as being the proper northern frontier of the Israelite dominions, though this is not entirely clear since the identification of the sites is far from certain. Nevertheless, in more than one place there is clear reference to the idea that the Israelite empire had a more northerly boundary than the traditional one at Dan.

This can be seen in the description of the "northern boundary" given in Num. 34 : 7–9, and again in Ezek. 47 : 15–17 and 48 : 1, and also in the statement that Jeroboam II "recovered for Israel Damascus and Hamath, which had belonged to Judah" (2 Kings 14 : 28; see also verse 25). A further reflection of the same idea is the claim made in 2 Chron. 8 : 4 that

Solomon "built Tadmor [i.e. Palmyra] in the wilderness and all the store-cities which he built in Hamath". It is true that this last statement seems to be taken from a passage in 1 Kings 9 : 18, in which it is said that he had built Tamar in the southern wilderness of Judah, but the fact that the change was made is itself evidence for the claim that the Palmyra line formed the northern boundary of the Israelite empire at its greatest extent.

Unfortunately the places mentioned in Numbers and Ezekiel can be at best only guessed at, but the possible identifications which have been made are along this line. Thus, "the entering in of Hamath" may be either a place name, Lebo-Hamath, probably to be identified with the modern village of Lebweh, north-east of Baalbek, or else it refers to the whole region on the border of the Hamath dominions. Zedad can be identified with some certainty as Sedad south-east of Homs, and Hazar-enan possibly with el-Qaryatein.[5] It is impossible to regard this line as an Israelite frontier except in the most optimistic sense and reflecting merely those very brief periods of maximum strength when Damascus admitted some kind of vassal position towards Israel, a position which she certainly rejected at the very first opportunity. However, it does seem to have formed a boundary zone between differing regions, historically just as much as geographically.

In this northern region by far the most important section from the biblical point of view was the wide area of steppeland plateau east of the River Orontes, for the marshes of the Rift Valley and the thickly forested Western Highlands formed so effective a barrier on the seaward side that the coast remained isolated from the interior. This isolation of the coast-land is reflected today in the existence in this area of a separate religious group, the Nuseiriyehs, a people who, it is interesting to note, still preserve the ancient Semitic custom of worshipping in groves.

On the plateau, however, movement was much less fettered, though the major route always seems to have swept far to the north, following the Euphrates to the very foot of the mountains before swinging south-ward to join the Orontes valley at Hamath. This is because the main wadi lines run from south to north across the plateau to join the Euphrates, and travellers from east to west are forced continually to toil across the ridges between them. Consequently, the line of least resistance was the long way round to the north, this being also the area of thickest population, and to places lying on this great northward curve there is frequent biblical reference. The piedmont region lying east of the River Euphrates, and especially on either side of its tributary, the Balikh, was undoubtedly Paddan-aram, or Aram-Naharaim, referred to in the patriarchal stories (e.g. Genesis 24 : 10; 25 : 20; 28 : 2 ff.; 31 : 18; etc.), and we now know the names of many of Abraham's family mentioned in Gen. 11 : 14–30 to be the same as names of towns in this area, e.g. Serug, Haran, Nahor. Later, as the great Assyrian steamroller pushed southwards towards Egypt, crushing all opposition in its path, the names of Calno, Arpad and Hamath along this road are quoted as evidence of Assyrian victories (Amos 6 : 2; Is. 10 : 9; 36 : 19). Hamath is one of the places from which the Assyrian king is reported to have brought men to replace the people of Samaria (2 Kings 17 : 24), and Avva in the same passage is identified by some, though dubiously, with Tell Kafr 'Aya close to the modern town of Homs. It was at Carchemish to the far north that the combined army of the Assyrians and the Egyptians was defeated by the Babylonians (2 Chron. 35 : 20), and at Riblah in the land of Hamath, not far to the south of Homs, that Pharaoh Necho had his camp earlier in the campaign (2 Kings 23 : 33). It was at Riblah finally that the unfortunate King Zedekiah was blinded, after having seen his sons killed before him, by the orders of the King of Babylon (2 Kings 25 : 6–7).

B. THE LEBANON–ANTI-LEBANON REGION

South of the great depression running from west to east through Palmyra the tendency of all the structural lines to run from south-west to north-east is very marked indeed, and these lines quite dominate the physical pattern. The north–south line, however, is not entirely absent, for it can be traced as an extension of the Jordan valley along the south-western edge of the Lebanese mountains until it runs out to sea in the headland at Beirut (the ancient Berytus).

The most striking feature of this region is the extraordinary height to which the mountains have been lifted up, for both ranges rise to over 8,000 feet. The coast plain is excessively narrow, and at times almost non-existent, and the mountains of Lebanon climb almost straight up out of the sea. Even the Rift Valley between them is over 3,000 feet above sea-level. It is not here, however, a true "rift valley", that is to say that it is not a depressed area between two parallel lines of faults. Instead, there is one major fault line, forming the steep eastern slope of the Lebanon. The Anti-Lebanon is a sharply tilted block with a steep scarp overlooking the eastern plateau.

The Lebanon range, being nearer the sea, naturally receives the greater rainfall, and was famous in ancient times for its rich forest cover (Jud. 9 : 15; 1 Kings 4 : 33; 5 : 6; 2 Kings 14 : 9; 19 : 23; Ezra 3 : 7; Ps. 29 : 5; 92 : 12; Song 3 : 9; 4 : 15; Is. 2 : 13; 33 : 9; Ezek. 27 : 5; Hosea 14 : 6; Nah. 1 : 4; Zech. 10 : 10; 11 : 1, etc.), but both are high enough to be thickly covered with snow in winter, and this remains in patches even during the summer, for it is not to be thought of that "the snow of Lebanon leave the crags of Sirion" or "the mountain waters run dry" (Jer. 18 : 14). "Sirion" is identified in Deut. 3 : 9 with Mount Hermon, and this would seem to be borne out by Ps. 29 : 6, where the voice of the Lord "makes Lebanon to skip like a calf, and Sirion like a young wild ox", for these two snow-covered giants may be seen clearly in winter from many places in northern Palestine. However, in the Song of Solomon three peaks, Amana, Senir (=Sirion) and Hermon, appear to be thought of separately (Song 4 : 8). If this is so, it is possible that Senir is the name of the whole range, and especially of the northern section, while Amana has been identified with Jebel Zebdani, a detached portion of the Anti-Lebanon slightly to the west, from which rises the River Barada (the Abana of the Bible—2 Kings 5 : 12). But it is possible that the words "and Hermon" in this verse are really an explanatory gloss meaning "that is to say Mount Hermon", and that therefore Amana is the name of the northern section of the range, Hermon being in the south (Fig. 6). This certainly seems more satisfactory.[6]

The cleft in the Anti-Lebanon range which is followed by the Abana river (the Pharpar is possibly the Nahr el-'Awaj from Mount Hermon) is of great importance. One of a series of north-west–south-east faults lying at right angles to the main direction of the mountains, it forms a valuable, though constricted, route from the interior valley to the eastern plateau, and the waters of the Abana, which follow its narrow and precipitous course, supply the magnificent oasis of Damascus at the foot of the dry south-eastern slopes. This city is an almost classic example of a site where all nature conspires to provide a place where men must live. The admirable water-supply alone would bring a city into being anywhere in the dry Levant, where "water" and "life" are almost synonymous

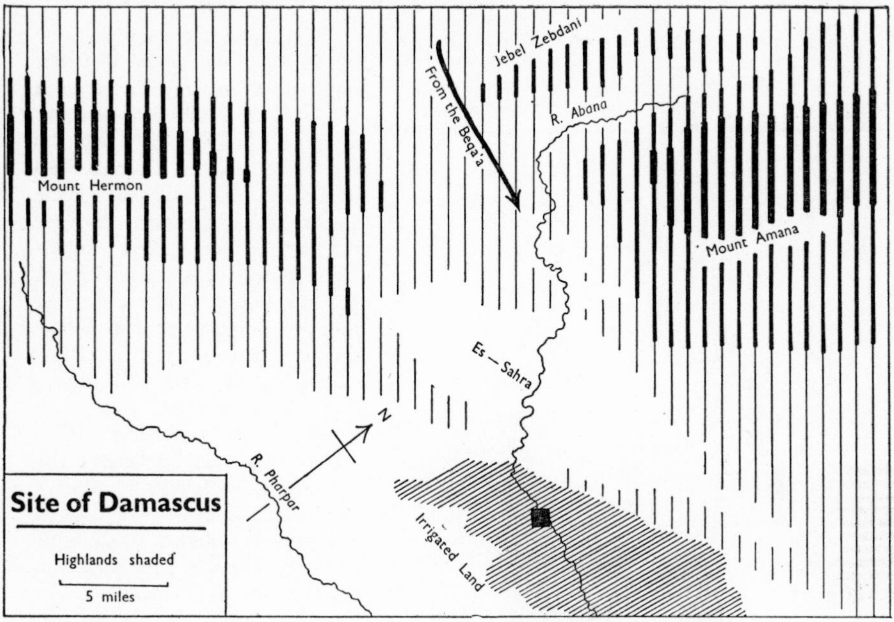

Fig. 6. The Site of Damascus

terms, but it is trebly valuable here where the dusty desert sweeps close to the bottom of the hills.

The orientation of the mountains and hills in this region is of great significance, for the higher land helps to "trigger" the rain from the dying Mediterranean storms, and the districts to the east of them are in their lee and therefore dry. It will be seen that north of the Abana gap the ridges fan out broadly like the fingers of a hand, and the SW–NE trend is very pronounced, not only in the Anti-Lebanon itself, but also in the lower parallel ranges to the east, such as Jebel esh-Sharq. To the south of the gap, however, the NW–SE faults which have developed transversely to the main trend are strongly in evidence, and these determine the direction of the great basalt outflows of the Jebel Druze, es-Safa, and el-Leja' (the Trachonitis district of Luke 3 : 1. Fig. 8). The desert plateau to the east of the Anti-Lebanon is therefore here enclosed within a right angle of higher ground with its apex at Damascus, and the caravan routes must consequently follow something of the same pattern.

Travellers would in any case swing round the edges of the desert, avoiding the treacherous "freshets that pass away", lest they "turn aside from their course" and "go up into the waste and perish" (Job 6 : 15–18).

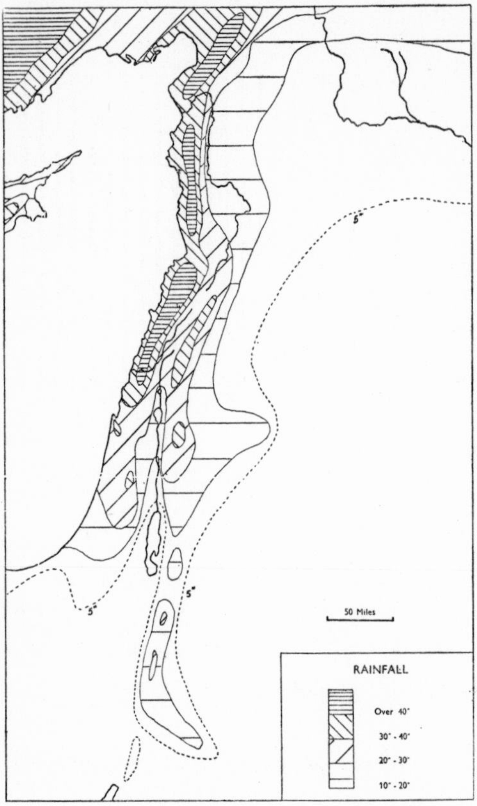

Fig. 7. Rainfall of the Levant

It is upon the rain that the whole life of the Levant depends, since irrigation from the rivers is possible only locally, and even this is ultimately dependent on the rain of the region. There are no large rivers such as the Nile, or the Tigris and Euphrates, drawing their supplies from distant mountains. Therefore a knowledge of the distribution of the rain is of the first importance for understanding the country.

(1) The rain falls only during the winter months, usually in torrential storms lasting for as much as three days or more. The prolonged gentle rain of western Europe is unknown. Summer is everywhere a period of absolute drought, but the length of this varies from five months in the south to two months in the north. It is useful to remember that Jerusalem has about the same average rainfall as London (25 in.), but only about fifty rainy days in the year.

(2) Rainfall increases towards the north, where it is both heavier and more assured. It decreases towards the east, and the eastern side of any hill or mountain is in a marked rain-shadow.

(3) Two things may "trigger" the rain, elevation or rising air currents, that is to say that the rain may be either *orographical* or *convectional*. The importance of elevation cannot be overestimated, and it is universally true that even a slight increase in height means an increase in the amount of rain. Convectional rain is largely confined to the beginning and end of the rainy season, and is particularly characteristic of the desert areas, where the heaviest falls often occur at these two periods. The start of the rainy season in about October is marked almost everywhere by striking thunderstorms as the cool, damp air is forced to rise off the still hot land. Convectional rain is usually very limited in extent, and so the beginning of the rain is often patchy, one place receiving enough for ploughing to start, while another, only a few miles away, remains obstinately dry.

(4) The extreme narrowness of the well-watered region should be noticed. It is only in the Syrian saddle in the north and in the region of the Jebel Druze further south that it extends much more than fifty miles from the coast.

(5) The Syrian saddle region is perhaps somewhat deceptive on this map, since it is better supplied than might appear, having enough rain for agriculture (i.e. more than 8 in.) over a wide area. The rain is here also much more assured than it is to the south.

(6) Really plentiful rain (i.e. over 30 in.) is confined to the mountains and coasts of the Phoenician region, with outliers on Mount Hermon, Gilead, and the Ephraimite Dome.

(7) Two anomalous extensions are of great importance: the long tongue of drought extending northwards along the Rift Valley, and the similar tongue of surprisingly heavy rain along the edge of the eastern plateau in the Edomite region to the south.

Yet the desert hills and valleys themselves point directly at Damascus, gathering not only the route from Palmyra, here turning south-westwards as the wadis dictate, but also the great Trunk Road from Calneh, Carchemish and Arpad. This is the road of the invader from the north, beaten out by the tramp of military feet, so that when "Hamath and Arpad are confounded, for they have heard evil tidings", Damascus also turns to flee (Jer. 49 : 23–24).

The southern line of hills is perhaps not quite so clear on the map, for volcanic outflows do not adopt the regular pattern of sedimentary strata, but the steps of the voyager are here even more rigidly confined. Basalt is a rude and cruel rock, blocking with rough boulders every line of approach, and cutting the feet of men and beasts that seek to cross it. Every caravan must skirt the region, and within are only the strongholds of those who seek refuge from authority. So it is that from the south as well every route is funnelled towards Damascus, which is "the head of Syria" (Is. 7 : 8) and the keystone of the Levant. It was by no accident that Elijah was told first to anoint Hazael, for the revolution which he wrought in Damascus brought in train the tumult which destroyed the House of Omri in Samaria and Jerusalem (1 Kings 19 : 15; 2 Kings 8 : 7–15; 9 : 1–37; 11 : 1–16).

Towering above Damascus to the west is Hermon, the majestic newel-post of Israel, whose northern boundary here turned southward, following apparently the line of volcanic cones which mark the edge of the eastern plateau (1 Chron. 5 : 23). "Baal-gad in the valley of Lebanon below Mount Hermon", which is claimed as the northernmost point of Joshua's conquests (Josh. 11 : 17; 12 : 7; 13 : 5; also possibly Baal-Hermon in Judges 3 : 3) has been placed by some at Banias, but this is hardly in the Valley of Lebanon, which is surely that uplifted part of the rift behind Mount Lebanon itself, and it must be looked for further north, though where is not yet certain.

This interior valley, the *Beqa'a* of today, is far more complicated than appears at first sight on the map. Though it must always have had importance as a corridor between the Lebanon and Anti-Lebanon, it is a rough and difficult passage, to which all three apparent entrances are in some sense blocked. In the north the valley of the Orontes is closed by a great dam of basalt, behind which has formed the Lake of Homs. This is the exit controlled by Riblah, and here the soil is but stony and infertile

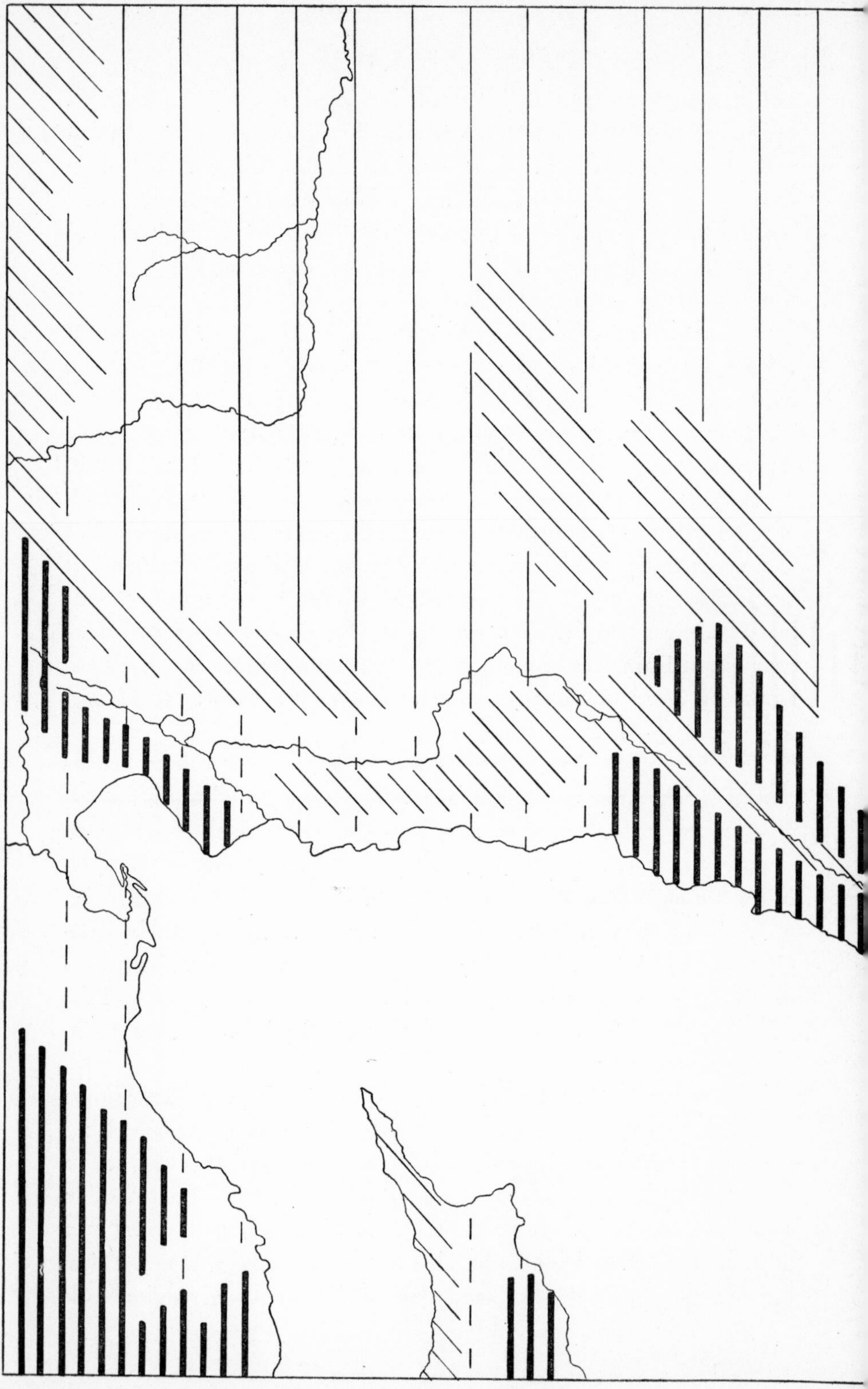

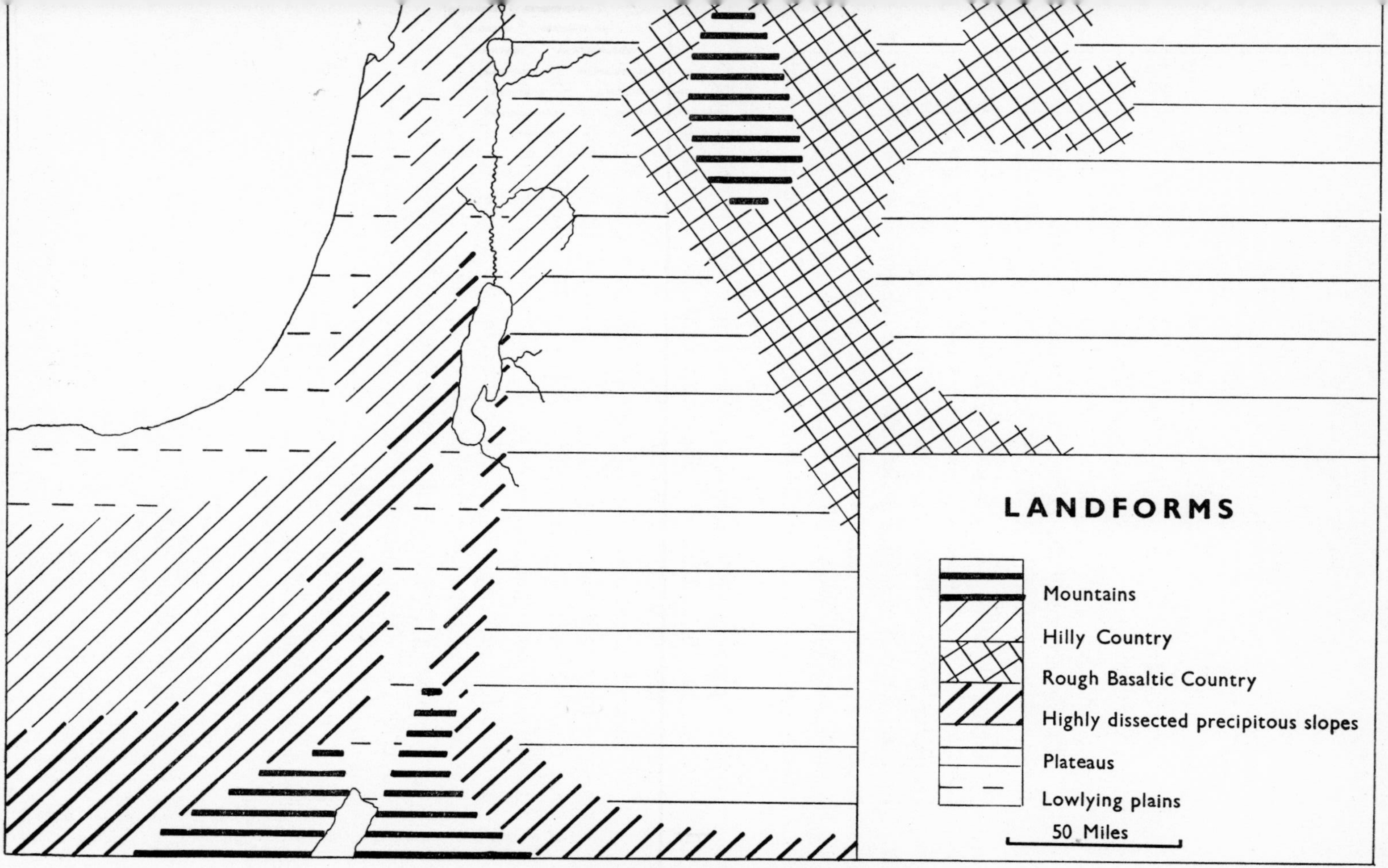

Fig. 8. Landforms of the Levant

and the region itself only thinly inhabited. In the south the Plain of Ijon (the modern *Merj Ayoun*) is much more fertile, but where it joins the north–south Jordan rift the flat plain temporarily disappears in a welter of broken rocks and a drop of some 1,500 feet. This plain seems to have been regarded by Israel as a kind of strategic apron, which they controlled whenever they could, but which was always the first to fall to any enemy from the north (1 Kings 15 : 20; 2 Kings 15 : 29; 2 Chron. 16 : 4).

The connections of the Plain of Ijon with the central section of the Beqa'a are almost as difficult, for the floor has been greatly disturbed by the sharply uplifted blocks which form the beginning of the Anti-Lebanon. It is these same hog-back ridges which make the gateway to Damascus by the Abana valley so much less simple than one would imagine, for they run athwart its course. The Litany, which drains the Beqa'a to the south, runs in a deep gorge of no value as a routeway and then turns sharply westward to the sea by one of that series of E–W faults which mark the southern end of the whole region. The Beqa'a remained therefore a strange, isolated region, with fertile patches and rich fruit-groves at the foot of the Lebanon, but invested with mystery, and a suitable home for the famous cult-centre at Baalbek, which later the Romans crowned with their vast temples.

This unexpected isolation of the Beqa'a, which on the map would seem to form so obvious a passage, must be held in part to explain the fact that so often it was under the authority of Tyre and Sidon, rather than of Damascus, despite the Valley of the Barada, as against the unbreached fortress of the Lebanon. The other, and more potent, explanation is that for all its isolation from the coast it remains a "Mediterranean" region, cultivating the crops of the coastlands, and bound to a Mediterranean way of life. Damascus, on the other hand, though set in its fabled gardens in which even the choosy olive will agree to grow, turns, nevertheless, its back upon the sea, and seeks to dominate the trade routes of the desert and the steppe.

2

THE SOUTH LAND

And she said unto him, Give me a blessing: for thou hast given me a south land; give me also springs of water.
(Jud. 1 : 15)

THE SOUTHLAND to which Achsah, the daughter of Caleb, was referring was the region of Debir, some fifteen miles south-west of Hebron, and falling, therefore, into the central of the three southern zones, though admittedly in the southern part of it. A more enthusiastic view of the Palestinian countryside is given in the Book of Deuteronomy, where it is described as "a good land, a land of brooks of water, of fountains and springs, flowing forth in valleys and hills, a land of wheat and barley, of vines and fig trees and pomegranates, a land of olive trees and honey, a land in which you will eat bread without scarcity, in which you will lack nothing" (Deut. 8 : 7–9). This is certainly more in accord with the traditional picture of the country as "a good and broad land, a land flowing with milk and honey" (Exod. 3 : 8; see also Exod. 13 : 5; 33 : 3; Lev. 20 : 24; Num. 13 : 27; 14 : 8; 16 : 13, 14; Deut. 6 : 3; 11 : 9; 26 : 9, 15; 27 : 3; 31 : 20; Josh. 5 : 6; Jer. 11 : 5; 32 : 22; Ezek. 20 : 6, 15), and in contrast with the desert this is the truer description.

Nevertheless the most important characteristic of the Palestinian world which needs to be borne in mind is the precariousness of the rainfall, and the increasing drought as one goes from north to south (Fig. 7). Well watered in comparison with the desert, it is in comparison with the more fortunate regions to the north a hungry land, gambling with the capricious rainfall in order to maintain its livelihood at all, and the southernmost section belongs to "that great and terrible wilderness" itself (Deut. 1 : 19). One must see it, therefore, as curiously balanced between famine and plenty. Throughout history it has remained unhaunted by the dread diseases of destitution, and the people are healthy peasant stock, despite their poverty—one must never confuse the *fellahin* of Palestine with the *fellahin* of Egypt—but for all this famine is a frequent visitor, and only in exceptional years does the end of the long dry summer find the farmer's family with more than just enough to eat.

Actual famine is mentioned only eight times in the course of Old Testament history,[7] which suggests that it was certainly not endemic, especially as some of these stories may not be historical (e.g. that of Ruth), and some of the other famines may be the result of war rather than the weather. Nevertheless, through the Old Testament references to famine are very frequent, which indicates that although famine may have reached catastrophic proportions only rarely, dearth was an uncomfortably common experience, and there was no natural security for the husbandman. It has been rightly pointed out[8] that even the longed-for peace did not come as an unmixed blessing, for when men were set free from the brutal demands of defence to beat their swords into ploughshares and till their neglected lands, the population tended to grow to a point where it exceeded the ability of the land to support it; a fact which does much to explain why the celebrated dream of every man sitting under his vine and under his fig tree with none to make him afraid (1 Kings 4 : 25; 2 Kings 18 : 31; Is. 36 : 16; Micah 4 : 4; Zech. 3 : 10) remained for the most part only a dream.

C. THE ISRAELITE ZONE

With this in mind, then, it is possible to descend from the heights of Lebanon to the more manageable landscape lying to the south of it. The descent is made in a series of steps, from the mountains to the highlands and from the highlands to the uplands. The first division is that which contains in succession the high fells of *Upper Galilee*, reaching over 3,000 feet in places, the *Lake Huleh basin* (Fig. 9) a little above sea-level, transitional between the uplifted plain of Ijon and the sunken Lake of Galilee, and to the east the highest part of the *Plateau of Bashan*, well over 3,000 feet above the level of the sea. Neither of the two highland areas comes greatly into the Old Testament story, and indeed so devoid are the historical records of any mention of this part of Trans-jordan that we are in doubt whether it ought to be included as part of Bashan at all, or whether it was a separate region with another name. Unlike Bashan proper it is far from flat, being interrupted frequently by small volcanic cones. There is a line of them along the edge of the plateau, known to the modern Arab as Tell Abu Nedd, Tell Abu el-Khanzir, Tell Abu Yusef, etc., and another group more centrally placed known as Tellul Sha'ar. Further east is the desolate and rocky region of Trachonitis (Plate XXVIII).

Various important roads radiate from Damascus across this region, splaying out among the volcanic hillocks between the towering barrier of Hermon and the equally impassable basalt of Trachonitis. One of them skirts the very foot of Hermon to enter the Huleh basin at Dan, which lurks like "a lion's whelp" (Deut. 33 : 22), as "a viper by the path, that bites the horse's heels so that his rider falls backward" (Gen. 49 : 17). Another is the great Trunk Road, which passes through the modern town of el-Quneitrah to cross the Jordan just south of Lake Huleh at the Bridge of Jacob's Daughters. It is interesting that although invasion came frequently along this road to Israel, there is no record of the Israelites' ever having fought back along it, so effective a barrier is the steep ascent of the plateau at this point. David, Ahab and Jeroboam II all claim to

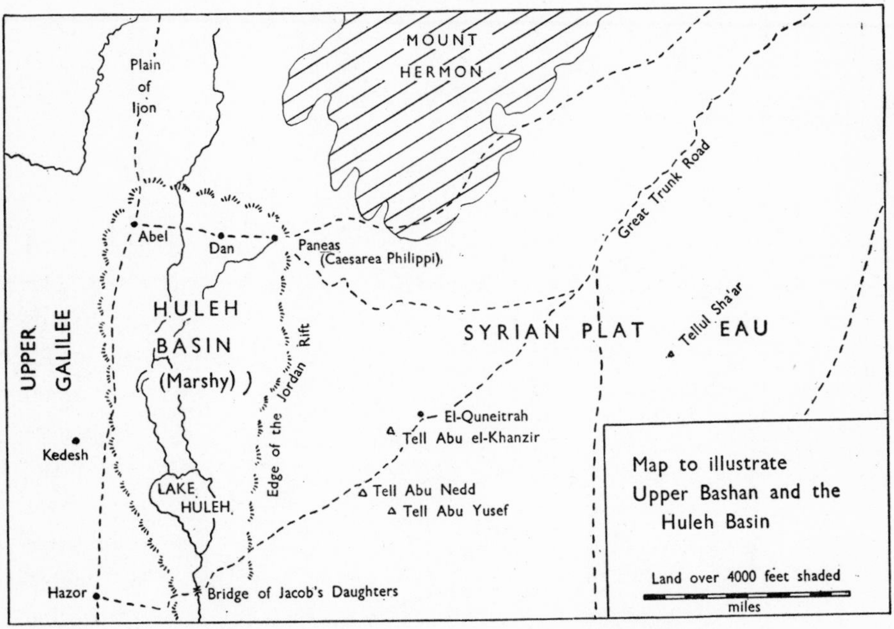

Fig. 9. Upper Bashan and the Huleh Basin

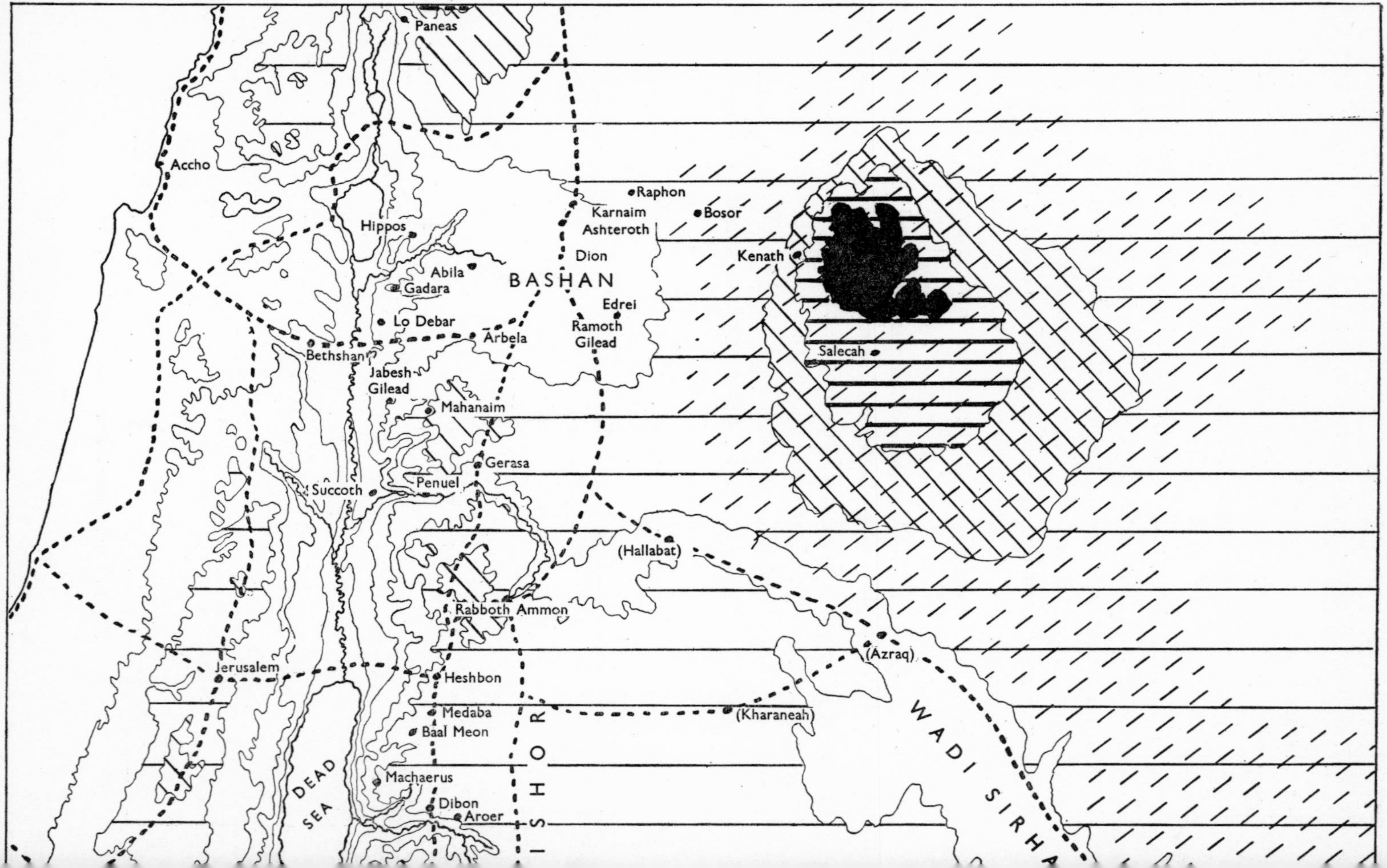
Paneas
Accho
Raphon
Karnaim
Ashteroth
Bosor
Kenath
Hippos
Dion
Abila
Gadara
BASHAN
Edrei
Ramoth
Gilead
Lo Debar
Arbela
Bethshan
Jabesh
Gilead
Salecah
Mahanaim
Gerasa
Succoth
Penuel
(Hallabat)
Rabboth Ammon
(Azraq)
Jerusalem
Heshbon
Medaba
Baal Meon
(Kharaneah)
DEAD SEA
Machaerus
Dibon
Aroer
ISHOR
WADI SIRHA

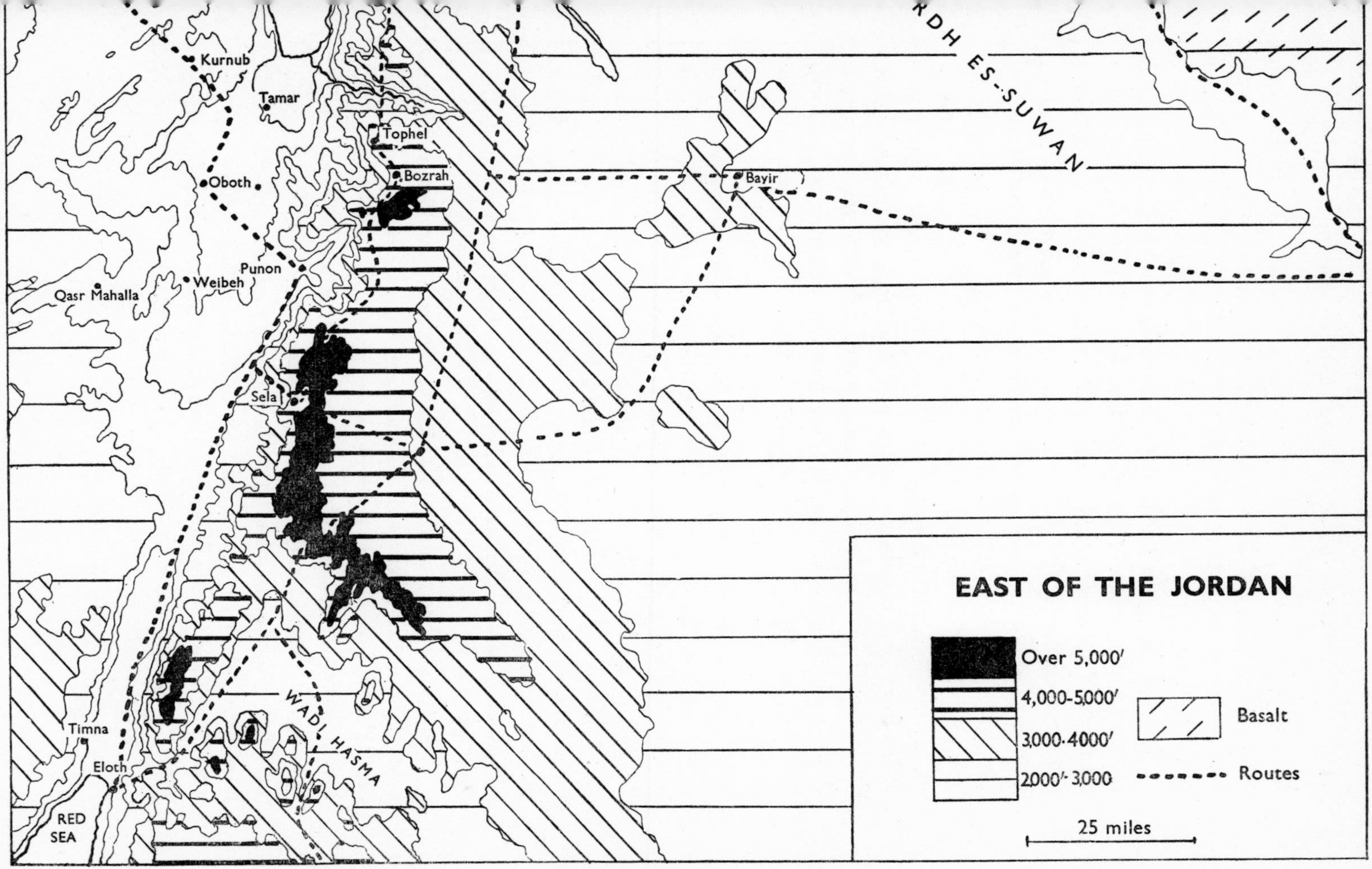

Fig. 10. East of the Jordan

have brought Damascus as a restive vassal within their imperial system, but nowhere is it said by what route they battled northwards. It may well have been across the much easier level country from Gilead further to the east.

The Rift Valley in this section receives far more constant mention, for it lay within the area claimed by the Israelites, and yet, by reason of its distance and isolation, must have been then as now essentially a defensive frontier zone. Indeed, its defensive character must then have been even more marked, for we must not picture the Huleh basin in ancient days as having the wonderful greenness which it has achieved in recent years. Instead, the 300-foot contour marked the edge of an impenetrable marsh, and the roads clung to the edge of the steep hillsides. One came southwards from Ijon, clambering down past Abel Beth Maacah to follow the foot of Upper Galilee, and another joined it from Syria, past Paneas (Caesarea Philippi) and Dan, crossing the northern edge of the plain. No road, apparently, skirted the eastern edge. The isolation, and the mysterious but wonderful water supply, of the northern edge of the basin, where alone there was room for huddled settlement, gave to this part of the country an aweful and a numinous quality. All the three places mentioned were cult centres. "They were wont to say in old time, 'Let them but ask counsel at Abel'; and so they settled a matter" (2 Sam. 20 : 18), and at Dan there was at first a famous graven image, which lasted "as long as the house of God was at Shiloh" (Jud. 18 : 31), and later the notorious golden calf of Jeroboam I (1 Kings 12 : 30). At Paneas (the modern Banias) the sacred niches may still be seen in the rock to this day.

The southern part of the Rift Valley, between Lake Huleh and the Lake of Galilee, is filled with an enormous mass of basalt, which has raised the level of the land to some thousand feet above the level of the Mediterranean Sea. Unattractive to settlement, it was likewise skirted by travellers, the road from the north still hugging the foot of the Galilean highlands until it could descend to the shore of the Lake, and the Trunk Road from Damascus crossing the Jordan between Lake Huleh and the basalt gorge, and joining the north–south road at Hazor, which "formerly was the head of all those kingdoms" (Josh. 11 : 10).

The highlands of Upper Galilee must for a long time have been covered with almost impenetrable forest, though they have long since been cleared of their trees and today have the aspect of a wild and windswept moorland, and they receive but scant mention in the Old Testament. Kedesh of Naphtali (Josh. 20 : 7; 19 : 37; Jud. 4 : 6) is undoubtedly Qadas which commands a small stretch of level land half-way down the eastern slopes, and overlooks Lake Huleh. Merom is equally certainly Meirun at the foot of Jebel Jarmak. The Waters of Merom, where Joshua is reported to have defeated Jabin, King of Hazor (Josh. 11 : 1–9), are the waters of the Wadi Lemmun which rises in a charming and shady wadi not far from Meirun, though it is probable that the battle was fought where the wadi debouches into the Plain of Gennesaret (see Map X) close to the Lake, for nowhere else would chariots have been usable. We must imagine, therefore, that the battle was the result of an attempt by Jabin to protect Hazor and the great Trunk Road from an attack from the south.

The upland region to the south of the Highlands will be dealt with more fully later on, when the military geography and the New Testament situation are discussed, and so a brief description here will suffice. Everywhere it is lower than the region to the north of it, and the dividing line is extremely clear. West of the Jordan a gigantic fault scarp (Fig. 11) marks the end of the forested plateau of Upper Galilee and the beginning of the hills and basins of Lower Galilee with their rich olive orchards and vineyards. This line of weakness is responsible also for the basalt outflows which cradle the Lake of Galilee in its rocky basin, and beyond the Lake the plateau of Lower Bashan is for the most part below 2,000 feet, and cut in two by the canyon of the Yarmuq.

The most complicated part of this section lies west of the Jordan where a number of cross-faults have created a series of down-faulted basins filled with fertile alluvium, which makes admirable wheat-growing soil when the ground dries out in the spring. In between these small basins are the hills, never as much as 2,000 feet in height, on whose slopes the olives and vines can be grown. They are not everywhere fertile, for Cenomanian limestone, with its valuable *terra rossa*, is found only in the centre. To the west, where the hills stretch out a narrow spur almost to touch the block of Carmel, the rock is the less fertile Eocene limestone, characteristic of the hills of the Shephelah further south, and indeed this part of the uplands, with their rocky slopes covered with rough woodland, might well qualify to be called the Galilean Shephelah (Map VIII). On

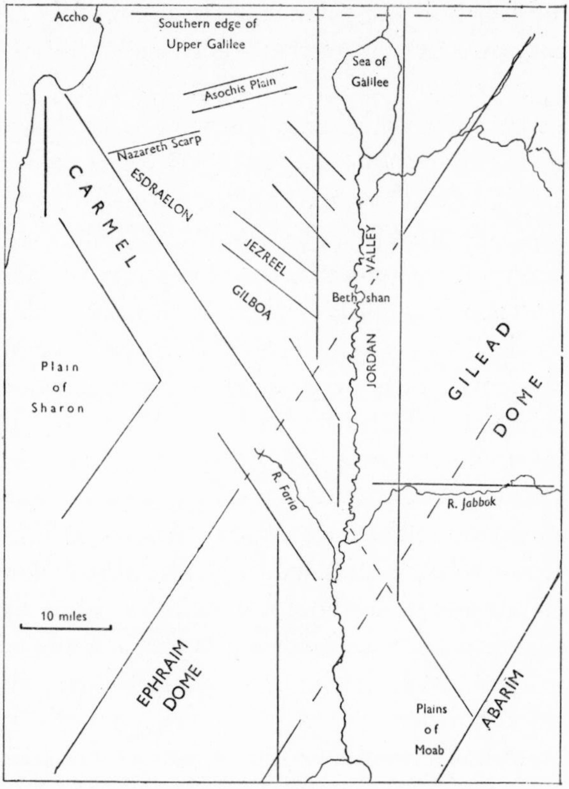

Fig. 11. Structural Elements of Central Palestine

the eastern side a great outflow of basalt has further confused the structure, and here again the sparse soil is of little value for farming. The basalt comes to an abrupt end in Mount Moreh, overlooking the corridor of Jezreel to the south.

This corridor is part of a feature which is not repeated across the Jordan—a series of minor rift valleys combining to make a passage of quite incalculable importance, which cuts right across the western hills, and touches 300 feet only in one or two places. This lowland corridor provides the most important transverse route in the whole country, since it leads from Accho on the Mediterranean, through the narrow gap which is guarded by Harosheth of the Gentiles (Jud. 4 : 2), into the broader triangular Plain of Esdraelon, and thence past Jezreel and the Spring of Harod into the narrow Valley of Jezreel between Mount

Moreh and Mount Gilboa, down to the Jordan valley. The junction of the two valleys is marked by a steep step leading down from Jezreel into the major Rift Valley, and upon this step stands the huge pyramid of *Tell el-Husn*, the site of the ancient Bethshan. This corridor was the territory of Issachar, "crouching between the sheepfolds; he saw that a resting place was good, and that the land was pleasant; so he bowed his shoulder to bear, and became a slave at forced labour" (Gen. 49 : 14–15). Pleasant though the land may have been, it was at the mercy of attack from every side.

To understand the physical pattern of the rest of this Israelite zone, it is necessary to grasp the nature of the underlying structure, for here all four of the major structural lines are strongly expressed (see Fig. 11). In one sense the dominant line is still the north–south direction of the great Rift Valley, which is the line also of the western highlands, and the edge of the eastern plateau. However, cutting across this is the great upwarp which extends from northern Judaea across the Jordan into the dome of Gilead, which forms the uplifted part of the eastern plateau south of Bashan. Directly at right angles to the Judah-Gilead upwarp, which runs from south-west to north-east, is the line of the Carmel range, running from north-west to south-east. Its direction can be seen very clearly marked indeed along the northern side of Carmel, and the Valley of Jezreel already discussed. It can be seen also in the minor rift valley which carries the little River Fari'a down to the Jordan slightly below the Jabbok confluence. The final structural direction, that from west to east, can be discerned in the faults which have produced some of the wadis flowing into the Jordan from the east, and especially the course of the Lower Jabbok.

Perhaps it will be easier to understand this rather complicated structure if one remembers that the Judah-Gilead upwarp is geologically the oldest, and therefore the least immediately obvious, since the others have been imposed upon it. Second in order of time comes the NW–SE Carmel line, complicating the previously simple SW–NE pattern. Then came the Jordan rift, cleaving its way right across the already existing hills and valleys, and imposing its north–south line as the dominant direction in this part of the country. However, where the Rift Valley crosses the two existing lines it is noticeably narrowed, and here, half-way between the Lake of Galilee and the Dead Sea, the mountains on either side close in upon the river. It is an important climatic divide also, because the part of the valley south of it is no longer steppe but desert. Finally came the E–W faults which have cleft the edge of the Trans-jordanian plateau.

The result of this criss-crossing of structural lines is to be seen in the present variegated physical pattern. First, we have to recognize the existence of two domes of valuable Cenomanian limestone, one to the west of the Jordan and the other to the east. That to the west is the territory of Ephraim, high and uplifted, and protected on every side by its precipitous limestone slopes. The Cenomanian limestone is the most important of all the Palestinian rocks and breaks down into a rich *terra rossa*, and here the height is enough to attract a usually sufficient rainfall. It is indeed "a land of hills and valleys, which drinks water by the rain from heaven, a land which the Lord your God cares for; the eyes of the Lord your God are always upon it, from the beginning of the year to the end of the year" (Deut. 11 : 11–12). The eastern dome is Gilead, cut in two by the valley of the Jabbok. Though the eastern slopes are in somewhat of a rain-shadow, and grade off fairly rapidly into the steppe, the summit and western slopes are admirably watered, and carry even today a cover of woodland. In ancient times this region was famous for its forest products (Gen. 37 : 25; Jer. 8 : 22; 22 : 6; 46 : 11; Ezek. 27 : 17; Zech. 10 : 10) and its sweet and delicate grapes have no equal in the world. It is the only region east of the Jordan where olives, grapes, and wheat will grow together, for the other parts are too open to the bitter east winds of winter, before whose blasts the olive cannot stand. However, this cannot have been a densely inhabited region, because of the thickness of its forests, and it seems to have remained a somewhat isolated frontier zone, often highly critical of the central government. Elijah, the enemy of Ahab, came from Gilead, and Jehu was acclaimed king by a dissident army group at one of its frontier posts (1 Kings 17 : 1; 2 Kings 9 : 1–10).

The central section, west of the Jordan, was the territory of Manasseh, which had managed to extend its authority also over the land of Gilead, once the heritage of Gad.[9] This is an altogether less satisfactory region strategically than that of Ephraim, and also, in its original area, less attractive agriculturally, for the chalk valleys which cut across it provide neither protection nor yet good soil. Moreover, the limestone hills are here of the less fertile Eocene type instead of the richer Cenomanian. The early history of Manasseh, therefore, was of subjection to Ephraim, on whose fortress heights at Shiloh the Ark was kept, and of determined attempts to find a satisfactory frontier. To this end she pushed outwards to include a great part of the central corridor, the passes across Carmel, the fords of the Jordan, and at least the western slopes of the great dome of Gilead beyond, dispossessing any of her weaker Israelite brethren who stood in her way. She thus became the strongest tribe in all Israel and consistently dominated the Northern Kingdom from the time of Jeroboam I onwards.

The long arm of Carmel extends north-westwards from Manasseh to end in the precipitous limestone headland just south of the bay of Accho. The rock here is the rich Cenomanian, and the closeness to the sea has meant an abundant rainfall, and an impenetrable forest cover, which, with the steep fault scarps on either side, defied penetration and settlement. Isolated, remote, and sumptuously wooded, Carmel was for long one of the homes of the gods, held in awe by Israelites and Phoenicians alike. It is not by accident that the bloody contest between the Tyrian Baal and the God of Israel was held to have taken place amid its mysterious forests (1 Kings 18 : 17–40), nor was it strange that it ranked with Lebanon in glory (Song 7 : 5; Is. 33 : 9; 35 : 2; Jer. 46 : 18; 50 : 19; Amos 1 : 2; 9 : 3; Nah. 1 : 4). The central section of the Carmel range is lower, but still steep sided, and because of the thick scrub woodland on the less fertile Eocene limestone difficult to cross. The passes by way of the narrow chalk valleys were therefore most important.

South of Carmel the narrow coastal strip widens out into the plain of Sharon, today green and fertile, but in ancient times clogged with thick oak forests and pestilent marsh, particularly at its northernmost point where the Crocodile river winds with difficulty across the sand dunes to the sea. The home of magnificent orange groves today, it was for the Israelites a grim and terrifying region, and they made no attempt to occupy it.

D. THE JUDAEO-MOABITE ZONE

As the northern end of the Dead Sea is reached the complicated structural pattern of the north is suddenly and unexpectedly simplified. The line of the Judah-Gilead Dome, it is true, is still apparent, but it is so dominated by the direction of the north–south rift that for our purposes it may be disregarded, at least for the moment. Here the western highlands have been pushed upwards in the Judaean block, which is outlined on either side by N–S faults into which the limestone strata dive headlong. The Rift Valley plunges dramatically to its greatest depth, nearly 2,700 feet below the level of the sea, though the bottom of the depression is filled by the heavy, saline waters of the Dead Sea, whose surface is 1,300 feet below that of the Mediterranean. Beyond, to the east, is the towering wall of the Moabite plateau, steadily rising towards the south, and exposing the ruddy sandstone precipices at its foot.

At each end of the Dead Sea "hinge-faults" curve obliquely into the highlands (Fig. 12) and mark abruptly the northern and southern limits of this section, being reinforced on the western side by a similar fault valley striking north-eastwards from the coast plain. Not only do these faults admirably define the region, but each has played its part in history.

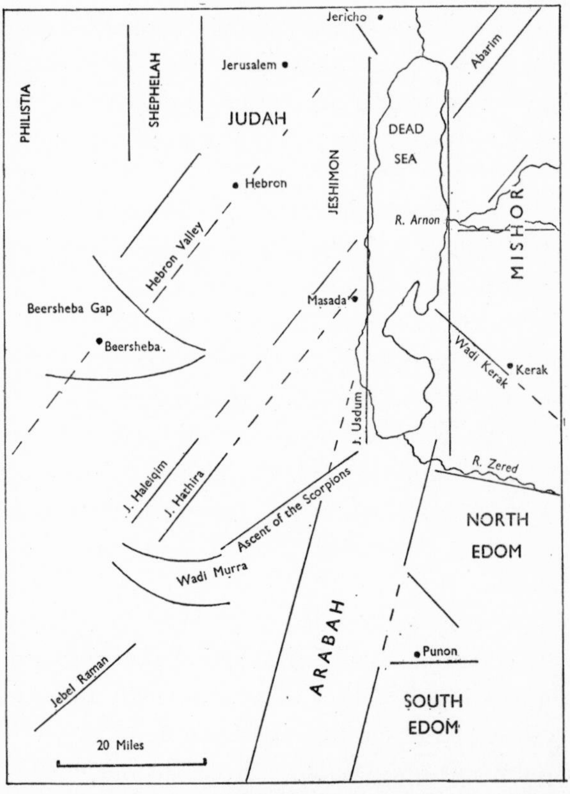

Fig. 12. Structural Elements of the Dead Sea Area

On the north-west the Valley of Ajalon provides the easiest route up into the mountains from the coast, and the Achilles' Heel of the Judaean defences. It is paralleled by another, though less dangerous, valley leading up from north of Jericho, and between the two lay the principal zone of movement across the plateau, the territory of little Benjamin.

The fault at the north-eastern corner of the sea created the Plains of Moab (Fig. 11) at its foot, where the Israelites encamped before crossing the Jordan (Num. 33 : 49), and can be traced further inland in the rich plain of the Beqa'a in southern Gilead (Plate XXII). The south-eastern fault is that which is followed by the line of the Brook Zered (Plate XXIII), the frontier between Moab and Edom, which seems to have been followed by the Israelites on their route northwards from Punon (Num. 21 : 12; Deut. 2 : 13, 14—it is called the Brook of the Willows in Is. 15 : 7, and is probably also the Brook of the Arabah in Amos 6 : 14). Similar hinge-faults may be traced also in the valley of the Arnon and its tributary, the Wala, as well as in the Wadi Kerak, leading down to the Dead Sea from Kir Haroseth (2 Kings 3 : 25), as well as in the line of some of the wadis to the east of it.

West of the Dead Sea (Plate XIX) the countryside falls into four clearly recognizable regions: Philistia, the Shephelah, Judah, and Jeshimmon. Philistia is the broad, open rolling lowland which here forms the coast plain, admirable barley country, but already feeling the effect of the increasing drought and therefore less suited to the other Palestinian products. It was occupied by the Philistines in the thirteenth century B.C. and served as the headquarters of their abortive attempt to dominate the whole country, and particularly the great Trunk Road which passed through their territory, here following the coast through Ashdod, Ashkelon, and Gaza, three of the five major Philistine towns. The other two were Ekron and Gath, which guarded the landward frontier. On the northern edge of the region were Joppa on the coast and Gezer further inland.

East of the Philistine plain, but west of the mountains, is a broad outcrop of the less fertile Eocene limestone, which forms a low and rocky plateau, rising in the south to 1,500 feet above sea-level. Economically unattractive, it was yet strategically of the first importance, for it formed the buffer zone between Judah and the Philistines, and was endlessly disputed between them (Map IX). Together with the territory of

Benjamin, it was the southern battlefield, the northern being the Accho-Bethshan corridor and the passes across Mount Carmel.

Judah, which rises steeply to the east, is divided from the Shephelah by a narrow but vitally important moat of chalk, which has been easily eroded to form a little valley. The highlands here are mainly of Cenomanian limestone, but the southward position has meant a lack of rain, and agriculture is increasingly difficult. The western valleys are too precipitous and rocky for cultivation, and do not form satisfactory routes, the roads in fact tending to keep rather to the spurs between them. On the plateau top, however, the slopes are not quite so steep, and can with care be coaxed into growing excellent grapes, which form the staple of this region. From north to south along the flat top of the plateau an important road follows the water-parting between the westward valleys and those which lead down to the Dead Sea on the east, and all the major towns are on this road—Jerusalem, Bethlehem, and Hebron, the road then swinging south-west towards Beersheba, an outpost of Judah at the foot of the hill-country. All the other villages and towns lie to the west of the road, for almost immediately on the east is the forbidding wilderness of Jeshimmon.

This fourth region owes its existence to the unhappy combination of two facts, the decreasing rainfall which always marks the eastward-facing slopes, and the dry and thirsty chalk which soaks up what little rain there is, and here is exposed over a very wide extent. The result is a desolation which has to be seen to be believed, starting with incredible suddenness almost on the edge of the water-parting road, and extending to the shores of the Dead Sea. No people have ever lived in this region, save for those who clung to its very edges, where some sustenance could be found, or the nomadic shepherds, poverty stricken even beyond their kind. Almost impossible to police, and seamed with caves, it has ever been the haunt of dissidents and rebels, with the hand of the government against them and living only by plunder (1 Sam. 23 : 15 ff.; 25 : 2 ff.; 26 : 1 ff.; Luke 10 : 30). Yet, at least upon the fringes, it has played a more constructive part in Israelite life, for Amos came from the borders of Jeshimmon to speak the Word in Bethel (Amos 1 : 1; 7 : 14–15), and it is to the hands of the desert-dwelling Essenes that we owe the famous "Dead Sea Scrolls".

The Essenes, it is true, lived rather in the Dead Sea region, where a few springs break forth at the foot of the barren slopes, and here also was Engedi (Josh. 15 : 62; 1 Sam. 23 : 29; 24 : 1; 2 Chron. 20 : 2; Song 1 : 14; Ezek. 47 : 10). Only those who have toiled through the dusty wilderness on foot can know what Engedi means, with its little vineyards, its tiny but verdant fields, and its wonderful spring of cool fresh water beside the mocking saltiness of the sea. On the other side of the sea there is in the south-eastern corner a broader stretch of irrigated coast, but it belonged to Moab and therefore excited less amazement. It may be, however, that we should put somewhere in this south-eastern corner the notorious Cities of the Plain, whose destruction was so long remembered (Gen. 18 : 16–19 : 28; Deut. 29 : 23; 32 : 32; Is. 1 : 9; 3 : 9; 13 : 19; Jer. 23 : 14; 49 : 18; 50 : 40; Lam. 4 : 6; Ezek. 16 : 46 ff.; Hosea 11 : 8; Amos 4 : 11; Zeph. 2 : 9; Matt. 10 : 15; 11 : 23; Luke 10 : 12; 17 : 28 ff.; Rom. 9 : 29; 2 Pet. 2 : 6; Jude 7; Rev. 11 : 8). The situation would well suit the battle of the four kings against five (Gen. 14 : 1–12), and it is certainly conceivable that the shallow southern basin of the Dead Sea may once have been dry land and watered by the River Zered. It must be admitted, however, that not one iota of proof of the site of these cities has yet been discovered.

Beyond the Dead Sea eastward (Fig. 10) the land rises steeply in rocky, inaccessible slopes to the broad tableland of Moab, which extends on either side of the deep canyon of the Arnon, despite the Israelite claim that the northern section belonged to the tribe of Reuben (Num. 32 : 37–38; Deut. 3 : 12; Jud. 11 : 26). The tribe of Reuben soon disappeared from history, and in the thinking of the prophets Heshbon and the surrounding towns are always Moabite (Is. 15 : 4; 16 : 8; Jer. 48 : 2, 34, 45; 49 : 3). This district seems to have had the regional name of *Mishor*, or "the Tableland" (Fig. 17), and was famous for its magnificent flocks of sheep[10] (Jud. 5 : 15–16; 2 Kings 3 : 4). There are also two other regional names which deserve attention. The first is *Abarim* which is applied to the last traces of the Gilead hills, as they trail off south-westwards towards the north-eastern end of the Dead Sea above the Plains of Moab. This same defensive approach to the plateau was known in New Testament times as the district of Perea and was under the control of the Romans (Num. 27 : 12; 33 : 47–48; Deut. 32 : 49). The other is *the Pisgah* (Num. 21 : 20; 23 : 14; Deut. 3 : 27; 4 : 49; 34 : 1) whence Moses viewed the Promised Land. It seems to have something of the same significance as the modern Arabic *neqb* (pl. *nuqūb*), which means a high, precipitous slope marking the edge of the plateau. "The top of the Pisgah", therefore, would have the same meaning as the Arabic *Ras en-Neqb*, or the edge of the plateau. To try to find an exact site for "Mount Pisgah" is consequently unnecessary, for the sense is rather that Moses was taken to the edge of the plateau, from which at any point the whole panorama may be seen.

The Mishor slopes off gradually towards the east, through the flinty *Ardh es-Suwan* to the lower-lying Sirhan depression. This is really outside biblical Palestine, but it is not without importance. Not a wadi in the normal sense of the word, but rather a shallow depression, it lies at the foot of the great outflow of basalt which stretches south-eastwards from the Jebel Druze. This is quite impassable, but along the Sirhan depression at its foot there are springs, and so an important desert route followed this line north-westwards towards Damascus.

E. THE NEGEB-EDOMITE ZONE

The last of the five major divisions of the Levant Coast which we have been considering is the most southerly one, and here the north-east–south-west structural trend is very strongly marked, even the great Rift Valley being twisted away from its north–south direction more towards the south-west (Fig. 12). The NE–SW line is most clearly evident in the Negeb of Palestine, between the Mediterranean and the Rift Valley, and here it dominates the structure. The backbone of this section of the country is formed by an unwarped region running north-eastwards from Jebel Khurashe (modern Israeli Har Horsha) on the Egyptian frontier about half-way between the Mediterranean and the Red Sea. It is not a simple structure, and is formed rather of a series of parallel ridges, several of which have been broken open to form the great cliff-enclosed "cauldrons" which characterize this part of the country.

This central backbone reaches its highest point in the extreme south-west, where Jebel Khurashe attains a height of 3,290 feet, and where the largest of the "cauldrons" is to be found, the gigantic Wadi Raman (Maktesh Ramon), which is crossed by the new road from Beersheba to Elath. Further north, however, the height declines and the ridges surpass 2,000 feet only occasionally, Jebel Hathira (Harei Hatira, 2,355 feet) being the highest, but the steepness of the slopes on the south-eastern flank, and the presence of the "cauldrons", make them far from easy to cross. The backbone finally runs out into the Dead Sea at Masada, where the Jews made their last stand against the Romans in A.D. 70. The line of it, however, may be traced in its continuation directly across the Dead Sea to the north-east, in the line of Abarim.

This backbone of higher land divides the Negeb into three unequal parts (Fig. 13): (a) The coastal lowlands, ending on the south-east at a line drawn through Beersheba, Khalasa and Nessana (=Arabic Auja el-Hafir, Hebrew Nitsana). The southern part of this section is covered with dune sand, and so only the northern triangle west of Beersheba is usable. This is the part of the Negeb which at present is being developed by the State of Israel. (b) A strip of gently rising land between the Beersheba–Khalasa–Nessana line and the crest of the backbone, some twelve miles in width. (c) The largest section lying south-east of the backbone. This is a wild and desolate region, with the characteristic *buttes* and *mesas*

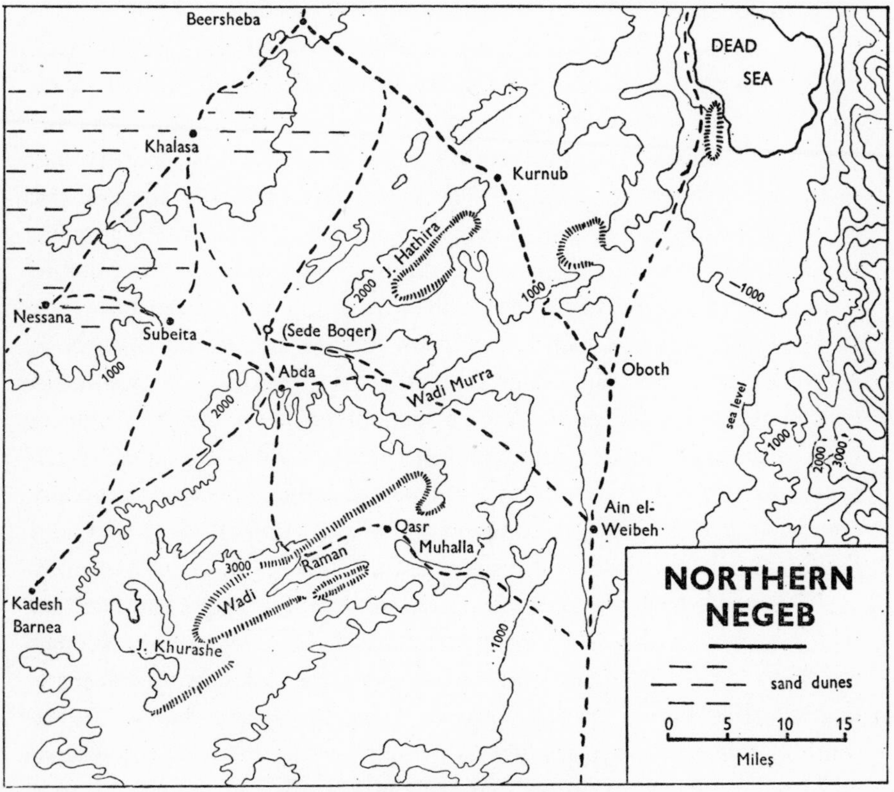

Fig. 13. The Northern Negeb

of a dissected desert landscape, and, when the Rift Valley is reached, sharply plunging strata emphasizing the steepness of the ascent.

Finally to be noticed is the huge sickle-like depression curving round south-westwards from the corner of the Dead Sea, and apparently part of a huge hinge-fault system, which cleaves its way right across the summit of the backbone. This is the Wadi Murra (Biqa'at Tsin), at whose head stands today the *kibbutz* of Sede Boqer.

Thanks to the prolonged researches of Nelson Glueck[11] we are learning much more about the use and occupation of the Negeb during the biblical period than we knew a few years ago, and as a result of the new Israeli roads famous Byzantine ruins, such as 'Sbeita and Abda, which until recently were "ghost towns" in the desert, have now almost a suburban character.

This change in fortune reflects the history of this region which has from time to time been brought under settlement and control, only to be submerged again by the relentless tide of the desert. Thus, Nelson Glueck has distinguished four periods of occupation: *c.* 3500–2900 B.C., the "Abrahamic" period of the twenty-first to nineteenth centuries B.C., the "Judaean" period from the tenth to sixth centuries B.C., and the Nabataean-Roman-Byzantine period from about the first century B.C. to the seventh century A.D. At such times, and especially the last, the Negeb was occupied by settled peoples and under the control of a strong government from one of the neighbouring kingdoms, sometimes that of Jerusalem when the House of David was strong enough to grasp the Red Sea port at Ezion Geber, but in the interval passing (at any rate in its south-eastern section) under the authority of Edom, ever jealous to control the trade routes and the copper mines of the Arabah. During these periods, it must be remembered, the south-eastern section, which everywhere has less than four inches of rainfall annually, was not generally cultivated, and the scattered settlements along the trade routes performed the function of fortresses and caravanserais.

These trade routes were three in number: the most important was that which led down the Wadi Murra and over a shoulder of the Raman upfold to 'Ain el-Weibeh ('Ain Yahav). This, the easiest of the routes, is that which is known to the Bedouin today as *Darb es-Sultan*. To the south of this was a road leading over the towering brow of the Raman cauldron and out through its exit at Qasr Mahalla (Metsad Mohila). It was particularly important in Roman times, and is followed in part by the modern road to Elath. The third road is that which led past Kurnub and down the steep "Ascent of the Scorpions" to the good spring at Oboth (Num. 34 : 4; Josh. 15 : 3; Oboth: Num. 21 : 10; 33 : 43). The most intensely cultivated section was naturally the small coastal triangle west of Beersheba, where the rainfall averages around eight inches, though it is highly precarious. The western slopes of the "backbone" were also cultivated, however, during the periods of settlement, and particularly by the Nabataeans.

The southern section of the Rift Valley is normally known as the Arabah, and it is, to the surprise of many people, almost as long as the section of the valley between the south end of the Dead Sea and the Lake of Galilee. A north-east–south-west upfold running across it raises the central part of the Arabah to 1,000 feet above sea-level, and then it sinks southwards again towards the Red Sea. Everywhere it is desert, save where occasional springs provide a welcome supply of water. However, historically it has had a double importance: as a trade route to the Red Sea and as a source of copper. This is found in the dark-red Nubian sandstone which outcrops particularly on the eastern, or Edomite, side of the rift. The most important of these copper mines was at Punon (the modern Feinan), almost certainly the place where Moses raised the serpent in the wilderness (Num. 21 : 4–10; 33 : 42–43). On the western side the copper-bearing rock outcrops only in the extreme south, and is being mined today at Timna, where also it was obtained in ancient times. This is the place known to the modern tourist as "King Solomon's Mines" (Deut. 8 : 9).

Across the Arabah is Edom, perched 5,000 feet above sea-level on the most uplifted part of the plateau edge, south of the Valley of the Zered. Here the great height of the plateau has resulted in a fairly plentiful supply of rain, which attains a yearly average of as much as twenty inches in places, though it is very restricted in extent and dies away rapidly as soon as the plateau edge is passed. The winters are bitterly cold, and the "King's Highway" (Num. 20 : 17) is often blocked by snow, though the summers are wonderfully cool and refreshing. There is but a single line of towns and villages along this road, the most important in the northern part of Edom being Bozrah (Jer. 49 : 13, 22; Gen. 36 : 33; Is. 34 : 6; 63 : 1; Amos 1 : 12), and the most important in the south being the

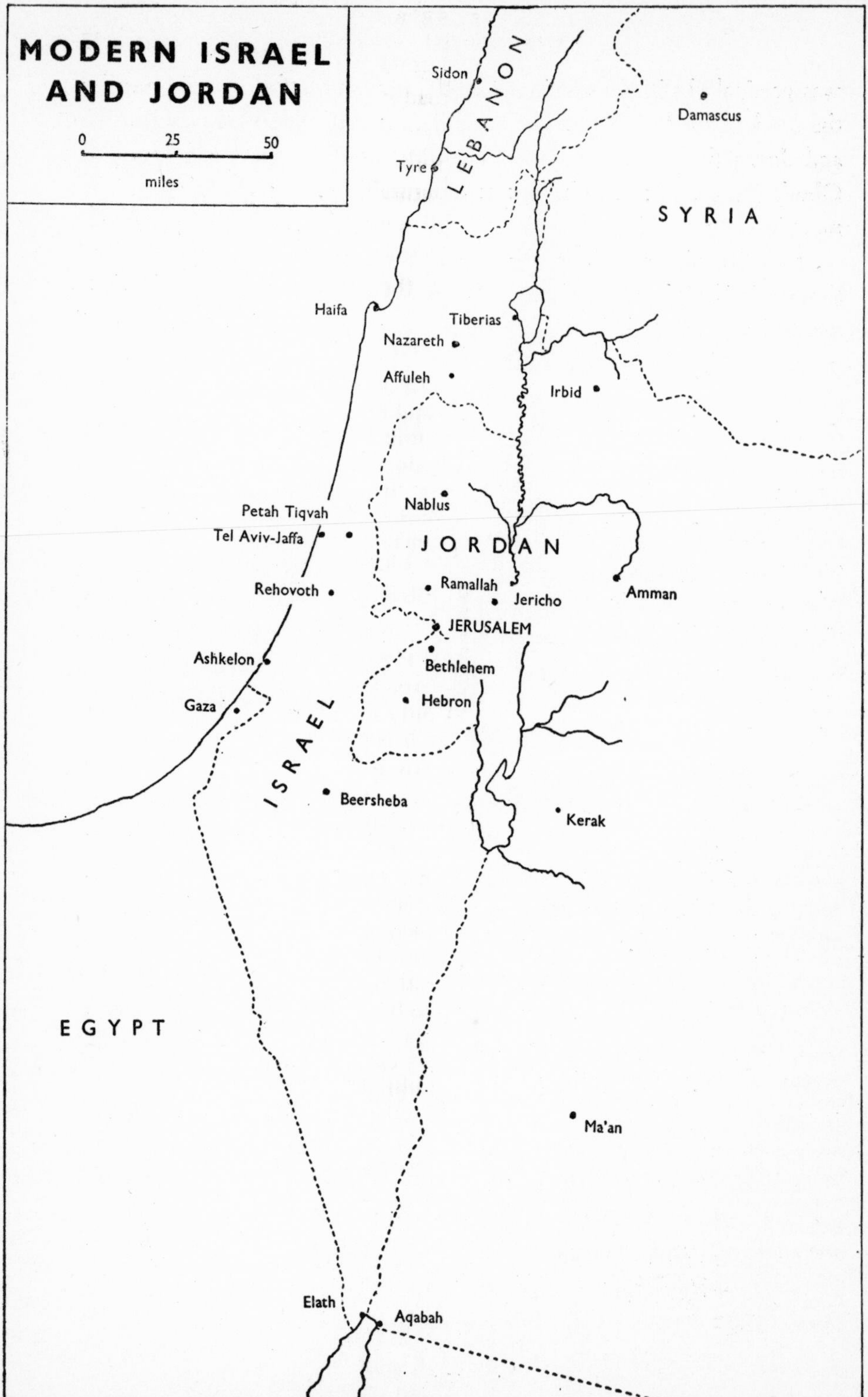
MODERN ISRAEL
AND JORDAN
0
25
50
miles
Sidon
LEBANON
Damascus
Tyre
SYRIA
Haifa
Tiberias
Nazareth
Affuleh
Irbid
Nablus
Petah Tiqvah
Tel Aviv-Jaffa
JORDAN
Rehovoth
Ramallah
Jericho
Amman
JERUSALEM
Ashkelon
Bethlehem
Gaza
Hebron
ISRAEL
Beersheba
Kerak
EGYPT
Ma'an
Elath
Aqabah

"strong city" of Sela, later the site of the great Nabataean trading city of Petra (Plate XII), carved out of the red sandstone (2 Kings 14 : 7; Ps. 108 : 10; Is. 16 : 1). Not far from Petra was Teman, the reputed home of Eliphaz (Job 2 : 11; see also Gen. 36 : 11, 34; Jer. 49 : 7, 20; Ezek. 25 : 13; Amos 1 : 12; Obad. 9; Hab. 3 : 3).

Edom comes to an end abruptly in the south, where a great fault cuts back from north-west to south-east, and marks the sudden termination of the Trans-jordanian plateau. Beyond is the fantastic Hasma, a sand-covered plain broken by towering crags of rock. On the west of it, and forming the edge of the southern part of the Arabah, is a huge wedge of granite, the so-called "Mountains of Midian", standing in places nearly 5,000 feet above sea-level. Across the Hasma, and round the south of the granite block by way of the Wadi Ytem, lay one of the Edomite routes to the Red Sea at Eloth.

Fig. 14. Modern Israel and Jordan

The most interesting thing to notice about this map is the extraordinary correspondence of the armistice line between Israel and Jordan with the ancient frontiers. Since the line represents the positions of the two armies at the end of the fighting, it demonstrates effectively the importance of the strategic geography discussed on page 78 following. The Jordanian territory west of the Rift Valley includes the hill country of Judah, Benjamin, Ephraim, and Manasseh before its expansion. Beersheba, which was a Judaean outpost, is outside the area, but the Jordanian salient down the Valley of Ajalon south-west of Ramallah should be noticed. Israel includes the Negeb, the Philistine territory (except Gaza, which, as so often in the past, has fallen to the Egyptians), the Shephelah, Sharon, the Carmel passes, the Accho-Bethshan corridor, and Galilee. The Valley of Jezreel is in Israeli hands, but the Mountains of Gilboa which overlook it on the south are, characteristically, in the possession of those who control the hill country. The effectiveness of the Judaean moat as a protection for the hills round Hebron is also well brought out. In other words, the west bank area of Jordan comprises, with singular exactness, the core of the ancient Israelite territory, to which they were confined in periods of weakness, e.g. during the latter part of Saul's reign. The only anomaly is the Israeli penetration up the Valley of Sorek to Jerusalem, of which they control the western section. This is a historical accident resulting from the fact that they were already established there before the fighting broke out. However, they were able to hold on to this corridor only with the greatest difficulty.

3

THE WHEAT AND THE BARLEY, THE OIL AND THE WINE

Now therefore the wheat, and the barley, the oil, and the wine, which my lord hath spoken of, let him send unto his servants.
(2 Chron. 2 : 15)

THE LAND of Palestine proper has been so frequently described by biblical scholars, learned travellers, and casual visitors that it is difficult now to find words to convey its peculiar quality and its singular mystery. Its face has been made so familiar by the Sunday School and the classroom, and more recently by the monstrous productions of Hollywood,[12] that it is almost impossible to divest oneself of the superimposed images of childhood and adolescence and imagine the country as once it was. Yet this must be done, for the endless processes of change have altered for ever the Palestinian environment, and to attempt to place

---

Fig. 15. Primitive Vegetation Regions

This map should be compared with the two climatic maps (Map II and Fig. 7), as well as with the physical maps (Map I and Figs. 2 and 8). The chief thing to be noticed is the very much greater extent of the forest, which now has almost completely disappeared. This forest was the remainder of the extensive forests which grew in this region during the very much wetter "Pluvial Period" which corresponds with the Ice Age in Europe. With the decrease in rainfall after the Pluvial Period, however, the Levant was on the extreme edge of the natural forest zone, and once the forests were cut down they did not re-establish themselves naturally. Traces of the ancient forests persisted until very recently, as for instance in the carefully protected rare patches of cedar in Lebanon and the oak forests of Gilead which still exist today. The isolated patch of forest in Edom was finally destroyed by the Turks during World War I, when they needed fuel for the Hejaz Railway. The continuous destruction of the forests over a period of nearly five thousand years is now at last being reversed by the extensive afforestation practised since World War II by the modern governments.

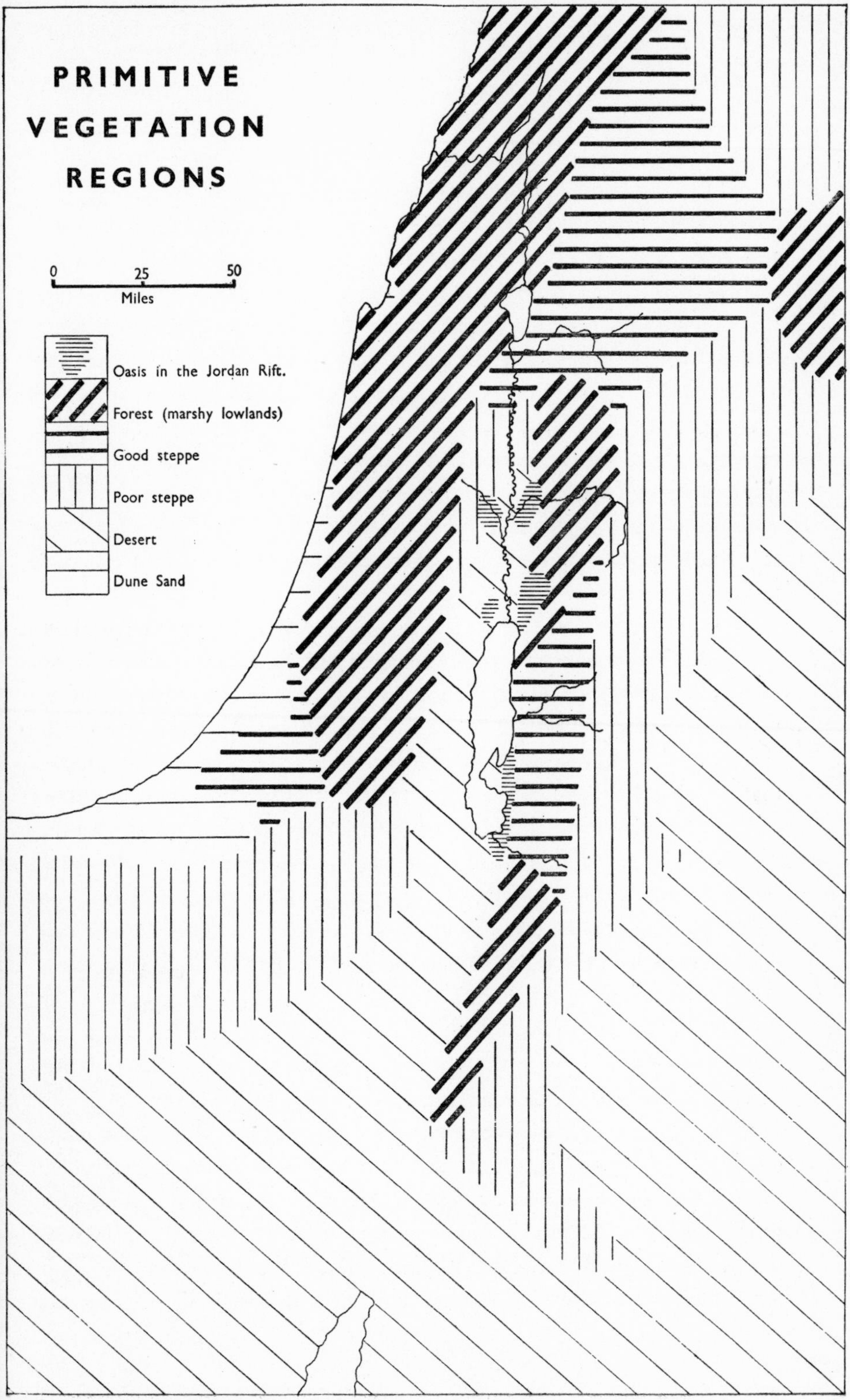
PRIMITIVE
VEGETATION
REGIONS
0
25
50
Miles
Oasis in the Jordan Rift.
Forest (marshy lowlands)
Good steppe
Poor steppe
Desert
Dune Sand

the biblical events in the setting of today, or even of the unwesternized Palestine of the Turks, is to court uncomprehension. One must strip the country of its orange groves, its hedges of prickly pear, its fields of tomatoes, and must clothe instead its hill country with forest (Fig. 15), clog much of its low-lying land with marsh, and wall up its little towns and villages, if one is to picture at all the Land of Canaan as the Israelites saw it when first they moved in from across the Jordan. Groves of olives, fields of wheat and barley, vineyards and fruit trees, were certainly there, then as now, but there was some difference in their distribution, for they had not at that early period begun to cover so much of the hills. Yet changes in the primitive landscape had already begun to take place. Herds of goats were engaged in the destructive consumption of everything they could see, and with the invention of the bronze axe-head some inroad had been made upon the woodland, the effects of it being apparently already noticeable in increased erosion as early as the third millennium B.C.[13]

To comprehend the effect of this new country upon the Israelites and upon their way of life, we are bound to ask what choices the environment placed before them as they moved slowly in, probably in several waves, and what restrictions it imposed. If we ask, for instance, to what extent it helped to determine where they were to live, we should discover that they had but little choice in the matter. The first chapter of the Book of Judges, with its revealing list of towns which the Israelites were at first unable to take,[14] makes it clear that the plains were closed to them (Fig. 16). Judah "took possession of the hill country, but he could not drive out the inhabitants of the plain" (Jud. 1 : 19), and the "Amorites pressed the Danites back into the hill country, for they did not allow them to come down to the plain" (Jud. 1 : 34).

Almost all the towns mentioned, it should be noticed, lie in the piedmont region between the still thickly forested uplands and the often marshy districts of the lower-lying plains, for here, where water is most easily available along the piedmont springline, and where movement is less hindered by the nature of the terrain, the greatest settlement had taken place. The only alternative, as Joshua is represented as making clear to the people of Manasseh and Ephraim (Josh. 17 : 18), was to wrestle with the only partly inhabited plateau. "The hill country shall be yours, for though it is a forest, you shall clear it and possess it to its farthest

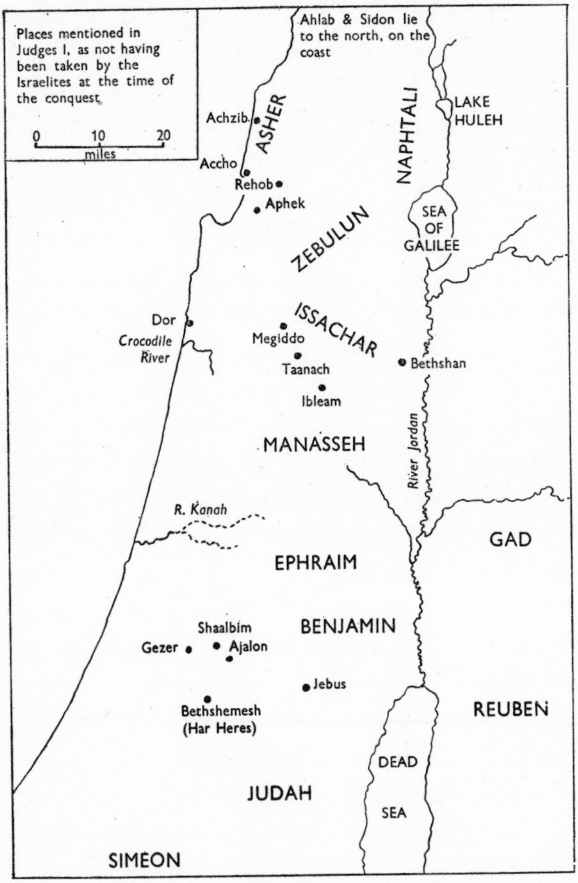

Fig. 16. Places Reported in Judges I as not having been taken by the Israelites

borders." The tribes that were able to do this were the tribes that most effectively survived.

As we imagine the Israelites settling down in the country, part of that endless process of transition from the nomadic, pastoral life to that of the settled farmer, whereby the wanderer first begins to cultivate, albeit shamefacedly, a little piece of land, returning to it yearly at seedtime and harvest, and then ceases to move his tent, and finally in the next generation builds a house for himself, we must ask still further what crops the land permitted him to grow. How far did it enable him, or even encourage him, to indulge in trade? What reflection of the environment is there in his literature, his thought-forms and his religion?

All these things are closely connected together, and we must understand the extent to which the total environment may colour the thinking of a people if we are to be on our guard against making what may be entirely false parallels between different cultures. We must not assume, for instance, that because we find in one area the apparent repetition of a cultic formula which we know elsewhere, therefore the significance of the formula is exactly the same in both places. Frankfort and Mowinckel are surely right to emphasize the very different concepts of the relationship of the king to the god, which resulted largely from the entirely different character of the Nile and Mesopotamian floods.[15] We know ourselves from our own experience that American and English people do not necessarily mean the same thing when they use the same words, and this was just as true of the two great riverine cultures of the ancient Middle East. It should warn us also against making a straightforward equation of the cultic formulae of the Ras Shamra tablets and similar expressions in Hebrew literature.

It is necessary for the student to know the environment intimately and personally, and in particular to be on his guard against transferring his own prejudices and reactions into the past. We take our conveniences of transport and housing so much for granted that we can hardly even imagine the problems which faced the ancient Israelites, or make the effort of getting inside their situation and looking outwards. Properly to understand biblical geography a man must walk over the country, and not only must he walk, but he must walk at all seasons, in all weathers and for days on end. He must never be content with a hurried visit to Petra in the spring, nor with a brief trip into the desert to see the Umayyad castles. He needs to stay in the desert, to pass his nights with the Bedouin and to look at Canaan with the eyes of Midian.

One could wish, certainly, that there were some easier discipline than this, some sort of "geography without tears", whereby the experience could be acquired without having to say, "By day the heat consumed me, and the cold by night" (Gen. 31 : 40), but this is not so. It is not until a man has toiled across it that he can grasp the character of Jeshimmon, which otherwise he will have driven through in less than an hour on his way to Jericho, "and take note of all the lurking places . . . and come back . . . with sure information" (1 Sam. 23 : 23). Nor will he understand why the Israelites found Tabor so impressive, though it is lower than the neighbouring hills, and why they were so much in awe of Carmel and Sharon. "As I live, says the King, whose name is the Lord of hosts, like Tabor among the mountains, and like Carmel by the sea, shall one come. Prepare yourselves baggage for exile" (Jer. 46 : 18 ff.); and the Psalmist does not shrink from classing Tabor with the majesty of Hermon, difficult though such a parallel would be for us today (Ps. 89 : 12). Only thus will he comprehend why Josephus thought that Jericho had the most wonderful climate in all the world,[16] or the exhausting effect of the sirocco, "a hot wind from the bare heights in the desert toward the daughter of my people, not to winnow or cleanse" (Jer. 4 : 11).

Yet, this is only one aspect of geographical thought and a fairly obvious one, after all. It is necessary also to ask what relationship the facts have to each other, and especially what relationship in space. This is the geographical question *par excellence* and it is, moreover, a three-dimensional question. Here it is important to know the exact height, and an impressionistic representation of relief will not do. It is significant, for example, that the rim of the eastern plateau is everywhere higher than its counterpart west of the Jordan, and Edom very much higher, towering more than 5,000 feet above sea-level, while opposite it the Negeb Uplands are no more than hills. The rainfall régime, upon which the whole life of the people depends, is governed by this fact.

The slightest variation in relief is important here, for Palestine stands at the very edge of the Mediterranean rainfall belt, and on the doorstep of the desert. Even a purely minor increase in height may be enough to trigger the much-needed rain (Plate XXII), while the shallowest of depressions may mean that the clouds pass over unaltered, like "a man who boasts of a gift he does not give" (Prov. 25 : 14). Thus, it always rains at Bethel before it rains in Jerusalem, only ten miles away as the crow flies but some 300 feet below it, and this fact was of no small significance in the rivalry between the two shrines, and a strong argument for those who said to the northern tribes, "You have gone up to Jerusalem long enough. Behold your gods, O Israel, who brought you up out of the land of Egypt" (1 Kings 12 : 28). It was not fitting for an upstart shepherd from the dusty wilderness, a mere dresser of the despised sycamore trees, to prophesy at Bethel, "for it is the king's sanctuary, and it is a temple of the kingdom" (Amos 7 : 13), justified moreover by its yearly effectiveness in the provision of more prompt and plentiful rain.

No frustrated farmer, waiting with empty cistern and unploughed fields for the storms without which he could not begin, could watch unmoved his more fortunate neighbours in the next village already sowing their grain, nor could he listen without bitterness to their taunts. It is surely not by accident that Amos, coming from the dry south to preach at Bethel, hammers relentlessly upon the precariousness of the rainfall even in well-watered Ephraim, and insists that Yahweh alone is responsible for famine or for plenty (Amos 4 : 6–8).

Even in Jerusalem itself the western half of the city is wetter than the eastern half, so close is the desert to the walls and so rapid the passage to the almost waterless Jeshimmon, and frequent are those days when one can see the rain of Jerusalem stop at the Mount of Olives only a couple of miles away. The orchards of Gethsemane may receive nourishment, while in Bethany "since there is no rain on the land, the farmers are ashamed, they cover their heads" (Jer. 14 : 4). The eastern slope of some little hill is always drier than the western slope, and the southern because of the greater evaporation drier than the northern. Whether on the forested heights of Carmel and Galilee or the barren slopes of the Wilderness of Judaea, this rule is absolute, and the vegetation and the farming are governed accordingly. Upon such small differences, which often one notices only on foot, the quality of the harvest depends.

But it is not enough to know merely the difference in height. One must know also how one place is related to another. This is the real difficulty of making a satisfactory map of Palestine, for it must, as far as possible, take account of the three essential aspects of the relief, which cannot easily be shown on one sheet of paper: the exact height above or below sea-level, the character of the slopes (i.e. steep, rocky, smooth, etc.), and the fact that a portion of the country is quite abnormal in being more than a thousand feet below sea-level (see Fig. 8). This is where the question of relationships in space becomes important, for the same area which in one relationship must be described as a low-lying plain, must in another be called an uplifted plateau. Thus, the upwarped region of the Negeb is, in relation to the coastal plain, a mere upland, with gentle and easy slopes, but relative to the depression of the Arabah it is mountainous, and the slopes are precipitous and rocky. Thus also in Syria, far to the north, Jebel Buweida would appear on most maps to be a mountain, for it is over three thousand feet above the level of the sea, but in relation to the already elevated plateau it has no more than the character of a hill.

This is clearly an important fact, but by itself it could be misleading, for it would suggest that the Negeb is more likely to be the domain of the dwellers on the coast, and Jebel Buweida no more serious than a minor obstacle, whereas again and again in history the Negeb has been under the authority of the inhabitants of distant Edom, and the hills which divide the Syrian desert have proved a singular barrier. To understand why this should be so, one must proceed further to a concept which is among the most suggestive of all geographic ideas, that of a "natural region".[17]

This is a technical term in geography, and it is approached by examining first other types of regions. Thus it is possible, and indeed necessary, to divide the whole area which is being studied according to a variety of criteria. One constructs maps of physical regions, geological regions, rainfall regions, temperature regions, soil regions, vegetation regions, crop regions, etc., etc. These must be closely compared with each other to see what measure of correspondence there is between them. There is, for instance, likely to be in Palestine a high degree of correlation between a particular type of limestone region, high plateaus, heavy rainfall, and thick woodland. One can begin, in fact, to recognize a similarity in the manner of life among people living in different regions of a similar type.

It becomes possible, then, to construct maps of what we call "natural regions", that is to say regions where one can recognize a *unity of life resulting from a unity of experience*. From this one can proceed to a study of the different natural regions, and try to distinguish the dominant factors. Now, this may sound very straightforward, and perhaps even very obvious. However, it is not quite as obvious as it sounds, for it was recognized very early by one of the fathers of modern geography, P. Vidal de la Blache,[18] that what geographers were laboriously trying to build up was often something which the ordinary peasants knew quite well, though naturally they could not explain it, and that the local district names often had an exact geographical significance, and persisted obstinately in use despite every administrative change and the drawing of new boundaries. He recognized this first in the Paris basin of France, which is divided by the local farmers into smaller regions such as Brie, Beauce, Champagne, Sologne, Gatinais, Oche, etc., so that they can always say exactly in which region a particular village stands. That they are able to do so is because they are forced to recognize the often minor differences in farming methods and results which spring from the difference in the environment. As a result of the study which he made such regions are called today by their French name, *pays*.

Further, and this is of considerable importance, the peasants tend to remain very much within their own *pays*, not moving out of it even to one that is apparently similar, so that the people of one *pays* often say that the people of another have a recognizably different character. There is, for example, a saying current in the Paris basin to the effect, "*Quatre-vingt dix-neuf moutons et un Champenois font cent bêtes*" (ninety-nine sheep and a man from Champagne make a hundred beasts).

The same phenomenon is known to occur elsewhere. One may think, for instance, of the *Veluwe*, or poor heathland, which in Holland is contrasted with the good land or *Betuwe*, of the *Polders* of Belgium, of the *Fens*, the *Weald*, the *Cotswolds* and the *Downs* in England, to name only a few, and it certainly seems possible to distinguish similar regions in ancient Palestine. Even the most cursory reading of the Old Testament makes clear that the writers knew of such different regions as the Arabah, the Shephelah, the Negeb, Carmel, Galilee, Jeshimmon, Abarim, and so on, and these are usually interpreted as having a largely physical significance (Fig. 17). However, there is occasional evidence that this is insufficient. The curious mention in Josh. 11 : 16 of "all the Negeb, and all the land of Goshen, and the Shephelah, and the Arabah, and the hill country of Israel and its Shephelah" certainly suggests that the writer recognized the similarity of the Eocene limestone landscape in the central Carmel region behind Megiddo and Jokneam and that of the true Shephelah near Judah. The mention of a district of Goshen in Palestine here and in Josh. 10 : 41 has baffled all commentators, and it must be admitted that we do not know where to place it.

Similarly, the dominant aspect of Sharon was not so much that it was lowland, but that it was clothed with almost impenetrable forest, and so it was classed with Lebanon and Carmel rather than with Jezreel or Dothan.[19]

There are many other regional names as well, such as Gilead, Bashan, and Argob, occurring in the Old Testament, and possibly also Pisgah and Mishor, but it will be noticed that all of them have a character which

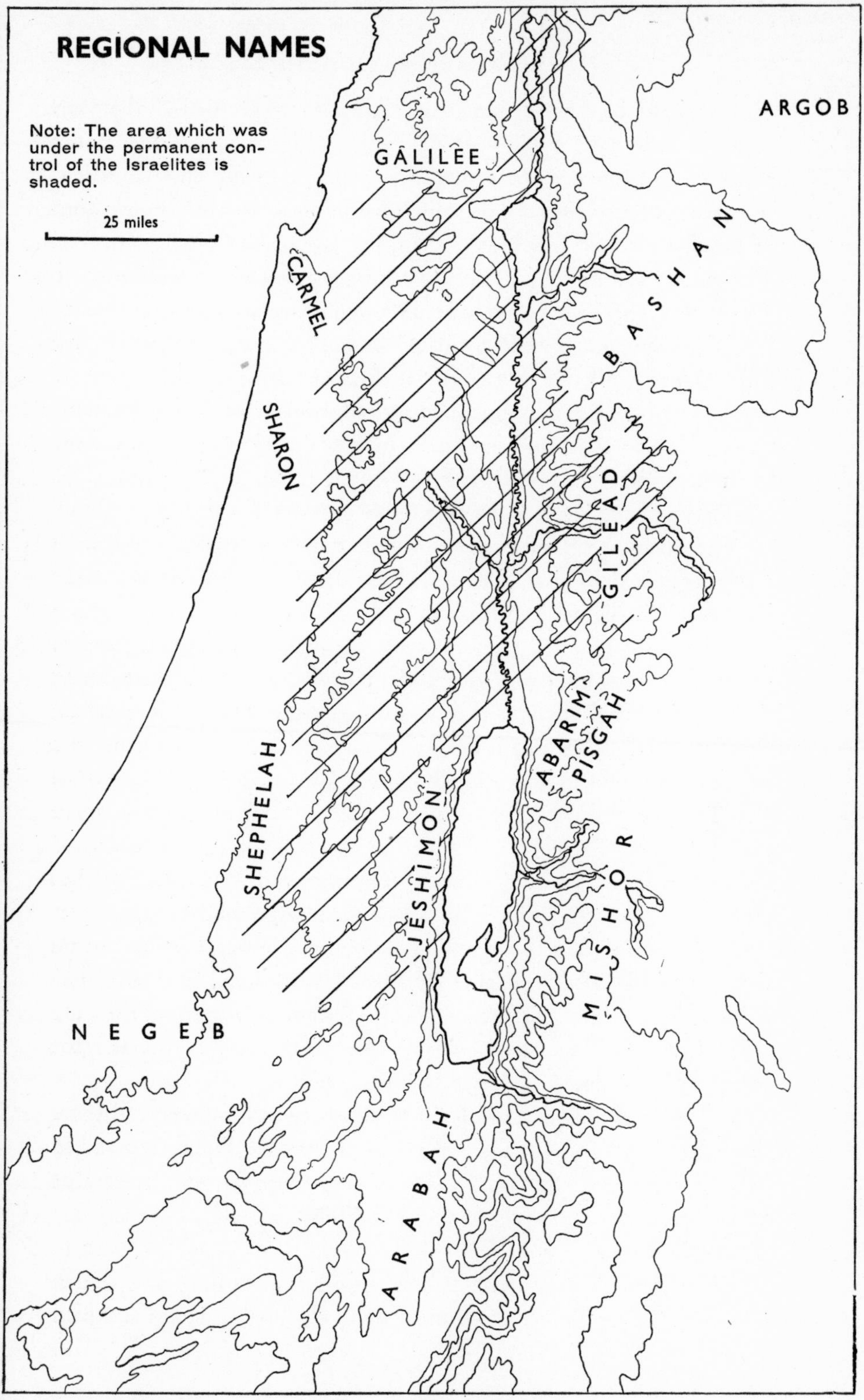
REGIONAL NAMES
Note: The area which was under the permanent control of the Israelites is shaded.
25 miles
ARGOB
GALILEE
CARMEL
BASHAN
SHARON
GILEAD
ABARIM
PISGAH
SHEPHELAH
JESHIMON
MISHOR
NEGEB
ARABAH

Fig. 17. Regional Names

may, perhaps, be described as "exotic". That is to say that all the districts which seem to have special regional names are districts outside the normal experience of Israelite life, sometimes because they are uninhabited, such as Jeshimmon and Sharon, or sometimes because they are on the borders of Israelite territory, such as Bashan, the Shephelah, Pisgah, and Argob. The name "Galilee" seems almost certainly not to have had in the Old Testament period such a wide connotation as we are accustomed to give it in the New, and should probably be kept for what we would today call "Upper Galilee" lying north of the great fault scarp between Acre and Lake Huleh.[20] It is noteworthy, for example, that no special regional name seems to have been applied to the plain which we call today the Plain of Esdraelon, and which is known in modern Israel simply as Ha-Emeq, or the Plain, and to the Arabs as Merj Ibn-'Amr.

The question therefore arises whether such natural regions were in fact recognized within the more populated districts of the Israelite heritage. It is highly improbable, in view of the very large number of clearly defined regional names outside the main Israelite areas, that such *pays* did not exist internally also, and it is probable that we must recognize them in the tribal districts, and regard the twelve tribal names as having equally a regional as much as a tribal character (Fig. 18). If this should be true, it would help to throw light upon certain vexed questions of Old Testament interpretation, such as the problem of whether the coast plain north of Carmel was known as the land of Asher even as long before the Exodus as the reign of Thutmose III in the early fifteenth century B.C., and the difficult matter of the tribal boundaries.

Before examining this question, however, it is necessary to recognize that the whole of the Israelite expansion was limited, not so much by political or strategic considerations, as by the effective limits of the Israelite way of life. Here we must rid ourselves of the very prevalent misconception that the most effective barrier to permanent expansion is likely to be a physical one, and must distinguish between military and strategic obstacles on the one hand, and those geographical phenomena which held in check the further expansion and colonization of an already settled agricultural people on the other. The two are by no manner of means the same.

The system of using river valleys, or crests of hills, or steep scarps as boundaries is a military or political method, for politicians and soldiers

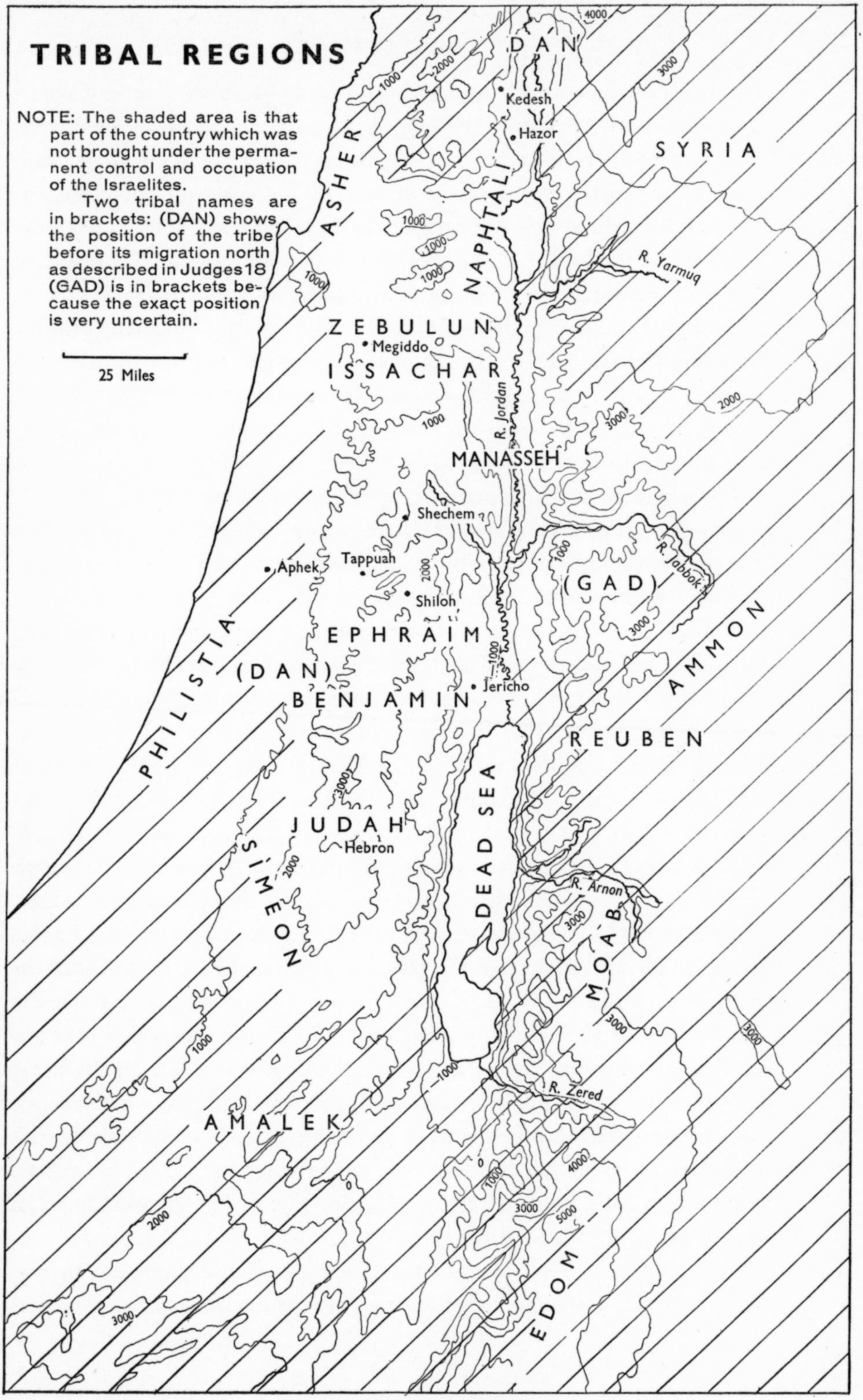

TRIBAL REGIONS
NOTE: The shaded area is that part of the country which was not brought under the permanent control and occupation of the Israelites.
Two tribal names are in brackets: (DAN) shows the position of the tribe before its migration north as described in Judges 18 (GAD) is in brackets because the exact position is very uncertain.
25 Miles
DAN
Kedesh
Hazor
SYRIA
ASHER
NAPHTALI
R. Yarmuq
ZEBULUN
Megiddo
ISSACHAR
R. Jordan
MANASSEH
Shechem
Aphek
Tappuah
Shiloh
R. Jabbok
(GAD)
EPHRAIM
AMMON
(DAN)
BENJAMIN
Jericho
PHILISTIA
REUBEN
DEAD SEA
JUDAH
Hebron
SIMEON
R. Arnon
MOAB
R. Zered
AMALEK
EDOM

Fig 18. Tribal Regions

have always had an unhealthy passion for clear-cut lines. Clear-cut lines, however, do not exist in nature, and it is this fact which makes political frontiers essentially unstable and the attempt to insist upon their permanence one of the major causes of war.[21] One is bound, therefore, to question the normal explanation that the Israelites owed their control of Gilead across the Jordan to the greater ease of communication across this section of the Jordan, for ease of communication seems to have played surprisingly little part in determining the question of permanent control. We have, for example, to recognize that the huge river canyons which cut back into the eastern plateau were often very ineffective barriers to movement, and that except for the Valley of the Zered between Moab and Edom, the frontiers lay along them only for brief periods.

Elsewhere what are, apparently, quite minor physical obstacles seem to have proved almost impassable barriers to expansion. So it is with the Hamath steppe north of Jebel Buweida. Characteristic of this region today are the curious "beehive villages" (Plate IX), which come, however, to an abrupt end both on the east with the very small descent from the plateau to the Euphrates, and on the south with the relatively insignificant hills of Jebel Bishri and Jebel Buweida. It is clear that the riverine way of life of the Euphrates valley is not that of the plateau, nor is the life of the Palmyra steppe that of the plateau of Hamath, similar though the two may appear to be to the uninstructed visitor. The physical problem is, in fact, secondary. The real obstacle is sociological and may be defined as the difference between the two ways of life. So Bashan extends across the Yarmuq to include the similar country to the south, and Gilead includes all the hill country on both sides of the deep gash of the Jabbok. To the south of this again is the pastoral plateau of Mishor, the ancient territory of Moab.

Throughout the eastern plateau only one region, Gilead, was at all suited to the Israelite system of farming, which was based on the production of the three staples, wheat and olives and grapes, which are so constantly mentioned together as to indicate their close connection in the Israelite mind (Gen. 27 : 28, 37; Deut. 7 : 13; 11 : 14; 12 : 17; 14 : 23; 18 : 4; 28 : 51; 33 : 28; 2 Kings 18 : 32; 2 Chron. 31 : 5; 32 : 28; Neh. 5 : 11; 10 : 39; 13 : 5, 12; Ps. 4 : 7; 104 : 15; Is. 36 : 17; Lam. 2 : 12; Hosea 2 : 5, 8, 22; Joel 1 : 10; 2 : 17–19; Hag. 1 : 11). These are all, unfortunately, somewhat particular plants, though none so much as the olive which will not ripen anywhere except in a pure Mediterranean climate, which here reaches its farthest extension to the south-east. Especially is it susceptible to any severe or prolonged frost and so the greater part of the high eastern plateau is closed to it, only the westward-facing slopes of the Gilead dome being sufficiently protected from the bitter east winds of winter to make large-scale olive production possible. Wheat is sensitive to a lack of moisture, and so in the hotter and drier areas it must be replaced by barley, which is extensively grown in the Philistine plain. Vines, it is true, are exceedingly hardy and will grow over a very wide climatic area. However, the quality of the grapes they produce is very variable, and even the slightest difference of soil or slope will affect them. In Palestine they are essentially a product of the hills, and the grapes of Gilead have long been famous for their outstanding excellence.

We must therefore imagine the Israelites confined to the hilly regions where this threefold system of agriculture was possible, and never effectively extending beyond it. Of course, from time to time they tried to expand further, but such extensions of power were political and strategic, and destined to be merely temporary, for the Israelites never colonized any region which they could not cultivate in the manner which they knew. This explains why the Negeb, both in the Old Testament and the New, was often the preserve of the people living on the Edomite plateau, though the people of Judah were so much closer and occasionally dominated it militarily. The physical barriers to Edomite expansion, though certainly very severe, were however less formidable than the invisible sociological obstacles to colonization from Judaea.

The same phenomenon explains the divisive rôle of the Shephelah, which is a very clear example of a true *pays*, though its character has often been misunderstood. It is rocky and infertile, and the celebrated sycamore trees of 1 Kings 10 : 27 must not be allowed to mislead us, for the word is assuredly as scornful as the "stones" of the previous clause.[22] The trees may well have been wild, but if they were cultivated it was because the more attractive products do not grow well here. The Shephelah is not suited either to the Israelite trio of wheat, vines, and olives, or to the broad open barley fields of the Philistine plain. Consequently, though both sides often overran it, neither side ever really made it their own.

The Israelite gods, according to the Syrians, were gods of the hills

(1 Kings 20 : 23), and for the Israelites to descend from the hills meant to encounter an alien culture in a foreign land. A small down-faulted plain among the mountains they could encompass, because it could be made part of their agricultural system, and of these the largest which they can be said ever to have fully incorporated is the triangular plain of Esdraelon. They do not seem to have controlled effectively any plain which was limited on even so much as one side by some feature other than mountains. One of the interesting problems of Israelite history, for instance, is the rôle in the Old Testament of the Lake of Galilee, which is mentioned only as a boundary (Num. 34 : 11; Deut. 3 : 17; Josh. 11 : 2; 12 : 3; 13 : 27. The town of Chinnereth in Josh. 19 : 35 is Tell el-'Oreimeh, and occurs merely in a list, and the Plain of Gennesaret, so famous in the New Testament, appears as the district of Chinnereth, one of the regions which fell to the invasion of Ben-hadad—1 Kings 15 : 20). The great Trunk Road, over whose control they were engaged in almost constant warfare, runs in one place close to the shore, and yet the Lake does not seem to come into their thinking. Moreover, none of the tribes who occupied level land, whether on the plain or on the plateau, managed to hold their own. Asher and Dan and Reuben were all dispossessed.

For the same reason it is necessary to ask whether we have not all accepted perhaps a little uncritically the classic explanation, as laid down by George Adam Smith,[23] for the Hebrew lack of interest in, and indeed horror of, the sea (see for instance Ps. 107 : 23; Is. 33 : 21; 57 : 20). The reason he gives is that the coast south of Mount Carmel is flat and sandy, and so it certainly is, but there *were* harbours and they *were* used. It would be more true to say that though the Israelites could see the sea from almost any point on the western edge of their hills, and sometimes from only a few miles away, they were shut off from it by this invisible barrier of a different way of life. Whenever they reached it, it was because of a temporary political explosion, and fairly soon they withdrew. They were not at home upon the sea because they were not at home on the coastal plain, and so from the known, familiar world of their cultivated hills, they gazed at the Mediterranean as the symbol of primeval chaos and the home of the dread Leviathan (Leviathan: Job 3 : 8; 41 : 1; Ps. 74 : 14; 104 : 26; Is. 27 : 1. For the sea as the symbol of chaos see e.g. Gen. 1 : 2; 7 : 11; 8 : 2; 49 : 25; Deut. 33 : 13; Job 38 : 16; Ps. 24 : 2; 42 : 7;

93 : 3–4; 104 : 6; Prov. 8 : 29; Is. 51 : 10; Ezek. 26 : 19; Amos 7 : 4; Hab. 3 : 8, 10).[24]

When we turn to the internal divisions of the Israelite territory we find the same ambiguity between the political strategic boundaries and the cultural or sociological divisions. Thus certain towns in Asher and Issachar are said to have been controlled by Manasseh (Josh. 17 : 11) and certain towns in Manasseh to have been in the hands of Ephraim (Josh. 16 : 9), which betokens a certain confusion over where the real frontiers lay.

Now it would appear that Judah, Benjamin, Ephraim, Manasseh in its original unexpanded form, as well as Naphtali, Asher, and possibly also Zebulun, are all of them authentic *pays*. This means that all the towns which are listed as being "in Ephraim" or "in Benjamin" appear to fall into a region which is geologically, morphologically, and agriculturally distinct from the surrounding regions. It is not suggested here, of course, that the tribes did not exist as tribes, but rather that each tribe absorbed territory to the limit of that type of agriculture to which it had become accustomed, and each had its own modification of the general bread-wine-oil pattern.

This may be seen as we examine Map V in which the distribution of the major crops is shown.[25] In Judah the dominant product is grapes; in Ephraim the great dome of Cenomanian limestone with its fertile *terra rossa* and the increased rainfall are the reason for the almost continuous olive orchards; in Manasseh the hills are less fertile, but the more frequent fault basins are floored with alluvium which lends itself to the cultivation of wheat. Benjamin is essentially transitional between the viticulture of Judah and the olive-yards of Ephraim, and in Philistia barley is predominant. Between these regions there was frequent movement, but very little permanent transference of population, and they remained resentful and suspicious of each other.

However, political necessity often demanded further expansion in order to give what was felt to be the necessary strategic security. Thus, Ephraim acquired a very strong frontier against Manasseh, and for this purpose included inside her territory an enclave of chalk which was essentially non-Ephraimite, but very typical of Manasseh. The very careful delineation of the boundary in the neighbourhood of Tappuah seems to make this clear (Josh. 16 : 5–8).

Manasseh, which was the least secure of all the great tribes, expanded steadily towards the north and west and east, though not on the south where Ephraim was expanding against her, in order to bring under her control all the approaches. She succeeded in doing so, but at the cost of including within her territory important areas of a non-Manassite type: part of the coast plain, or region of Asher, the region of Issachar in Esdraelon, and at any rate the western slopes of the region of Gad or Gilead. This last is a distinct *pays* of its own with very few similarities to the Manasseh type of landscape, but far more likeness to Ephraim. It may be that we have here the explanation of the battle between David and Absalom, which was fought east of the Jordan in the "forest of Ephraim" (2 Sam. 18 : 6), meaning that it was a forest of an Ephraimite character.

This expansion involved Manasseh in a serious geo-political problem, for whenever expansion has proceeded so far that regions of a different type are included inside one political unit, the question arises where the line is to be drawn. The different regions are seldom assimilated to each other, and this leads to internal dissension and a consequent tendency to expand still further in order to provide greater security, with, however, the inevitable result of over-expansion and a constantly restless frontier. This was undoubtedly the great unsolved political problem of both the Assyrian and the Roman empires, and, in her own small way, it was equally the insoluble problem for Manasseh. The impatient military intervening to provide a strong ruler for a disunited and unbalanced state—how often have we seen this in the new countries of the post-war world, and how often did it happen both in Israel and in Rome![26]

If this thesis is sound, then it behoves us to reconsider the nature of the tribal boundaries as they are usually shown in biblical atlases, where the tendency is to accept the political and strategic line as authoritative and permanent, and in cases where the boundary is uncertain to draw it in the best strategic position. On the basis of the geographical evidence, this would seem a dangerous procedure. In particular must one view with suspicion a river frontier, for river frontiers almost never occur in nature, though politicians are especially partial to them, since, on paper at least, they seem to admit of so little argument. In actual fact rivers tend to unite rather than to divide, and so, when we are told that the frontier between Manasseh and Ephraim was the River Kanah until it reached the sea (Josh. 16 : 8), we should surely be cautious. It has all the sound of a political expedient, and if the formation of the Kingdom had not made such an expedient no longer necessary, it might well have proved just as temporary as the Arnon frontier was for Moab.

Similarly, in drawing the eastern boundary of Asher, it would probably be more correct to keep it at the foot of the Galilean hills instead of carrying it further inland, for none of the places mentioned in Joshua 19 : 24–26 seems to be more than about 300 feet above sea-level. The name itself apparently refers to that narrow coast plain, never more than five miles wide at the most, which extends from the Crocodile marshes at the end of Sharon northwards into Phoenicia. If this is the correct regional interpretation of the name, whatever the tribal significance may have been, it would explain why Dor was considered to be in Asher (Josh. 17 : 11), and why Asher is said in one place to extend northwards as far as great Sidon, which is surely political nonsense (Josh. 19 : 28). The whole narrow region is characterized by one very important feature, which differentiates it from all the really Israelite territory: communication here was much easier by sea than it was by land, and for this reason it was soon taken over by the Phoenicians, as far south as the Crocodile river beyond the headland of Carmel.

So it seems advisable in drawing a map of the tribal regions to leave the limits undefined. One might, it is true, essay a definition on the basis of the soils instead of strategy, but even this would be insecure, for we no longer know for certain where the forests were, and these must have been highly important in dividing the tribes from each other.

4

KINGS GO FORTH TO BATTLE

And it came to pass, after the year was expired, at the time when kings go forth to battle, that David sent Joab, and his servants with him, and all Israel; and they destroyed the children of Ammon, and besieged Rabbah.

(2 Sam. 11 : 1)

NO ONE can read much of the Old Testament without becoming aware of the extent to which it is concerned with war. The almost idyllic pastoral picture of the Patriarchs is disturbed, very soon after the story has begun, by the account of the battle of the four kings against five (Gen. 14 : 1–12), the earliest record that we have of Mesopotamian penetration into Palestine, and Jacob complains that his name has been made odious in the land by the brutal and treacherous capture of Shechem by Simeon and Levi (Gen. 34 : 30). These two stories are but a portent of what is yet to come, for when the Israelites enter Canaan after the Exodus, it is under the banner of a God who "is a man of war" (Exod. 15 : 3). Only by the arbitrament of battle do they attain their inheritance, and by battle only do they sustain it, for almost yearly are their armies commanded to march forth either for conquest or defence. So familiar to the inhabitants of a city was the sight of a troop sallying out to do battle on their behalf that it has been argued that whereas the phrase "all who went in at the gate of his city" (Gen. 23 : 10, 18) must refer to all those who have a voice in the affairs of the community, the apparently parallel phrase, "all who went out of the gate of his city" (Gen. 34 : 24), means rather all those young men who are capable of bearing arms.[27] "Happy is the man who has his quiver full of them!

He shall not be put to shame when he speaks with his enemies in the gate" (Ps. 127 : 5).

The student of biblical geography, therefore, must turn his attention to the question of how far military strategy was the result of geographical considerations. To do this he needs to ask two primary questions: (a) What overall pattern of military activity does a study of Old Testament Palestine reveal, and (b) what particular areas, if any, require special study as being repeatedly the scene of decisive fighting? It has already been suggested that within the area of Israelite occupation such persistent battlegrounds are two, the northern being the vital Accho-Bethshan corridor and its approaches across Mount Carmel, and the southern being the region round the Valley of Ajalon, extending on the one hand across the mountains in the territory of Benjamin, and on the other southwards into the Shephelah. Before considering these two districts in detail, however, it is necessary first to examine the more general question of the overall pattern.

It must be remembered that throughout the period of the Old Testament there were no made roads and no bridges, but only rough tracks, of varying width and difficulty. Consequently, what would appear on the map or even on the ground today to be no hindrance at all provided for the ancient fighter an unmanageable obstacle, and even a slight difference in elevation would serve as an admirable defence, if the slope were steep and the vegetation thick. Marsh was the worst of the problems (see Fig. 19), and the barrier to movement that it formed was absolute. Even those low-lying plains which tended to become waterlogged in winter were a major difficulty, and so were those depressions in the road where water might collect, and which for some reason or other could not be avoided. Almost as difficult as marshland was a really thick and impenetrable forest, such as those of Sharon, Carmel, and Upper Galilee, and we know of at least one fiercely contested battle in which "the forest devoured more people than the sword" (2 Sam. 18 : 8). It was not necessary for the trees to be of great height for the army to be baffled; a thick scrub of Mediterranean *maquis* with its entangled, thorn-covered bushes could effectively prevent any penetration, and so confuse the warrior that he lost all sense of direction.

In comparison with the obstacles of an adverse vegetation, those provided by the physical landscape were less severe, steep slopes and rocky

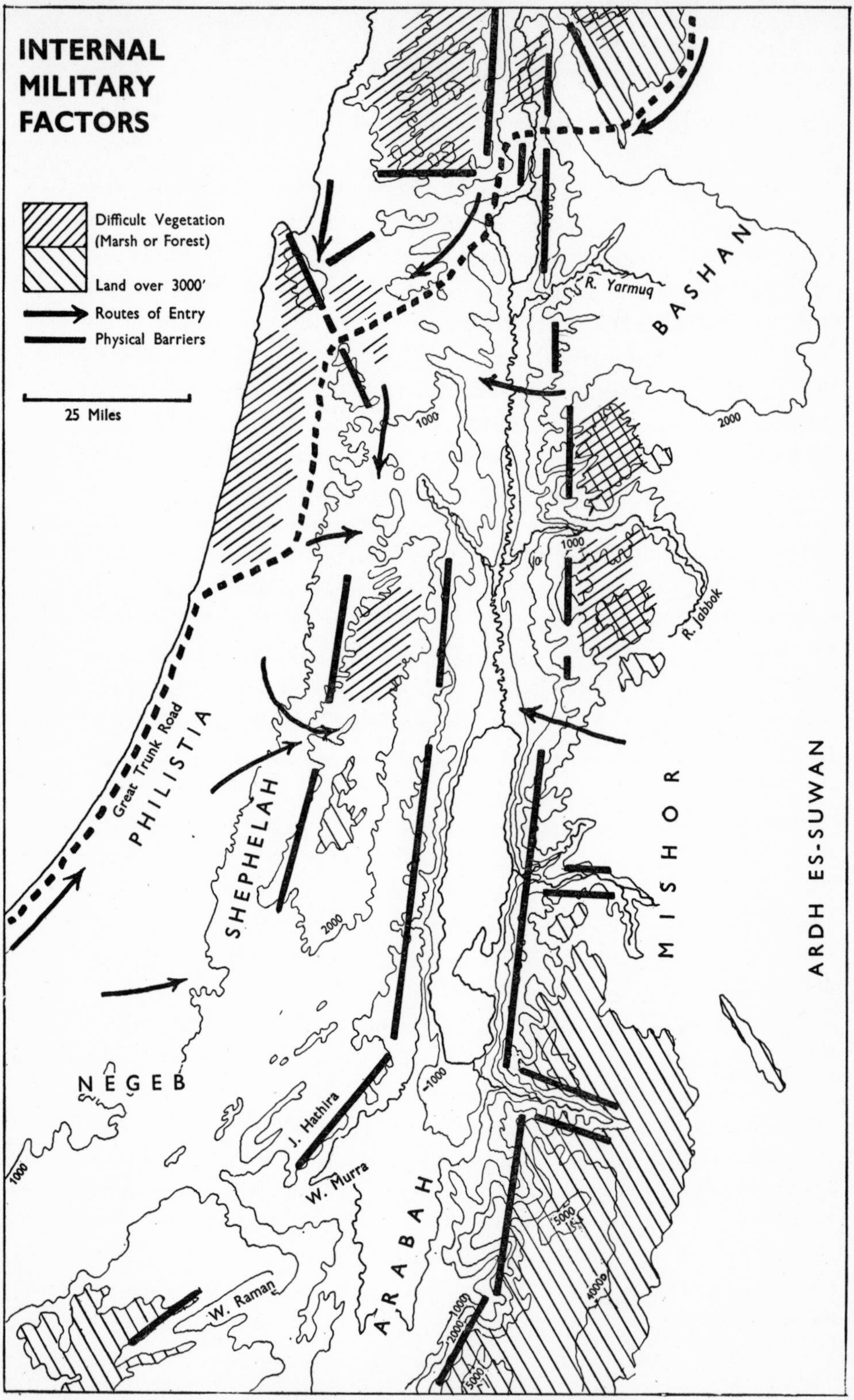

Fig. 19. Internal Military Factors

ground being the chief among them. The soft and friable Nubian sandstone is easily worn away to form gentle slopes in the wetter north, where it is exposed in the Jabbok Valley, and offers relatively easy passage. But in the dry south it stands up in huge, forbidding cliffs which seem to defy every attack, and so the pride of the Edomite heart deceived them and they thought that no one could bring them down to the ground (Obad. 3–4). The visitor to Petra today, seeing the narrow approach through the winding *Siq*, and the towering cliffs of the Edomite citadel of Sela, is apt to think that here, if anywhere, is the unconquerable city. Its defences were certainly admirable, but dry rock does not provide the same problems as forest or marsh, and it is always possible for a few bold men to climb the crags and overwhelm an unsuspecting garrison. So it was that Amaziah "took Sela by storm" (2 Kings 14 : 7), and more than once in its proud history the rock-cut city fell.

Nevertheless, such exploits certainly are not common, and an army will normally avoid precipitous and rocky bastions such as those provided by the sandstone in the south, and the Cenomanian limestone almost everywhere it appears. The Eocene limestone of the Shephelah was apparently less difficult, for it is less steep and normally less thickly forested. However, it could carry a very obstructive *maquis*, and the roads usually skirted the Eocene outcrops. For this purpose the chalk valleys were of immense importance. Easily eroded to form low-lying dales and passes, never obstructed by boulders, never waterlogged, and with only a minimum of vegetation, chalk is the rock of the ancient Palestinian roads. Only in Jeshimmon, where it is combined with the plunging slopes of the Rift Valley and the fierce drought of the desert, does the chalk hinder rather than encourage movement.

"If you have raced with men on foot, and they have wearied you," the Lord asked Jeremiah, "how will you compete with horses? And if in a safe land you fall down, how will you do in the jungle of the Jordan?" (Jer. 12 : 5). Not only must we take account of the differences of vegetation and terrain, but also of the weapons of war. There is a clear distinction again and again in the Old Testament between those who fought on foot and those who used horses and chariots, the latter being the stronger in the plain, but quite unsuited to manœuvre in the hill country. Yet another warrior was the desert raider on his swift dromedary, sweeping in from the east for pillage and plunder, and returning before he could be caught. It would appear that the camel was not sufficiently tamed for this purpose until the end of the second millennium B.C. and the yearly raids of the Midianites and Amalekites which reduced the land to such a plight in the days of Gideon (Jud. 6 : 1–6) seem to have been the earliest example of this form of warfare. An even more exotic animal appeared in the days of the Maccabees when Antiochus Eupator brought elephants[28] to battle against Judas Maccabeus (I Macc. 6 : 28–47), but this is outside our period, and does not really concern us.

With all this in mind, it is possible to look at the map of Palestine and estimate something of the problems which it posed for the military mind, problems which, despite the changing methods of war, proved in 1948–49 to have changed surprisingly little in the course of millennia. To the east was the plateau of Trans-jordan, and in the steppelands of Moab, Ammon, and Bashan movement was extremely easy. Indeed, every mention of military activity in Bashan in the Old Testament is an account of an unhindered advance, from the time that the four kings swept through it into Gilead (Gen. 14 : 5), to the victorious campaign of Judas Maccabeus in the same region (I Macc. 5 : 24–52: see also Fig. 20). One of the most triumphant of the Israelite memories was that of their overwhelming success against Og, king of Bashan, when first they came into the country, for "there was not a city which we did not take from them" (Deut. 3 : 4. See also Num. 21 : 35; Josh. 9 : 10; Ps. 135 : 11; 136 : 20). Yet, the plateau was not everywhere easy, for further to the east lay the difficulties of the desert, and the even more terrifying basalt, while on the edge of the plateau were the forested hills of Gilead and the proud heights of the Edomites. The steep plateau edge itself, of course, was a major obstacle, and there is no record of any frontal attack ever having been made upon the plateau regions directly from the west. The invading army always had to look for a way round (2 Kings 3 : 8).

Fig. 20. Maccabean Palestine

This map illustrates the Maccabean campaigns as they are described, mainly in the First Book of the Maccabees. The distribution of the places mentioned should be noticed, since they reflect the typical Palestinian military pattern of a rebel group entrenching themselves in the rocky hill country of Judah and Benjamin, from which they could conduct effective guerilla warfare. From there they harried the Trunk Road in the old Philistine region. As they became stronger they thrust outward towards the Negeb and across the Jordan.

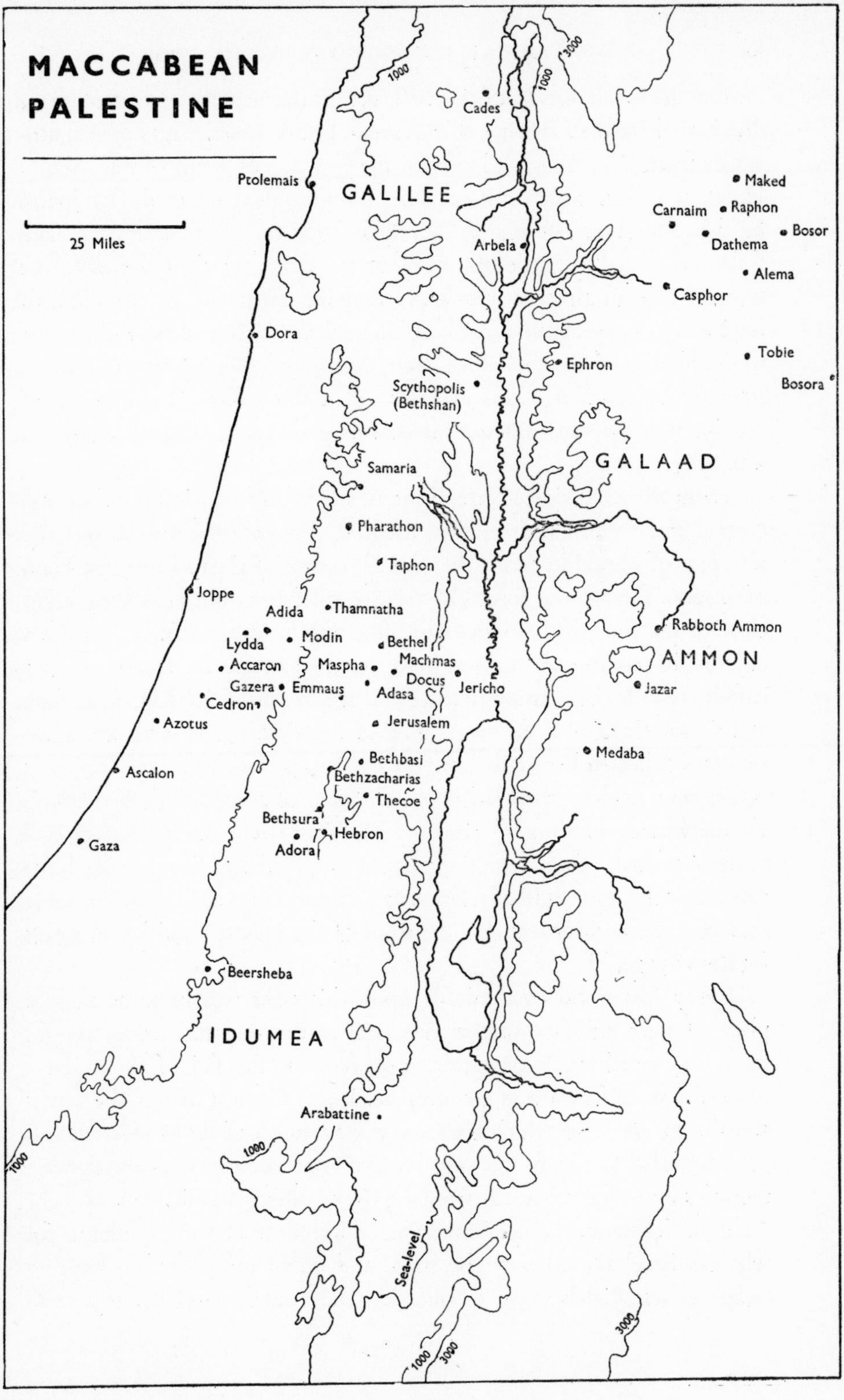

MACCABEAN
PALESTINE
25 Miles
Ptolemais
GALILEE
Cades
Maked
Carnaim
Raphon
Bosor
Dathema
Arbela
Alema
Casphor
Dora
Ephron
Tobie
Bosora
Scythopolis
(Bethshan)
GALAAD
Samaria
Pharathon
Taphon
Joppe
Adida
Thamnatha
Rabboth Ammon
Lydda
Modin
Bethel
AMMON
Accaron
Maspha
Machmas
Docus
Gazera
Emmaus
Adasa
Jericho
Jazar
Cedron
Azotus
Jerusalem
Medaba
Ascalon
Bethbasi
Bethzacharias
Thecoe
Bethsura
Hebron
Adora
Gaza
Beersheba
IDUMEA
Arabattine
Sea-level
1000
3000

On the western side of the Rift Valley the military geography was dominated by the existence of the great Trunk Road. This came southwards from Damascus, and crossed the Jordan just south of the Lake of Huleh at a place which still bears the picturesque name of the Bridge of Jacob's Daughters. It joined the road from the north at Hazor, and followed the edge of the hills as far as the Lake, which it skirted in the region of Gennesaret, only to leave it again at Migdal (the Magdala of the New Testament), and climb up through the Valley of the Robbers on to the plateau of Lower Galilee. Both Hazor and Migdal were important strategic points, and it was at the head of this valley, at the Horns of Hattin, that Saladin inflicted his smashing defeat on the Crusaders in A.D. 1187.

From thence it skirted round the northern side of Mount Tabor and crossed the Plain of Esdraelon to Megiddo, whence it climbed over the low pass of Megiddo across the central section of Carmel into the Plain of Sharon. Here it was forced by the Sharon forests and marshes to cling close to the foot of the Samaritan hills, but at Aphek (the modern Ras el-'Ain) it was able to turn south-westwards towards the sea. Thereafter it followed the coast, through the Philistine towns of Ashdod, Ashkelon, and Gaza. Gaza was the beginning of the desert, and here the great caravans collected before making the difficult passage to Egypt. This was where men loaded "their riches on the backs of asses, and their treasures on the humps of camels" (Is. 30 : 6). Those who know *Eothen* will remember that "Gaza stands upon the verge of the Desert, and bears towards it the same kind of relation as a seaport bears to the sea. It is there that you *charter* your camels ('the ships of the Desert') and lay in stores for the voyage."[29]

Every town and every defile upon this road was in some sense a place of stern military importance, and as the imperial troops fought their way northwards or southwards along it the fall of these places marked a stage forward in the advance. But it was not merely the towns actually on the road which attracted the attention of the invader; it was necessary also to ensure the long lines of communication as the delicate tentacles extended outwards from Egypt or Mesopotamia. This was the difference between the northern Israelite kingdom and the southern; for whereas Israel lay athwart the road, and could not therefore hope to escape attack, Judah stood to one side and could reasonably expect to maintain some show of independence by a careful, if unheroic, policy of non-interference. This was the advice of Isaiah, who urged the "scoffers, who rule this people in Jerusalem" (Is. 28 : 14) to undertake every possible internal reform, designed to strengthen the kingdom, but to avoid all foreign entanglement. Even the militarist Assyrians would think twice about detaching part of their forces to subdue a petty principality on a difficult hillside away from the road, but should the Jews try to descend from their hills they must entertain no hopes of mercy.

The military situation of the Hebrews was, of course, markedly different before and after 1000 B.C., that is to say before and after the establishment of the Davidic monarchy, for in the earlier period they were on the defensive and every approach to their territory was assaulted and put to the test, "that the generations of the people of Israel might know war, that he might teach war to such at least as had not known it before" (Jud. 3 : 2. See also Map IV). The shadowy "Cushan-rishathaim king of Mesopotamia" represents the persistent pressure from the north along the trade route, which the Israelites were, to their cost, to come to know so well in later years (Jud. 3 : 7–11), and the stories of Sisera (Jud. 4 and 5) seem to reflect two other lines of attack, one from the powerful fortress of Hazor, which controlled the trade routes, and the other from the coast through the narrow Kishon river gap, which divides Carmel from the Galilean Shephelah. The story of Gideon which follows (Jud. 6 : 1 – 8 : 32) portrays an invasion through the eastern gate into Esdraelon, that area which is protected by Bethshan, a city which at that time the Israelites did not control. Jephthah in his turn defended the Gilead hills from the pressure of the Ammonite steppeland to the east, a pressure which was to be maintained throughout history (Jud. 11 : 1–33; 1 Sam. 11 : 1–11; Amos 1 : 13–15). The attacks of the Moabites across the Jordan towards Jericho had already been recounted in Jud. 3 : 12–30, where they are associated both with the Ammonites and with the Amalekites, who belonged properly speaking to southern Cis-jordan, and threatened not Jericho but Beersheba. Their downfall is recorded in 1 Sam. 15 : 1–9.

The last of the approaches was that from the coast plain and the route of any enemy who controlled the southern part of the Trunk Road. In the early period the danger came from the Philistines, but in still earlier years the Egyptians had thrust northwards along this road and were to do so again in the time of the kingdom (1 Kings 14 : 25; 2 Kings 23 : 29). There were three main points of entry: by the valley of Ajalon and the Ascent of Beth-horon to the hills near Bethel; by the low-lying chalk valleys which lead into Manasseh; and across the passes of Carmel into the plain of Esdraelon.

The continued pressure of the Philistines, which led to the establishment of the monarchy and finally to their own defeat, reveals a feature of Palestinian military geography which is still potent today. Though the Philistines seem to have been immeasurably stronger, by reason of their more effective organization and weapons[30] so that they were able to penetrate even into the fortress of Ephraim itself and destroy Shiloh (1 Sam. 4 : 1–11; Jer. 7 : 12), they were never able to bring the whole land effectively under their control. They might terrify the inhabitants, and drive the refugees, or at their most powerful even the rump of the government, across the Jordan into Gilead (1 Sam. 13 : 6–7; 2 Sam. 2 : 8–9), but they could not stamp out the guerilla warfare, which spread unchecked like sparks among the stubble, and to which the limestone hills with their cliffs and their caves were so admirably suited. The same problem baffled Saul when a rival arose to challenge his leadership, and much, much later troubled also the British Government, who packed the land with troops but could not reduce it to order.

When the kingdom was established, the Hebrew armies sallied out by the same gates which once they had so desperately defended to attack and harry the surrounding nations, but an examination of their policy in this connection must be left to the next chapter. Suffice it for the moment to say that whenever in subsequent years the government at home was weakened and the outward pressure was perforce relaxed, the old dangers were once more renewed and the same places had to be defended again. In the confusion which followed the division of the kingdom Jeroboam seems to have been forced to leave his first capital at Shechem and rule temporarily from across the Jordan (1 Kings 12 : 25). It is not known what danger in the west caused him to do this (if indeed this is the correct interpretation of the verse), but it is at least possible that the Philistines were trying to get their revenge, for there is no doubt that the Israelites had fairly constant trouble with them later (1 Kings 15 : 27; 16 : 15).

The Northern Battlefield (Map VIII)

"For they are demonic spirits, performing signs, who go abroad to the kings of the whole world, to assemble them for battle on the great day of God the Almighty . . . And they assembled them at the place which is called in Hebrew Armageddon" (Rev. 16 : 14, 16). The use of this name, which from this verse has passed into common English speech as symbolic of the decisive battle which shall mark the end of the world, seems to come from the fact that at Megiddo the hopes of Judah were extinguished in the days before the Exile. It was there that King Josiah, who had been responsible for the great Deuteronomic reforms, and of whom it was said that "before him there was no king like him, who turned to the Lord with all his heart and with all his soul and with all his might, according to all the law of Moses; nor did any like him arise after him" (2 Kings 23 : 25), was slain by Pharaoh Necho en route to the support of the Assyrians (2 Kings 23 : 29; 2 Chron. 35 : 22). "All the singing men and singing women have spoken of Josiah in their laments to this day. They made these an ordinance in Israel" (2 Chron. 35 : 25), a yearly lamentation which seems to have become confused with the weeping for Tammuz (Ezek. 8 : 14), and to which there is apparently a reference in Zech. 12 : 11.

Be this as it may, there can be no doubt of the appropriateness of the symbolism, for there is no place in the whole of the Israelite territory where their fate was more constantly placed in jeopardy. It is a small, very roughly rectangular, plain, extending from north-west to south-east along the north-eastern side of the Carmel range, no more than twenty miles in length by six miles wide. Enclosed as it is by hills on almost every side, which in ancient times must have been fairly well covered with forest, or equally discouraging scrub, the points of entry are of great importance. These are:

(a) *The Tabor Gate*, about the middle of the north-eastern side of the rectangle. This is a broad extension of the plain, some two to three miles wide, lying between the steep scarp of the Nazarene hills on the north, and the ancient volcano of Mount Moreh on the south. About seven miles along this corridor is the isolated hill of Mount Tabor, rising some 1,000 feet above the level of the plain. A narrow valley, the Wadi Bira (=modern Hebrew Valley of the Tavor), leads down to the Jordan from the foot of Mount Tabor behind Mount Moreh, but it is rocky and difficult and does not seem to have played an important rôle as a route-way, though in Crusading times its exit was controlled by the castle of Belvoir. The real importance of this gate was that it was possible to go round the foot of Mount Tabor north-eastwards towards the Lake of Galilee, and this was the route taken by the main Trunk Road.

(b) *The Valley of Jezreel*, which joins the rectangle at its north-eastern corner. This, again, is a broad gateway, some three miles wide, and about eleven miles long. It descends steadily, but not steeply, and at the exit from the plain passes almost immediately below sea-level. Bethshan, which guards the entrance to this gate at the south-eastern end, is about 500 feet below the level of the Mediterranean, and here there is a very clearly marked step, 250 feet in height, where the geological fault marking the edge of the Jordan valley cuts across the minor rift valley of the Jezreel corridor. The mountains of Gilboa on the south-western side rise very steeply from the valley floor to a height of 1,500 feet above sea-level, but the slopes of Mount Moreh on the other side are neither so steep nor quite so high.

(c) *The Ascent of Gur*. The remaining gateways into the plain are all very narrow, and this, which joins the plain just beside the town of En-gannim (the modern Jenin), is the first of four which cross the uplands of Carmel into the Plain of Sharon. The name is known only from 2 Kings 9 : 27, and the exact site of Gur is as yet unknown.[31] There is a narrow defile immediately south of En-gannim which opens out after about a couple of miles into the little Plain of Dothan (Gen. 37 : 17; 2 Kings 6 : 13), near the town of Ibleam (Josh. 17 : 11; Jud. 1 : 27). From the Plain of Dothan it is possible either to descend into Sharon or go southwards into the hills towards Samaria and Shechem.

(d) *The Pass of Taanach*. The most difficult of the Carmel passes, being both narrow and steep, and rising to 1,250 feet above sea-level, this was nevertheless used on occasions, and in the famous inscription of Thutmose III at Karnak, it was suggested by the officers of Thutmose as a safer alternative to a frontal attack on Megiddo.[32] W. F. Albright has shown that there were times when Taanach replaced Megiddo in importance,[33] and presumably during these periods this pass was more in use.

(e) *The Pass of Megiddo*. This was, without doubt, the most important of all the Carmel passes, and it is followed today by the modern road from Affuleh to Hadera. It is one of the two chalk valleys which cut across the central section of Carmel, and nowhere does it reach as much as 1,000 feet above sea-level.

(f) *The Pass of Jokneam.* This is the second of the two chalk valleys which lie on either side of the Eocene limestone outcrop, known as the Israelite Shephelah (Josh. 11 : 16), and also the second of the two alternative routes suggested by the officers of Thutmose, though they describe it as coming out at an unknown town of Djefti, probably somewhere near Jokneam. It is actually lower than the Megiddo Pass, but it is less central and offers a less direct crossing of the plain.

(g) *The Kishon Gate.* This is the exit in the north-west into the coastal Plain of Accho, where the tiny stream of the Kishon leaves the plain through a gap, which at its narrowest is less than a quarter of a mile wide. This is the gap which was controlled on its seaward side by Harosheth of the Gentiles (Jud. 4 : 2).

The excessive narrowness of this exit, through which the plain is drained, has meant that the Kishon is but an ineffective agent in carrying off the floodwaters which pour down into the plain from every hillside during the torrential storms of winter. Yet it is the Kishon which has to bear the whole of the load, for the waterparting which divides the Mediterranean streams from those flowing to the Jordan lies well to the south-east near Jezreel. The result is that almost the whole of this lowland below the 250-foot contour rapidly becomes waterlogged during the winter months, and before the introduction of modern drainage was likely to remain in this state for weeks or even months on end. Every road, therefore, must skirt its edges, and the route from Accho to Beth-shan clung closely to the foot of Carmel, even as the modern road still does today.

Yet there was one point where the plain could be crossed, and that was in its centre, where a narrow causeway of volcanic rock extends north-eastwards from Megiddo in the direction of Mount Tabor. This provided the only possible direct route across the plain during all the flood season, and was consequently of quite vital importance. We must consequently trace the Trunk Road from Mount Tabor across this causeway to Megiddo, which thus stood at the most important crossroads of the plain, which by reason of its central position it could easily command. It must be classed with Hazor in the far north, and Gaza in the south, as one of the three key points to the control of the Trunk Road as it ran across the narrow Palestinian bridge.

It seems to have been along this causeway that the battle between Barak and Sisera was fought (Jud. 4), though it is possible that we have here a conflated account of two battles, one against Sisera attacking through the Kishon Gate in the north-west, and another against Jabin, pressing southwards from his headquarters at Hazor towards Tabor, by way of the Trunk Road. Moreover, it is doubtful whether the Kedesh of verse 11 is the same as Kedesh of Naphtali near Hazor in verse 6, and whether it should not rather be identified with Tell Abu Qudeis near Megiddo. However, the battle against Sisera seems fairly clear: the Israelites had gathered near Mount Tabor, since it was a sanctuary of some importance, and then they drove south-westwards along the road to meet the more heavily armed troops of Sisera, who had swung round to cross the Kishon by the causeway. However, the downpour in which the battle was fought (Jud. 5 : 20–21) had so swollen the river that it was impassable to chariots even at this point, and the Israelites were able to force the enemy to abandon their armour and flee back on foot along the road by which they had come. It was near Megiddo that Sisera went to his death in the tent of Heber the Kenite.

The same road must have been used time and again by the invading armies from the north, but Megiddo is not mentioned further in this connection until the unhappy death of Josiah who tried here to check Pharaoh Necho as he pressed northwards in the opposite direction.

The Jezreel gate, however, recurs more than once in the military history of Israel, for whoever had mastered the plain must also master this corridor if they were to be secure. So we find in pre-biblical times the Egyptians in control of Bethshan, and in the time of Saul the Philistines in possession of the same city (1 Sam. 31 : 10). Nevertheless, the corridor had one weakness in that it was dominated by the steep hillside of Gilboa on the southern side, and whoever could make their way along the ridge which connects Gilboa with the hills of Samaria to the south could threaten the army encamped in the valley. On two occasions at least this happened. The first was when the Midianites swept in on one of their annual raids (Jud. 6 : 1–6) which seem to have penetrated across Carmel well into the coastal plain; and the other was in the final years of Saul's reign, when the Philistines had gained the mastery of the whole

Trunk Road and its approaches (1 Sam. 29 : 1). On each occasion the Israelites were engaged in the desperate guerilla warfare to which their rocky hills were so well suited, and under Saul they had pressed down the spur which leads to Jezreel. In this second battle, however, they had to meet the better disciplined and better organized army of the Philistines instead of the loosely controlled camelry of a Bedouin *ghazzu*, and so it was that under Saul they were defeated in the same place where under Gideon they had been the victors. The route of the vanquished, however, was the same, for they fled whither the refugees of Palestine must always flee—across the Jordan into Gilead (Jud. 8 : 4; 1 Sam. 31 : 7).

It was from Gilead also that came the third of those bloody events which mark the history of this gate, the lightning onslaught of the usurper Jehu against the house of Omri (2 Kings 9 : 14–37). Both Joram and the dread Queen Mother, Jezebel, were killed in Jezreel itself, but Ahaziah of Judah, on a visit to Joram at the time (for which the Chronicler, who has a rather different account of his death, primly rebukes him —2 Chron. 22 : 7–9) fled southwards towards En-gannim,[34] and was slain, apparently, in the narrow defile which leads up to the Plain of Dothan.

THE SOUTHERN BATTLEFIELD (MAP IX)

This battlefield is physically different from the northern one, but in fact bears a curious resemblance to it, in that the existence of both has been largely determined by the relation of the chalk valleys to the Eocene limestone. The chalk here is found in the broad, down-faulted basin of the Valley of Ajalon, which marks the southern end of the Dome of Ephraim and the beginning of the Shephelah, but it extends also a long and narrow tongue southwards between the Shephelah and the Judaean hills, which, especially in the south, rise very steeply from it on the east. The Shephelah itself is composed of the rough, infertile Eocene limestone, which must in biblical days have carried the same tangle of scrub which was so prohibitive of movement on its northern counterpart. It is probable that it was prohibitive of movement here also, and much of the strategic importance of this region lay in the fact that it constituted a notable obstacle to each of the two bitter enemies who inhabited the land on either side of it. However, the passes across it were both more numerous and easier, being all of them reasonably wide lowland valleys in place of the constricted passes across Mount Carmel.

By far the most important of these was the broad Valley of Ajalon at the extreme northern end of the region, important not only because of its openness, but because it led up into the easiest of all the approaches to the highlands, the famous Ascent of Beth-horon. Further to the south lies the Valley of Sorek (Jud. 16 : 4) renowned for the exploits of Samson against the Philistines, almost all the places mentioned in the story lying on either side of it. Further south still is the Valley of Elah, where David slew Goliath not far from Azekah (1 Sam. 17 : 1–2). Its outlet into the coast plain is protected by the strong fortress of Libnah, which was captured by the Assyrians as part of their drive to protect their lines of communication for the attack on Egypt (2 Kings 19 : 8). Still further south again is the Wadi Zeita, controlled by Mareshah, where Asa is reported as having beaten off a strong Ethiopian attack (2 Chron. 14 : 9–14). Finally comes the Wadi Qubeibeh, dominated by Lachish and Gath.

The effectiveness of these valleys as lines of attack on Judah was strictly limited by the fact that they all led into the Judaean moat, the north-south chalk valley which lies at the foot of the Judaean hills, and any army which had penetrated thus far would be forced to turn northwards and use the Valley of Ajalon as the means of ascent into the hills. It is true that the three prongs of the Valley of Sorek, which penetrate almost to the gates of Jerusalem, look extremely tempting on the map, but they are narrow and rocky, and could not accommodate more than a small raiding force. There is no record of this approach ever having been used for an attack on Judah, though it was followed by the cattle drawing the Ark on a more peaceful occasion (1 Sam. 6 : 1–7 : 2), and may have been used as an exit from the hills by the ill-fated Amaziah going down to battle at Beth-shemesh (2 Kings 14 : 11). In the time of Samson the tribe of Dan was still living here and the Philistines had not yet begun to penetrate the hills.

The overwhelming importance of the Ajalon approach is the explanation of a short passage in Isaiah which has often puzzled the exegetes (Is. 10 : 27b–32). The tenor of the passage seems to indicate the approach of the dreaded Assyrian army, but the direction of the approach from the north has led some scholars to suggest that it must refer to the Syro-Ephraimite alliance of 734 B.C.[35] However, this is unnecessary, for even though the Assyrians were besieging Libnah and Lachish to the south

(Is. 36 : 2; 37 : 8) they would have had to have used the Valley of Ajalon and the Ascent of Beth-horon in order to bring anything like a sizable army up on to the plateau, and they would therefore have borne down upon Jerusalem from the north.

The strategic rôle of this valley was a very simple one. It was the only point of real danger in the Judaean defences, and the warring armies either pressed straight up or straight down it (Josh. 10 : 10–15; 1 Sam. 14 : 31; 1 Macc. 3 : 13–24). So dangerous a salient demanded very careful protection by the people of Judah, and Solomon is reported to have "built Upper Beth-horon and Lower Beth-horon, fortified cities with walls, gates, and bars" (2 Chron. 8 : 5). His successor, Rehoboam, bereft not only of the Northern Kingdom, but of all the Judaean dependencies, and besieged in his own capital city by Shishak of Egypt (1 Kings 14 : 25), wisely fortified the whole of this valley and the length of the Judaean moat, as well as the defences of Judaea on the eastern side (2 Chron. 11 : 6–12). "He put shields and spears in all the cities, and made them very strong. So he held Judah and Benjamin." Ajalon, however, was lost by the feeble Ahaz (2 Chron. 28 : 18), and this is the measure of his weakness.

5

ISRAEL AMONG THE GENTILES

Israel is swallowed up: now shall they be among the Gentiles as a vessel wherein is no pleasure. For they are gone up to Assyria, a wild ass alone by himself.

(Hosea 8 : 8, 9)

THE RELATION of the Israelite kingdoms with the surrounding nations is exceedingly complex, and justice cannot be done to it in the space of a few pages. It might, perhaps, be treated schematically under the separate headings of commercial dealings, offensive and defensive warfare, and the cultural inheritance, but this would be merely a convenience. In actual fact these three aspects of the question are closely interrelated, and should be thought of as all part and parcel of an involved and complicated unity. This network of warfare, trade, and interlocking culture long pre-dates the Bible, for we are now taught to think of a situation nine or ten thousand years ago in which Palestine contained towns "almost modern, or at least medieval in appearance", needing to defend themselves against well-organized external attacks more serious than the sudden incursion of the desert raider, trading with other towns at a considerable distance.[36]

Certainly by the time that the biblical history begins the pattern was already established, and is by no manner of means merely of antiquarian interest. It has been held by some[37] that the characteristic Old Testament concept of the meaning of history, upon which so very much of the prophetic argument is based, belongs to the very earliest stratum of biblical thought. Upon this view the patient editors who, under the impact of the dread events of the later Israelite years, collected and arranged the patriarchal stories, were faithful interpreters of a process of thought which had begun with the Patriarchs themselves.

This process of thought had a double character, for it was the product of a continual debate, developing through the centuries, between those who accepted and drew their strength from the culture in which they lived, and those who, jealous for the Lord of Hosts, stood over against the culture and opposed it. As the biblical heritage has been transmitted to us, there can be no doubt that the dominant tone of the Old Testament is one of cultural rejection, and of a stern intolerance of the idols of the Gentiles, which "are silver and gold, the work of men's hands" (Ps. 115 : 4); and as the Church learned again under the pressure of the Nazi tyranny, if one is driven to make a choice, this in the last resort is always the choice which one must make. Yet, the evidence of biblical archaeology is increasingly to the effect that this choice does not have to be made all the time, but only in extreme cases, and indeed we are continually becoming more aware of the extent to which even those who opposed the culture were in fact its debtors.

As a result of the extensive research which has been carried on, and the almost overwhelming discoveries that have been made, the tablets from Mari, from Cappadocia, from Nuzi, from Alalakh, and from Ugarit, to name only some of the tens of thousands of texts which have been brought to light in the past decades, we now know how faithfully the patriarchal stories preserve for us the culture and customs of the first half of the second millennium B.C. And not only that, but the Psalms and the prophetic books speak again and again in terms of the mythology which the true follower of Yahweh was bound to abhor; they use its language, paraphrase its hymns, and reflect in countless ways its thought-forms and its patterns of behaviour. Even the famous Solomonic Temple itself was almost a slavish copy of Phoenician and Syrian originals.[38]

Nor was it only the nearer countries of the Levant which lent their ideas to the people of Palestine; Egypt and Mesopotamia also greatly coloured their thinking, and there is hardly a psalm, among all the hundred and fifty which we sing in church today, which does not reflect the thinking, not merely of the ancient Israelites—that, after all, is to be expected—but of the whole Middle Eastern world in which they lived.

Easily pre-eminent in this world were the two rival empires of the Nile and the Tigris-Euphrates valley, whose rivalry has persisted in the antagonism of Nasser and Kasim, and has owed its intensity in no small measure to the geographical differences between them. The two maps (Figs. 21 and 24) may help to make this clear. They are drawn from a somewhat unusual angle in order that the differences between the two regions may become apparent. In each the mouth of the river is at the bottom of the map, and the observer is looking up the valley from its entrance to the sea. He is standing, moreover, at about the same latitude in both cases, for Cairo is almost parallel with Basra, both being 30 degrees north of the Equator. There, however, the likeness ends.

When one stands at the mouth of the Nile and looks up the valley one is looking towards the south, in the direction of the humid tropics which lie beyond the vast Saharan desert, and beyond them again towards the high equatorial plateaus of eastern Africa. It is a prospect so distant, and involves a journey so difficult, that it was not until the mid-nineteenth century that men knew for certain where the river began, and even then they did not discover this by proceeding up the Nile itself. Until the journey of Speke and Burton inland from Zanzibar in 1856 the secret remained effectively preserved by the immense marshes of the southern Sudan.

It is these marshes also, together with the staggered flooding of the Abyssinian rivers, which are responsible for the remarkable nature of the Nile floods, so fantastically regular that it is possible to predict within a day's error the date of their beginning, and so carefully prolonged that the beneficial waters remain on the land for weeks on end, and are then but lethargically withdrawn. No tributary joins the river after it enters Egypt, and only the rarest and most occasional shower ever falls to add to its supply. Beyond question the most important fact about Egypt is that the life of every single one of its millions of people depends upon a water supply which enters the country through one only pipeline, and rises and falls with a quite hypnotic regularity. It is not surprising, therefore, that Frankfort should say of them, "The Egyptians had very little sense of history or of past and future. For they conceived of their world as essentially static and unchanging . . . only the changeless is truly significant."[39]

Moreover, the Egyptians were singularly unthreatened by external enemies. As one gazes up the river from the delta there is on the right the sandy Saharan waste, inhabited by nomadic peoples it is true, but so

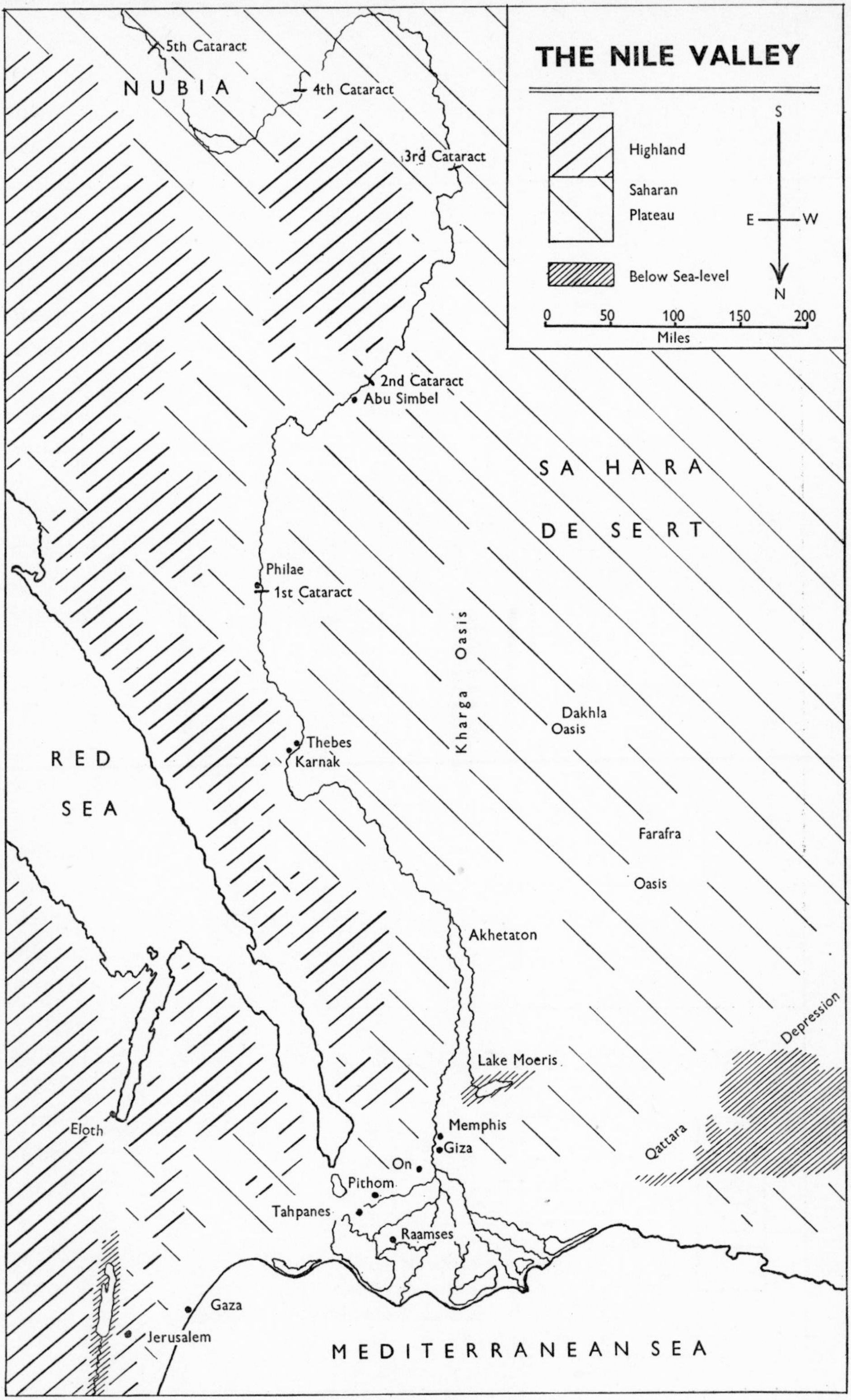

Fig. 21. The Nile Valley

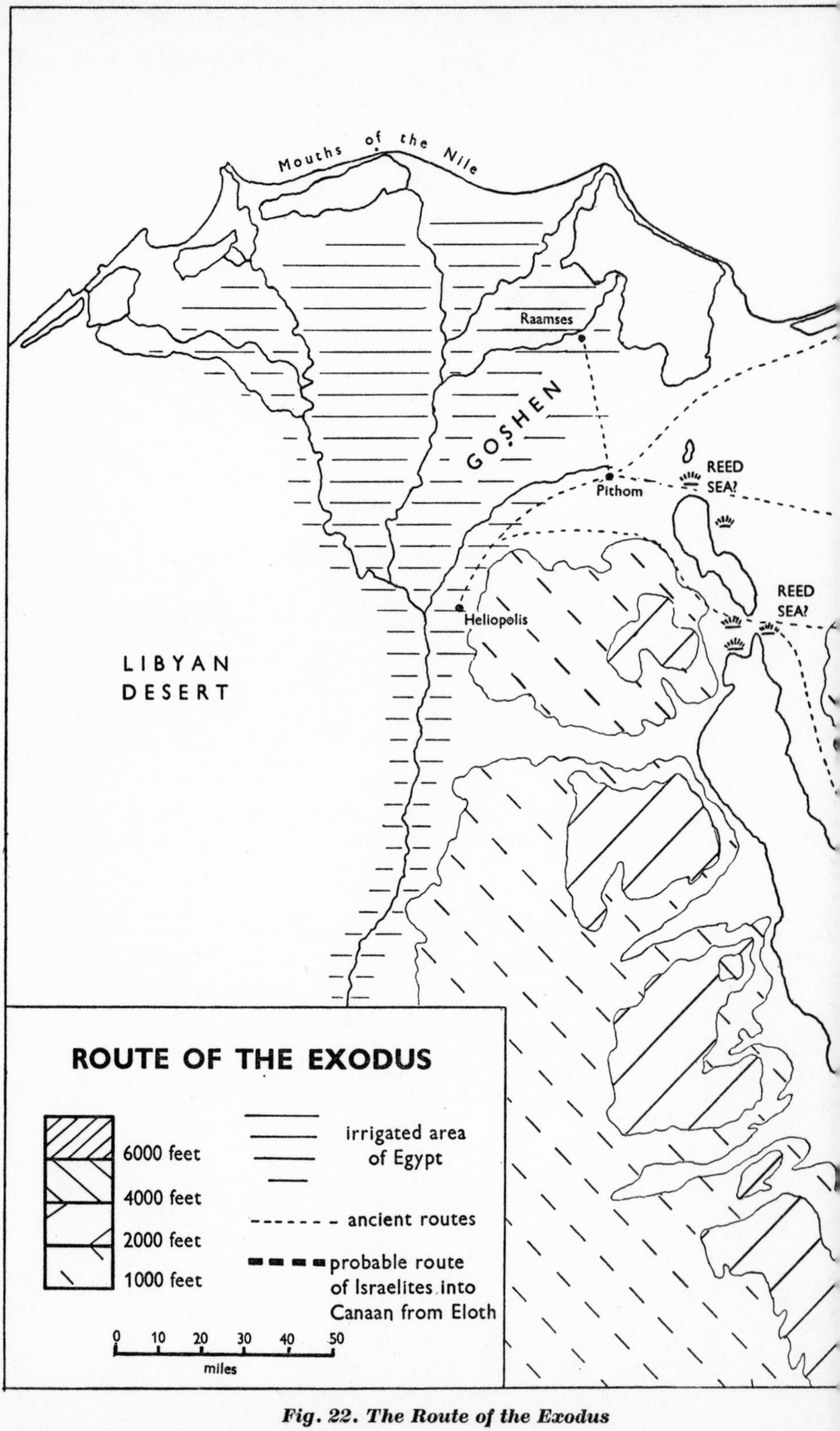

Fig. 22. The Route of the Exodus

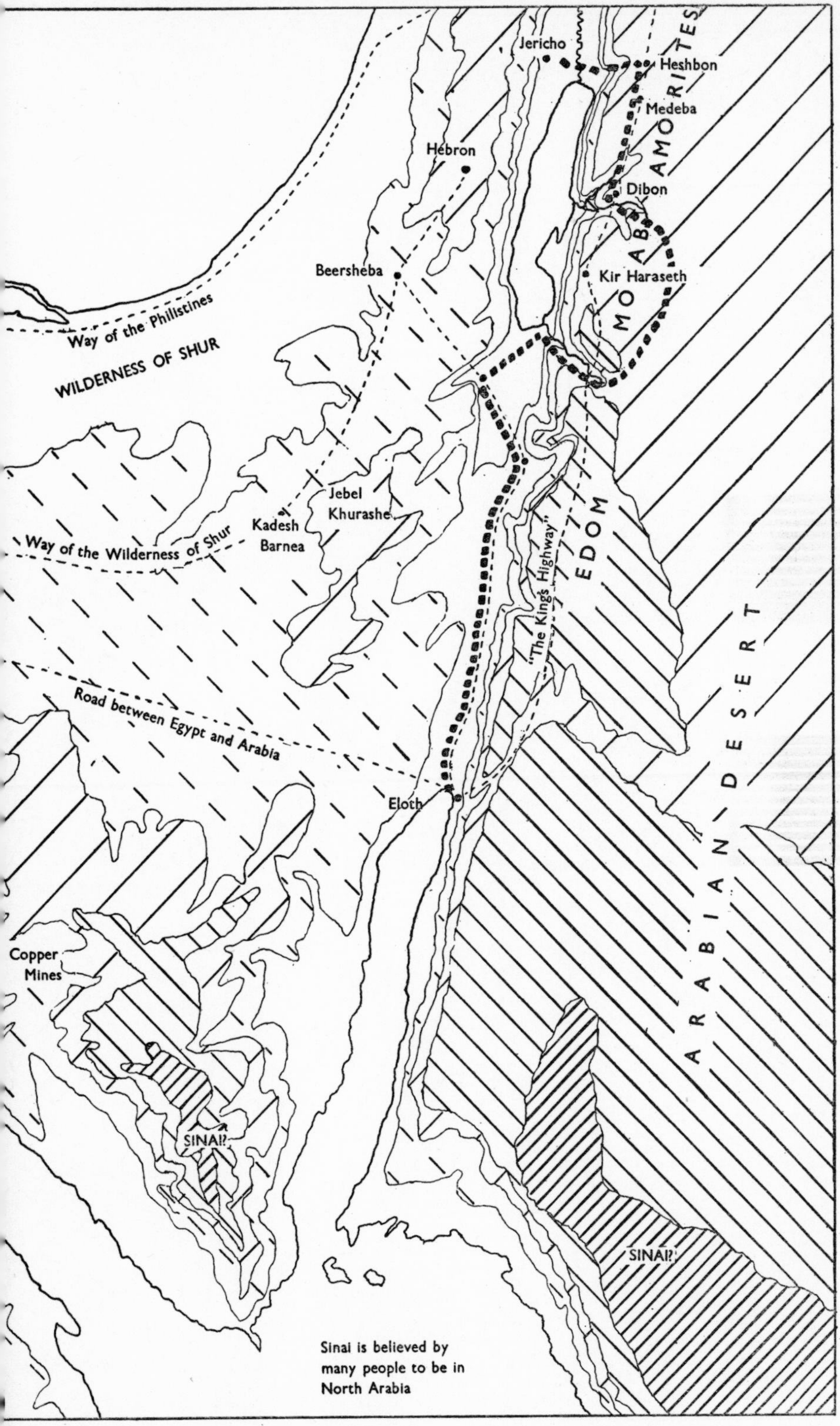

Jericho
Heshbon
Medeba
AMORITES
Hebron
Dibon
MOAB
Beersheba
Kir Haraseth
Way of the Philistines
WILDERNESS OF SHUR
Jebel
Khurashe
EDOM
Kadesh
Barnea
Way of the Wilderness of Shur
"The King's Highway"
ARABIAN DESERT
Road between Egypt and Arabia
Eloth
Copper
Mines
SINAI!?
SINAI!?
Sinai is believed by
many people to be in
North Arabia

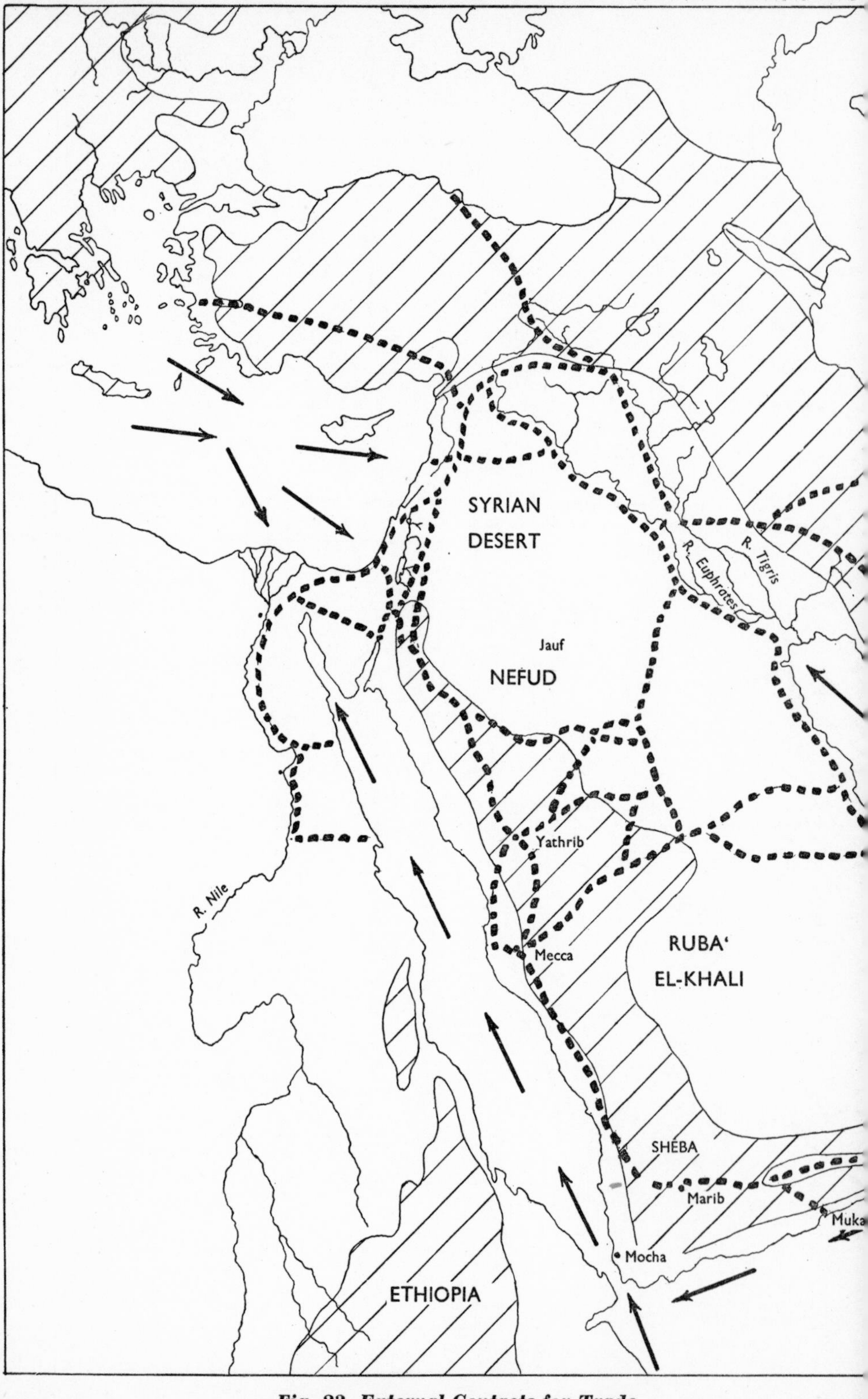

Fig. 23. External Contacts for Trade

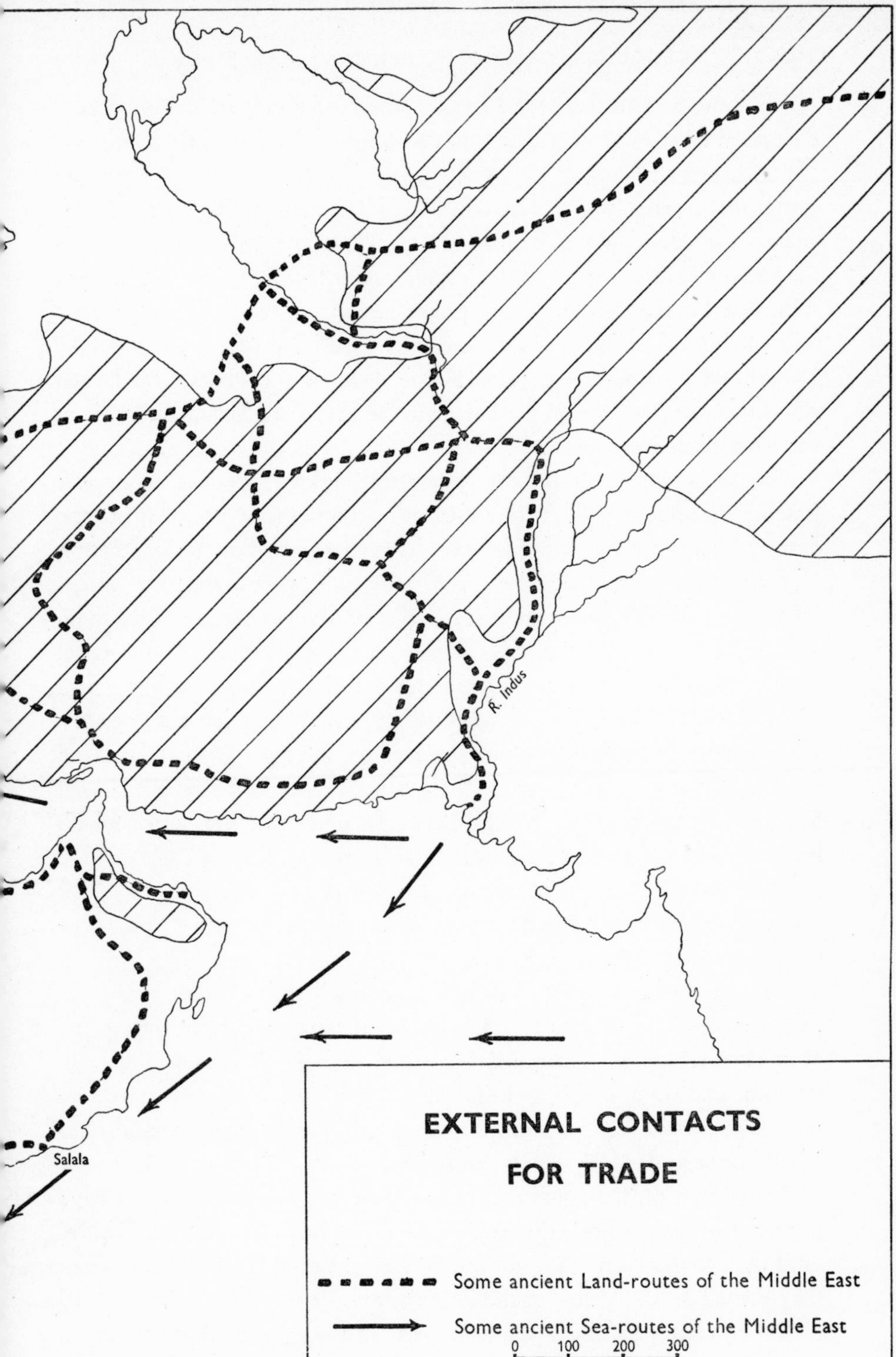
R. Indus
Salala
EXTERNAL CONTACTS
FOR TRADE
Some ancient Land-routes of the Middle East
Some ancient Sea-routes of the Middle East
0
100
200
300
Miles

much more severe than the "tame" desert of northern Arabia that it contained no trading cities, and no great tribes waiting to descend upon the rich riverine lands. It is a world enclosed upon itself, and it is perhaps symptomatic that of the two oases called *Kharga* (outer) and *Dakhla* (inner) the second should be further away from the Nile. To the left lies the narrow eastern desert, with its single mountainous ridge, and beyond it the Red Sea trough. The only menace came from the continual pressure northwards of the Ethiopians, and the possibility of attack from the Levant, which once took place in the days of the Hyksos, and then not again for a thousand years when the Assyrians invaded Egypt in the seventh century.

Tagging along behind the successful Hyksos invasion came the Israelite tribes, part of that continual pathetic movement from the desert towards the Nile of those who have succumbed to the temptation of the "cucumbers, the melons, the leeks, the onions, and the garlic" (Num. 11 : 5). We know that they settled on the very edges of the delta in the north-east (see Fig. 22), and we are fairly certain of the cities which they were forced to build, Pithom and Raamses (Exod. 1 : 11). We know something also of the route by which they left the country, when finally in desperation they packed up their baggage and moved out into the cruel desert again, for it is almost certain that the "Reed Sea", whose crossing they remembered for ever, was the marsh which lay once where now the Suez Canal has been cut, and the "Way of the Land of the Philistines" (Exod. 13 : 17) which they rejected is without doubt the main Trunk Road towards Gaza. But we do not know where they went after that.

The problem, of course, is the site of Sinai, and whether we are to look for it in the peninsula which bears the name today or among the volcanic mountains of northern Arabia. The evidence remains singularly tenuous, and though it is common in most biblical maps still to adhere to the traditional site,[40] it seems better to leave the route unmarked until Eloth on the Gulf of Aqabah is reached.[41]

From then on the route is reasonably clear, since they seem to have pressed northwards along the Arabah valley, by way of Punon and Oboth, until they found their way blocked by the waters of the Dead Sea. Then they turned up the Valley of the Zered seeking a way round. The refusal of the Moabites to allow them to pass through their territory caused them to move round the desert frontier of Moab and then turn westwards down the Valley of the Arnon, but once again the road was blocked, this time by the precipitous cliffs of the lower Arnon valley, and so they were forced to join battle with the Amorites, who then controlled the northern flank, and they won the resounding victory which is recounted in the twenty-first chapter of the Book of Numbers (Num. 21 : 21–30).

Mesopotamia (Fig. 24) is very different from Egypt. If one stands there at the mouth looking upstream one is confronted not with one river but two. On the right are the towering mountains of the Zagros ranges, with behind them the high plateaus of Persia, and to the left are the deserts of Arabia. Part of this is the *Nefud* (Fig. 23), a sand desert it is true, but it is not here as large or as serious as the vast *ergs* of the Sahara, and much of the country is stony *hamada*, over which the Arabian tribes range in search of pasture. The Arabian plateau is tilted towards the east, and the high western edge is mountainous where it overlooks the Red Sea. Here the rain is rare, but it is sufficient for there to be a line of trading cities and the great incense route which led from south to north of the peninsula. All the long wadi-lines run eastward from these mountains, and there is an important group of them in the centre of the peninsula, between the *Nefud* in the north, and the far more terrifying *Ruba' el-Khali* (the "Empty Quarter") in the south. Here it is possible to cross the whole width of Arabia following the oases from Mecca in the west to the shore of the Persian Gulf and the Mesopotamian delta in the east.

Moreover, as one stands at the delta mouth one looks not south but north, away from the summer rains of the Tropics towards the cold winters and heavy snows on the mountains of Anatolia, those mysterious northern heights where dwelt the council of the gods. Everything about Mesopotamia was different. The floods came at the end of winter instead of at the beginning, and burst with a sudden, unpredictable fury upon a terrified plain. The Euphrates is like the Nile in that it receives no tributaries in its lower section, but unlike it in that everywhere there is a little rain, and occasionally bitter cold.[42] The Tigris, however, receives tributaries from the swift mountain streams right until the mouth is reached, and so rapid is the descent of the flood water that the river at Baghdad is apt to rise six feet in a few hours. Until very recent years no permanent bridge had been built there, and the transpontine traffic was maintained

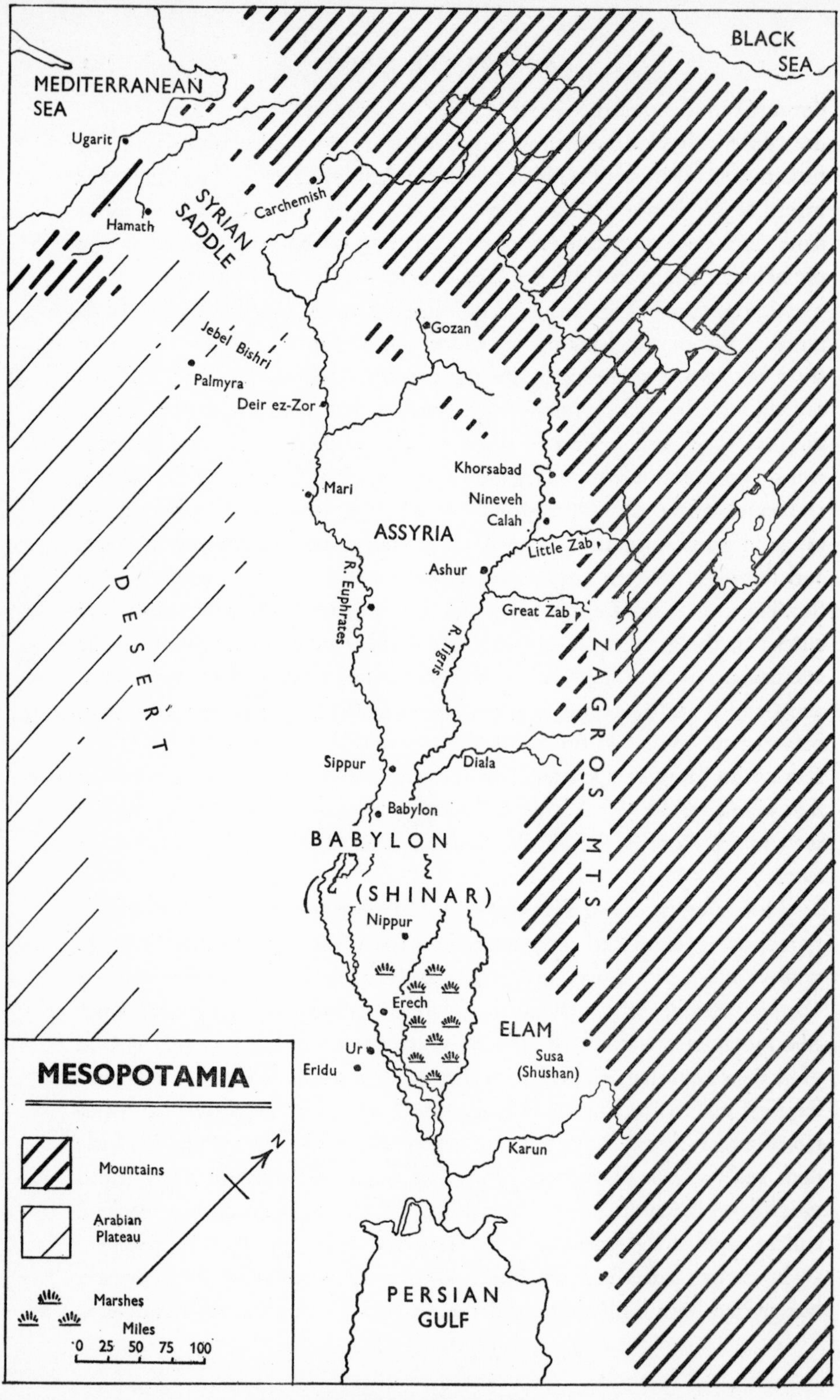

Fig. 24. Mesopotamia

during the drier part of the year by a bridge of boats. Another feature of the Mesopotamian plain which is quite unknown in Egypt is that the final tributary of the Tigris, the Karun, which enters close to the delta, brings down from the mountains such a quantity of silt, and so effectively clogs the course of the slower moving major rivers, that they are ponded up behind it and deposit their own sediment in the vast and desolate marshes which form the southern part of the country.

Where Egypt, then, is unchanging Mesopotamia is erratic, and where Egypt is secure Mesopotamia is threatened; where Egypt was united under the double crown Mesopotamia was plagued by the endless struggle between Assyria and Babylon. The beneficent river of Egypt, steadily rising and falling year after unchanging year, is replaced in Mesopotamia by the treacherous dual floods, whose waters have to be passed from one to the other, as first the Euphrates, and then the Tigris, and then the Euphrates again flows at the slightly higher level. "Small wonder, then, that the boldness of those early people who undertook to found permanent settlements in the shifting plain had its obverse in anxiety; that the self-assertion which the city—its organization, its institutions, citizenship itself—implied was overshadowed by apprehension. The tension between courage and the awareness of man's dependence upon superhuman power found a precarious equilibrium in a peculiarly Mesopotamian conception. It was a conception which was elaborated in theology but which likewise informed the practical organization of society: the city was conceived to be ruled by a god."[43]

These were two ways of life, two entirely different approaches to the problems of existence, essentially as different from each other as Communism is from Capitalism, and they could not agree to co-existence. They were bound to come in conflict, even as Iraq and Egypt must come in conflict today. Superficially the Iraqi revolution of July 1958 may seem to repeat the pattern of the Egyptian revolution of July 1952, but the likeness is only on the surface, and it was only to be expected that Abdul Nasser, who had so often summoned the Iraqis to revolt against their rulers in the Egyptian manner, should within a week be found vilifying the people who had done so. Given their so separate worlds, he could hardly help himself.

In ancient times, as in the modern world, the theatre of their conflict was the Levant. The United Arab Republic, the Greater Syria Plan, the

Fertile Crescent Scheme—these are but the modern equivalents of the ancient struggle between Egypt and Assyria for the Levantine hegemony. Within this vice Palestine was caught, and only in moments of purely temporary balance could she manage to assert herself, and establish with tragic optimism an imperial pattern of her own. (See Map VI.) In such a situation her choice was always the same, for steadily the same possibilities presented themselves. There were first her immediate neighbours, Philistia, Ammon, Moab, and Edom, and in any conflict in which they could not appeal for the support of some external colossus the Israelite kingdom, once established, was the stronger. Once master of the Trunk Road at Megiddo she could from the security of her mountain heights dominate the Philistines, whose only possibility of expansion was along that road. That she could bring Moab and Ammon under her authority was without question, for neither possessed that centre of power from which imperial expansion was possible. Her only serious threat was the commercially powerful Edom, which could afford to pursue a somewhat independent line. However, the Edomite control of the desert trade routes, which included also the Red Sea passage, was exercised from a very constricted base, strong though it was, and it was not impossible for the government at Jerusalem, in periods of its greatest power, to cut the trade routes, and isolate the base.

Beyond these immediate, and smaller, kingdoms lay the three greater ones of Syria, Phoenicia, and Egypt, for we must imagine that at such times the Assyrian thunder, though rumbling endlessly upon the distant horizon, gave no threat of an immediate storm, and could therefore be neglected. It was clearly impossible for the Israelite ruler, despite his great accession of strength, to do battle with Damascus, Tyre, and Thebes all at the same time, and he had to decide with whom he would fight, and with whom he would make an alliance, even though he had to pay the cost of it. All three coveted some part of the Israelite possessions, and those which could not be fought would have to be bought.

The decision was as much a commercial as a military one, for the strength of every Levantine state depended upon her ability to trade, and to bring in from without that which by nature the land itself could not provide. Conflict with Egypt was therefore ruled out, not merely because of the traditional military glory of Egypt, which at this period was sometimes more fabled than real, but because it was possible to come to terms commercially with a country for whom international trade was not a primary necessity. The Egyptian Pharaoh held all foreign trade in his own hands as a royal peculiar; his people lived from the chocolate-coloured silt.

With the two northern kingdoms, however, it was different, since trade was there part of the life of the state. There was, nevertheless, this distinction between them: Phoenicia looked outwards to the Mediterranean, upon whose distant shores she had already in the days of David and Solomon begun to establish her far-flung colonies, while Damascus was a station upon the same Trunk Road as Megiddo. Phoenician and Israelite trade could be therefore thought to be complementary, and some agreement reached between them, but with Syria there could be no lasting covenant. The question of which of them should have the longed-for mastery of the road was not to be settled without bloodshed. So we find the strong rulers of Israel endlessly at war with Damascus, but purchasing the friendship of Egypt and Phoenicia at a price.

The pattern was first established in the reigns of David and Solomon, about whom we know more than any of the other kings, but it would seem that a similar policy was followed in their turn also by Omri, Ahab, and Jehoshaphat, and later by Jeroboam II and Uzziah. Both David and Omri sealed the treaty of friendship with Phoenicia by the marriage of their son to a Phoenician princess, and David's son, Solomon, was able to achieve the almost unparalleled distinction of marriage with one of the princesses of Egypt, who were hardly ever married outside their own country (1 Kings 3 : 1; 11 : 1; 16 : 31).[44] The price they had to pay for such alliances, however, was heavy, since they were forced to renounce all thoughts of expansion in that direction and even be prepared for loss of territory (1 Kings 9 : 11–13). The whole of the plain of Asher as far as the Crocodile marshes seems to have passed for ever out of Israelite hands at this time, and during Solomon's reign much of the Philistine plain must have been under Egyptian control, for Pharaoh was able to give Gezer as dowry to his daughter when she married Solomon (1 Kings 9 : 16). The almost complete dependence of Israel upon Phoenician workmen during the empires of David and Solomon and of Omri and Ahab seems to have been the means whereby the friendship was kept sweet. Solomon's alliance with Egypt was less fortunate, for it did not prevent Pharaoh from giving asylum to Hadad, the claimant to the

Edomite throne (1 Kings 11 : 14–22), and to the rebel Jeroboam (1 Kings 11 : 40) or from attacking the weakened dominions of his son (1 Kings 14 : 25).

The importance of the foreign trade is the reason why David placed military governors in both Damascus and Sela, "establishing garrisons throughout both Syria and Edom" (2 Sam. 8 : 6, 14), but seems to have been content merely with exacting heavy tribute from Moab and Ammon, who were less likely to disrupt his commerce (2 Sam. 8 : 2; 12 : 31). But the garrisons were ineffective in preventing the early revolt of both Syria and Edom during the reign of Solomon (1 Kings 11 : 14–25). For the same reason much attention was given to the great strongholds on the Trunk Road, which were fortified by Solomon (1 Kings 9 : 15), and later by Ahab and Jeroboam II.[45]

If that for which the kings of Israel fought the kings of Syria was the immensely valuable transit trade across the Palestinian bridge, of which there is some mention in 1 Kings 10 : 28–9, the trade for which David and Solomon, and later, Jehoshaphat and Amaziah of Judah, battled with the Edomites was the equally tempting traffic along the incense routes to southern Arabia. These were the routes by which the frankincense and myrrh were brought to the countries of the Mediterranean.[46]

The oft-quoted statement by Pliny that a whole year's supply of Arabian frankincense was burnt at the funeral of Poppaea, Nero's wife, is an indication of the immense importance of the Arabian incense trade in the time of the Roman empire, but it had developed long before that. It seems probable that we must date the rise of the kingdom of Sheba and the growth of the desert trade routes back to the latter part of the second millennium B.C., when the camel was tamed and the Arabian world was first provided with an adequate means of transport for extensive journeys through the desert. Certainly by the time of Solomon the trade was well established and the famous visit of the Queen of Sheba (1 Kings 10 : 1–13) was clearly an economic mission to arrange terms with the new power which had arisen at the north end of the route and which, by virtue of its fleet of ships (1 Kings 10 : 11–12), was threatening the south Arabian monopoly.

An interesting, and so far unique, confirmation of this trade has recently come to light in the temple at Bethel, where the fragment of a south Arabian clay stamp was discovered in the course of the 1957 campaign.[47] "A multitude of camels shall cover you," said the Prophet of the Exile to Jerusalem, "the young camels of Midian and Ephah; all those from Sheba shall come. They shall bring gold and frankincense, and shall proclaim the praise of the Lord" (Is. 60 : 6), and Jeremiah had earlier asked in scorn, "To what purpose does frankincense come to me from Sheba, or sweet cane from a distant land?" (Jer. 6 : 20). But this is so far the only direct evidence of the trade in the Iron Age Israelite kingdoms. (See also Ps. 72 : 10, 15; Ezek. 27 : 22; 38 : 13.)

The caravans, "coming up from the wilderness like a column of smoke, perfumed with myrrh and frankincense, with all the fragrant powders of the merchant" (Song 3 : 6), did not bring only the incense which was needed for the Temple worship (e.g. Exod. 30 : 34; Lev. 2 : 1, 15, 16; 5 : 11; 6 : 15; 24 : 7; Num. 5 : 15; Neh. 13 : 5, 9), and the myrrh for cosmetics, perfume, and medicinal purposes (Exod. 30 : 23; Esth. 2 : 12; Ps. 45 : 8; Prov. 7 : 17; Song 3 : 6; 4 : 14; 5 : 5, 13; Matt. 2 : 11; John 19 : 39) but also spices from the Indies, and pearls from the Persian Gulf. Cinnamon, which must have come from Ceylon, was apparently among the items imported into Egypt in the early fifteenth century B.C., and possibly somewhat earlier, for the coastwise trade, which made use of the alternating winds of the Monsoons, seems already to have been established by that time, and long antedated the beginning of the camel caravans.

The antiquity of trade, and of intercourse between one distant region and another, is a fact which receives continual confirmation as archaeological research progresses. It has already been said that the coastal trade with India and Ceylon preceded the use of the camel for desert transport, but communication between the Fertile Crescent and the Indian peninsula must be carried back even further to nearly five thousand years ago. Somewhere around 2500 B.C. there was already communication between Mesopotamia and the Nile valley on the one hand and the civilization in the Indus valley on the other, and it is probable that it did not begin at this date.[48]

Any attempt by the Palestinian kingdoms to dominate the trade routes came to an end with the establishment of the great imperial systems of Assyria and Babylon, and the even greater empire of Persia which succeeded them, though the Edomite dominion over the desert routes was revived by the Nabataeans in the first century B.C. During their brief period of authority they even succeeded in exercising some form of control over Damascus (2 Cor. 11 : 32), but all was brought to an end with the Roman conquest of Petra in A.D. 106. This was in its way as inevitable as the Assyrian conquest of Israel, for so valuable, and indeed so vital, a trade route could never be allowed by the Romans outside their own system, with all the attendant instability which the relative independence implied. So also was Egypt doomed to be delivered into the hands of Britain as soon as the Suez Canal was built.

This brings us to the last of the features of the Israelite relationship with the surrounding nations, and the beginning of a change in the pattern, which is shown by the maps of the Assyrian empire (Fig. 25) and of the Levant at the end of the eighth century B.C. in the time of Isaiah (Map VII). The dominant fact at this time, and for the rest of the Old Testament period, until the entry of Rome on the scene in 63 B.C., is the disproportion between the tininess of the kingdom of Judah and the terrifying immensity of the successive empires. It first becomes apparent with the haunting question of Amos, "O Lord God, cease, I beseech thee! How can Jacob stand? He is so small!" (Amos 7 : 5), though there is scant evidence that at so early a date the inhabitants of Israel themselves were aware of their own littleness. But with the fall of Samaria in 722 B.C. no one left in the kingdom of Judah could fail to be conscious of it, and one cannot begin to comprehend the political problems of Isaiah's period, if one is not able to stand in Jerusalem, and watch the unhindered advance of the Assyrian steamroller.

Fig. 25. The Assyrian Empire

This map should be compared with that of the Persian empire (Fig. 26). The Assyrian empire was essentially based on the Fertile Crescent, with an expansion northwards up into the mountains, in order to bring under control the people of the intermontane plateaus who were continually harrying the Assyrian frontiers. The short-lived Babylonian empire, which succeeded the Assyrian one, was not very different in extent, and so no separate map of it is shown.

The Persian empire, however, was vastly more extensive and included the Fertile Crescent as only one part of the Persian dominions. This was because it had started, not from a centre within the Fertile Crescent, for which the surrounding mountains provided an *enclosing* barrier, but within the intermontane plateau, for which the mountainous rim served rather as a temporary obstacle limiting expansion into the rich and tempting land beyond. There was a similar expansion on the north side into the Oxus plain of Russian Central Asia.

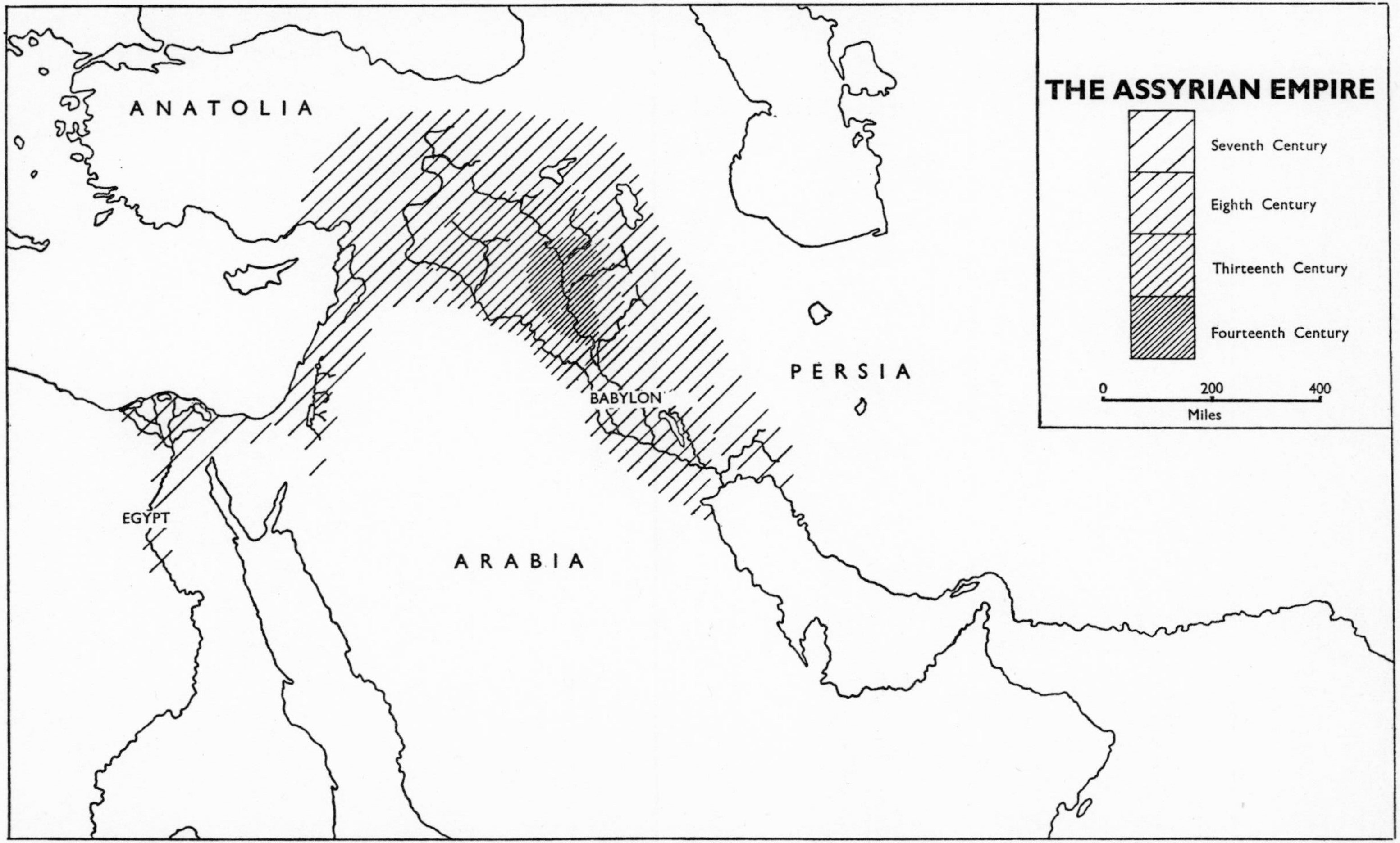
THE ASSYRIAN EMPIRE
Seventh Century
Eighth Century
Thirteenth Century
Fourteenth Century
0
200
400
Miles
ANATOLIA
PERSIA
BABYLON
EGYPT
ARABIA

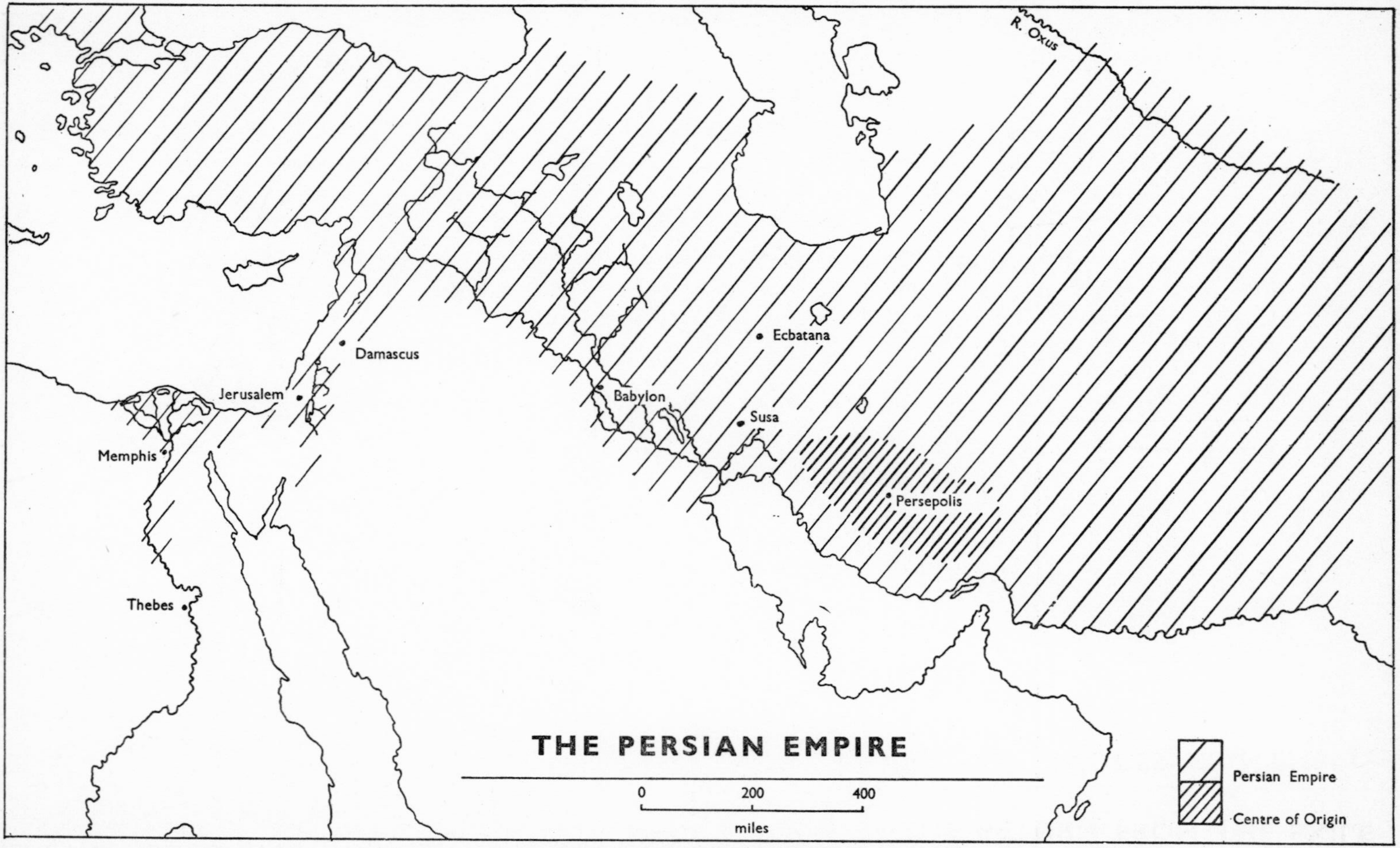

Fig. 26. The Persian Empire

THE RETURN FROM THE EXILE
Lod
Valley of the Craftsmen
Bethel
Beeroth
Mizpah
Ramah
Michmash
Geba
Gibeon
Jericho
Chephirah
Azmaveth
Kiriath Jearim
Anathoth
Nob
JERUSALEM
Zorah
Bethhaccerem
Ananiah
Jarmuth
Azekah
Zanoah
Bethlehem
Netophah
Adullam
Harim
Tekoa
Keilah
Nebo
Bethzur
Elam
Lachish
HEBRON
3000
2000
1000
sea level
DEAD SEA
I D U M E A
Ziklag
Madmenah
0 1 2 3 4 5
Miles
Sidon
Tyre
Accho
Damascus
Road from Babylon
Rabboth Ammon
Jerusalem
Gaza
Land over 3000 ft
District of Judah

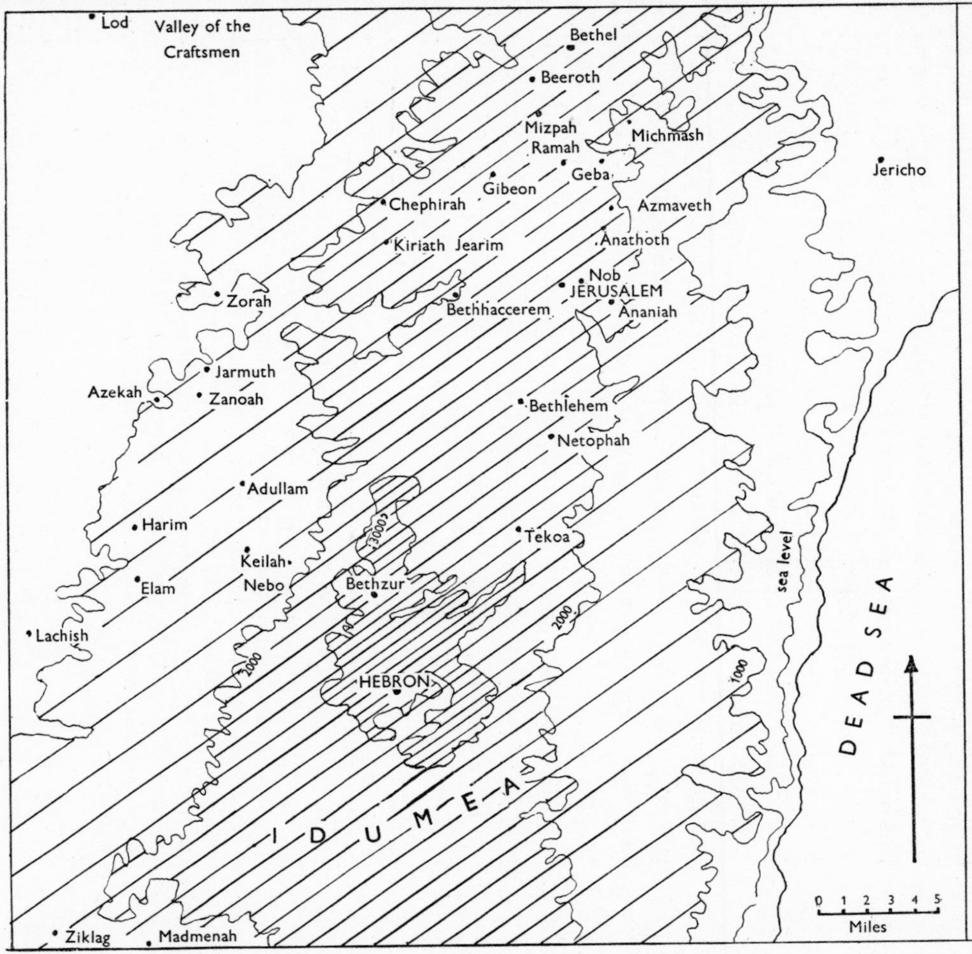

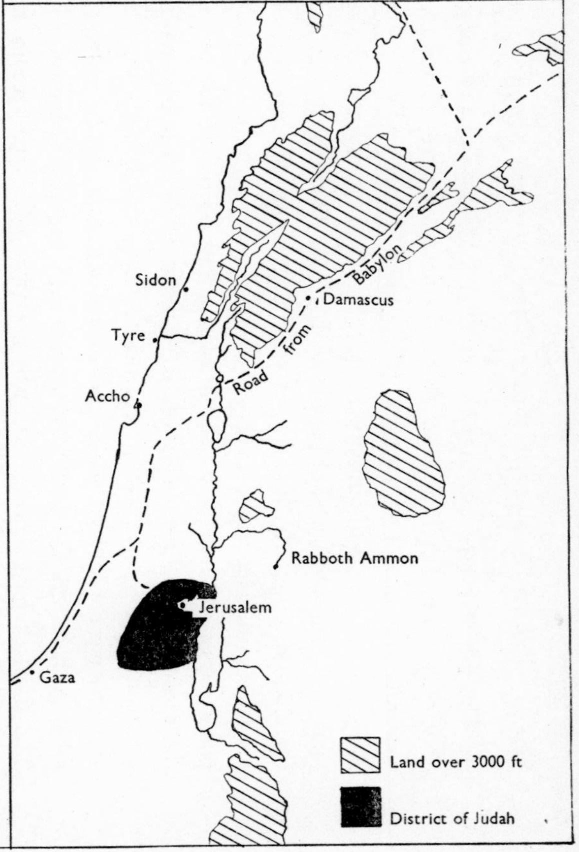

There is, it must be admitted, a tendency among some writers aware of it only academically to play down the sense of terror in the city and therefore the sense of incredible relief when it was not sacked by the Assyrian army, and the inhabitants were not led out with hooks in their noses, like the unfortunate people of Lachish. They see in the fact that Hezekiah undoubtedly had to pay tribute (2 Kings 18 : 13–16), and that his successor, Manasseh, managed to preserve the tenuous semi-independence of Judah only by the most steadfast obedience to Assyria and the most ruthless suppression of any opposition to his policy within the kingdom (2 Kings 21 : 1–18), evidence that the Jerusalemites were making altogether too much of the events of 701 B.C. But this is not to see the relation between the historical events and the psychological realities. The siege of Jerusalem in 701 was no more of a true victory for the people of Judah than Dunkirk in 1940 was a victory for Britain; but in both cases the event (though serious enough in all conscience) was so much less than the imagining, that the delirious rejoicing of the city, which earned the scathing condemnation of Isaiah (Is. 22 : 1–14), though it may have been short-sighted in view of the future which the people had to face, must not be considered surprising.

From now on the political glory had departed from Jerusalem, and though there was a brief attempt at a renaissance under Josiah, and a still brief though certainly more effective one much later under the Maccabees, never again in the whole of history could there be any hope that the city might exercise imperial authority. The exiles who returned from Babylon came but to a tiny territory (Fig. 27) and were made heirs only to a token state. It had been made clear that the triumph of Jerusalem would have to take another form.

Fig. 27. The Return from the Exile

The places marked on this map are those listed in Ezra 2 : 21–35 and Nehemiah 7 : 25–38. According to these lists the places mentioned are those from which the refugees had originally come, but it seems likely that they indicate rather the places to which they returned when they were resettled after the Exile, though it is not impossible that every effort was made to allow people to resettle in their family homes. The concentration of places in Benjamin and northern Judah should be noticed, which suggests that the region between Bethel and Hebron was the extent of the district of Judah after the return.

6

THE WORLD IS GONE AFTER HIM

The Pharisees therefore said among themselves, Perceive ye how ye prevail nothing? behold, the world is gone after him.

(John 12 : 19)

When Popilius Laenas, in 168 B.C., drew a circle on the ground round Antiochus Epiphanes, and told him not to step out of it until he had said whether he would have peace or war with Rome,[49] there began for Palestine a new era which has persisted until the present day. In 171 B.C. Antiochus had marched along the Palestinian bridge in imitation of many others before him, and had invaded Egypt, forcing Ptolemy to surrender. However, the situation demanded his return in 169; and it was while he was in Egypt on this occasion that Popilius presented his ultimatum, to which Antiochus had to agree, forfeiting thereby the chance of annexing Egypt to his empire, a triumph almost within his grasp. From now on the Palestinian bridge no longer dominates the history of the country, as it had been doing for millennia.

The bridge did not disappear, of course, and it was still important in World War II, when troops were brought northward from Egypt for the invasion of Syria. It is still important, for that matter, today, though it is as it were a broken bridge, and the Syrian Region of the United Arab Republic had in its day no direct communication by land with the Egyptian Region to the south. Yet, with the appearance for the first time in history of a great power to the west, this feature of Palestinian space relations becomes subordinate to the fact that thereafter Palestine has been condemned to lie between what the West either most desperately wanted or what it most urgently feared. The bridge between north and south has been replaced by the stepping-stone between west and east.

Beyond the forbidding Arabian desert the West has glimpsed the gorgeous East, and has heard tales of the amazing treasure which it contained—incense from the southern shores of Arabia, silk from distant Cathay, spices from the Indies and Ceylon, and, in the modern world, oil from the Persian Gulf, once famous for its pearls. It is impossible to exaggerate how passionately the West has desired these things, and how convinced it has been that life itself depended upon their possession. Yet equally it has seen beyond the Syrian coast the strongholds of some enemy—the Parthians, whom the Romans fought but could never defeat; Chosroes who menaced the Eastern empire and sacked even Jerusalem itself; the Muslims with whom the West was to fight for over a thousand years; and now the dread and terrifying Russian Bear. These visions have ever had a somewhat fabulous quality, a reputation of being larger than reality, and both of them have tempted the West from time to time into adventures beyond its strength.

At certain periods the West has tried not to become directly involved, and has endeavoured to work through a friendly eastern power which would keep the peace, after the manner of nineteenth-century Britain, bolstering up the tottering Turkish empire for her own purposes. However, the endemic instability of the area has always frightened the West, which has seen its own wellbeing threatened by the Levantine confusion, and so from time to time the dominant western power has taken the matter into her own hands, and has established a beach-head in Syria from which the turbulence could be controlled—the Provincia Arabia, or the Latin Kingdom of Jerusalem, or the Mandatory system, with its successor in the State of Israel.

Unfortunately for the West, Arabia shares with Russia and China the ability to resist in depth, and to withdraw into her impenetrable interior, trading space for time. To maintain the beach-head, therefore, the West must continue endlessly to pour in new blood and fresh resources, in order to maintain a position of strength in an area which is as endlessly harried on its undefinable landward frontiers by an enemy beyond the western reach. In the eleventh and twelfth centuries this supply of men soon dried up, and the Crusaders could hold out against the Saracens only by virtue of their gigantic castles. Today the same need exists, and Ben Gurion's controversy with American Zionism stems from his conviction that without two million *western* immigrants the country will go under.

Such was the insoluble problem which the Roman intervention in the Middle East first introduced to the world political scene. The policy of indirect control was initiated by the ultimatum of Popilius, and a century later the beach-head was established, when Pompey strode into the Holy of Holies in 63 B.C. to find "not a single image of a god, but an empty place and a deserted sanctuary".[50] Of this violation of the sanctity of God's House Josephus says, "Among the disasters of that time nothing sent such a shudder through the nation as the exposure by aliens of the Holy Place."[51] It was admittedly no new event in the long history of Jerusalem that in distress of heart men should cry to the Almighty, "The enemy has destroyed everything in the sanctuary! Thy foes have roared in the midst of thy holy place" (Ps. 74 : 3, 4), but on previous occasions it was an enemy that had done it. Pompey, however, had been invited into the country by both of the rival Hasmonean claimants, Aristobulus II and Hyrcanus, though he had had to fight for Jerusalem, whose conquest took him three months to complete, and it was under the guise of friendship that he established Hyrcanus as a semi-independent Ethnarch. It was the beginning of that bitter sense of betrayal which even now characterizes the Palestinian attitude towards the West.

It was in this surprisingly modern political world that Jesus spent His earthly life, being born during one of the experiments at indirect rule, and dying in one of the times of direct Roman control. No one who lived for any length of time in Palestine under the Mandate could fail to be aware of the extraordinary similarity between the situation of the Gospels and the situation of twentieth-century British Palestine, the same political pressures producing the same results. The Pharisees were replaced by the Husseinis, the party in strongest opposition to foreign rule; the Herodians by the Nashashibis, who were prepared to work more closely with the government; and the Zealots by the "rebels" (or later the *Irgun Zwei Leumi*), those who held that only by violent methods could the hated foreigner be driven out.

It was even a "partitioned" country, this being the futile expedient, born of political frustration, whereby a foreign government attempts to bring history to heel, and keep the ancient enemies from each other's throats. The map of Roman Palestine is therefore a patchwork. Judaea, with its fanatical inhabitants, was separated from the territory of Samaria, "for Jews have no dealings with Samaritans" (John 4 : 9), and the much

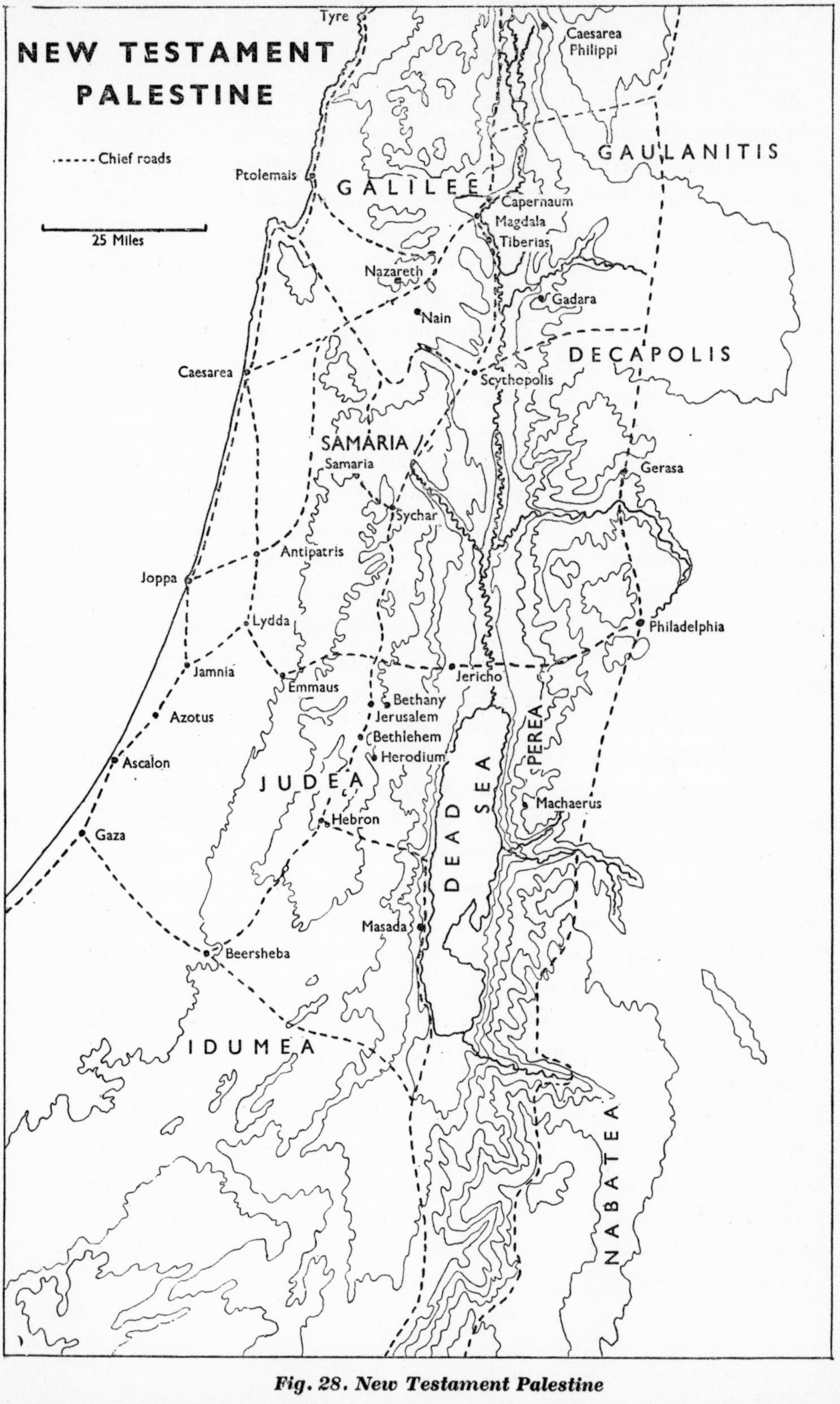

Fig. 28. New Testament Palestine

more Hellenized, and therefore supposedly more amenable, northern section was separate again. This was the Tetrarchy of Herod Antipas, which included also Perea, on the westward facing slopes of the Transjordanian plateau, the ancient Abarim. The tetrarchy of Philip lay across the Lake of Galilee in the pagan world of southern Syria, which had on its southern side the rather vaguely defined region of the Decapolis (Matt. 4 : 25; Mark 5 : 20; 7 : 31).

This was a loose federation of independent Greek cities with no clearly demarcated frontier, extending from Scythopolis (Bethshan) in the west to Canatha (modern Kanawat, ancient Kenath, Plate XXVIII—Num. 32 : 42) in the east, and from Raphana (Raphon) in Bashan in the north to Philadelphia (Rabboth Ammon) in the south, that is to say comprising most of Gilead and the southern section of the Syrian plain, or Lower Bashan. Scythopolis was the only city of the Decapolis lying west of the Jordan, but it is probably a mistake to draw a sharp frontier around it, as is done in many biblical atlases, so that Herod Antipas' territory is cleft in two. It is more likely that there was effective communication between Perea and Galilee, and that Scythopolis was a somewhat isolated outpost. Equally pagan from the Jewish point of view was the region of Tyre and Sidon (Mark 7 : 24) or the Province of Phoenicia, which extended, much as the ancient kingdom of Phoenicia had done, along the coast beyond Mount Carmel, and as far south as the Crocodile marshes. It was the most thoroughly westernized section of the whole country.

We would like, of course, to know very much more than we do about the movements of Jesus, as "he went throughout all Galilee, preaching in their synagogues and casting out demons" (Mark 1 : 39), but it has to be admitted that we know almost nothing. The Gospels are no more intended to serve as a *vade mecum* for a pious pilgrimage than they are to provide the material for a biography, and one must protest, therefore, against the repeated attempts to draw maps which show the itineraries of Jesus according to the various evangelists. One may not have to go all the way with the extremists of the form critical school, and deny any trustworthiness to the details of the Gospel accounts, but in the matter of the journeys of Jesus we must certainly echo the regretful words of Lightfoot, "[the Gospels] yield us little more than a whisper of his voice; we trace in them but the outskirts of his ways."[52]

The Old Testament is the history of a *people*, and for this reason geography has much to contribute to the understanding of their experience; but the New Testament is concerned with a *person*, and concerning him the geographer inevitably has much less to say. Such light as he can throw concerns, not the exact identification of a journey, for which there is no evidence, but the relationship of one region to another, and the manner in which this coloured the thinking of the people of the time. Thus, it is a geographical fact, of which the author of the Fourth Gospel was very well aware, that in travelling from Judaea into Galilee by the direct route one "had to pass through Samaria" (John 4 : 4), but it was also a humiliating fact for a Jew, and this compulsory journey therefore provides for St. John one of the illuminating little details whereby he underlines the parallelism between the meeting with the Samaritans and the Passion narrative.[53]

Mark is equally conscious of the relation between one part of the country and another, and it is false to say that "he was certainly unfamiliar with the geography and topography of northern Palestine".[54] His thought is in terms of regions rather than of itineraries, but he is always aware of the countryside, and he never propounds impossible journeys. Even the famous statement that Jesus "returned from the region of Tyre, and went through Sidon to the Sea of Galilee, through the region of the Decapolis" (Mark 7 : 31), which has disturbed so many commentators, is perfectly possible. It is emphatically not "equivalent to saying that a man leaves Chester and goes through Manchester to the Wash, by way of Essex".[55] There is a road leading inland from Sidon across the mountains to the central valley to the modern town of Jezzine. It would have brought Jesus round by way of the Plain of Ijon, whence He could have easily and naturally gone through Caesarea Philippi, and from there on to the eastern plateau, and so to the further side of the Lake of Galilee. This would have brought Him "through the region of the Decapolis".

This is not to say, of course, that the journey actually took place, but it is the kind of journey Mark had in mind, as he arranged the material for the "Gentile section" of his Gospel, a section which is of fundamental importance to his argument. It is a circuitous, but entirely reasonable, diversion which would keep Jesus continuously in pagan country until He could get into the boat and be ferried back to the Jewish town of Magdala (Mark 8 : 10.)[56]

The extraordinary *foreignness* of the other side of the Lake is an aspect of New Testament Palestine which needs to be emphasized, for then, as now, it divided the Jews from the Gentiles, and those on the western side could not but be conscious, as they looked across the water at the twinkling lights only five miles away, that on the other side there was a *different* people, a people who did not keep the feast. One may compare it, perhaps, with the feeling of those who live on the islands of Chios or Samos, and gaze across the strait at the towns and villages of those for whom Easter has no meaning, or with the inhabitants of Kinglake's Belgrade, for whom the people on the other side of the Danube were "compromised".

Those who have never lived so close to such a frontier may find difficulty in believing that the mental impression of it can be so powerful, for a merely political boundary has no such oppressive effect, even when it is a boundary dividing enemies. The mind learns to live with, and to discount, the chance of merely physical danger, if only because one has to cease to be afraid if one is to go about one's daily tasks. But the question here is not of physical danger, since the people of Capernaum could have had no conceivable fear that the men of the Decapolis would attack them, but rather of a strange, incomprehensible *otherness*, of a wholly different way of life, which is fascinating just because it is different. Thus, a whole coach-load of people in an Israeli train will stand up as one man, when they approach the armistice line near Tulkarm, or, as an Arab in the present divided Jerusalem once whimsically expressed it, "We cannot help looking across the line occasionally to see whether the people on the other side have really got tails!"

Every New Testament mention of "the other side of the sea" has this sense of exotic difference, which was enhanced by the fact that even in the sophisticated New Testament world the little Lake of Galilee still held something of the significance of the great and terrifying "Deep". We must surely read Mark 4 : 35–5 : 20 in this light, and understand how for anyone who knew and had experienced the Lake of Galilee it was not absurd to see in these events the person of Him "who dost still the roaring of the seas, the roaring of their waves, the tumult of the peoples; so that those who dwell at earth's farthest bounds are afraid at thy signs" (Ps. 65 : 7, 8).

Although it is true that one can no longer trace the journeys of Jesus and His disciples, yet it is impossible not to be struck by the manner in which tradition confines these to the villages and smaller towns (Map X).

Nazareth itself was a village, and though from the hills above it one may certainly see the plain of Esdraelon or Megiddo, across which passed much of the most important traffic of the country, and in the northern direction the smaller Campus Asochis (=Sahl Battauf), which carried the main road inland from the port of Ptolemais, no road ran through Nazareth itself. Jesus grew up in a little pocket away from the great commercial highroads, and yet they were all around Him, and in the course of His ministry He must have used them or crossed them again and again. The only two other places which He is reported to have visited in Lower Galilee were villages also: Cana, which was not at the traditional site of Kefr Kanna, but lay on the northern slope of the Campus Asochis, almost due north of Nazareth, and Nain, which was further south, on the northern flanks of Mount Moreh (John 2 : 1; 4 : 46; Luke 7 : 11).

His headquarters seem quite clearly to have been at Capernaum, which both in the Synoptic Gospels and in St. John receives more frequent mention (Matt. 4 : 13; 8 : 5; 11 : 23; 17 : 24; Mark 1 : 21; 2 : 1; 9 : 33; Luke 4 : 23, 31; 7 : 1; 10 : 15; John 2 : 12; 4 : 46; 6 : 17, 24, 59), but one or two other places beside the Lake also occur in the records. Chorazin, overlooking the Lake from the basalt dam to the north of it, and Bethsaida, which lay on the north-eastern shore, are both condemned with Capernaum for not having repented at the teaching of Jesus (Matt. 11 : 20–24; Luke 10 : 13–15), and they were certainly more than villages, though hardly important cities, which honour must in this region be kept for Tiberias, a town that Jesus apparently never visited. It is quite true that He may have gone there on a visit of which we have no record, and it is perhaps too easily taken for granted by some commentators that He avoided Tiberias because it was Gentile, since certainly (as far as we know) He went to Gentile territory across the Lake; but in the absence of any evidence we must probably assume that He confined His activity on the Jewish side of the Lake to the Jewish towns.

Two suggestive points may be noted in connection with the ministry of Jesus beside the Lake of Galilee. The first is that it was commercially a much more important region than it is today, and the lakeside towns exported a large amount of fish[57] and had also a lively transit trade in wheat from Bashan. One may perhaps be justified, therefore, in arguing that the refusal of these towns to hear the Word was in part the result of their wealth. The second point is that the shores of the Lake have long been famous for their hot springs, which attract a large number of invalids. They are found on both sides of Tiberias, those at Hamath to the south being particularly important, and there are others at Hamath Gader in the lower part of the Yarmuq valley. The warm winter climate also makes this part of the country very agreeable to those whose health cannot stand the severer temperatures of the hills, and it is not unreasonable to see in these facts a connection with the tradition of the large number of miraculous cures which Jesus performed here (Mark 1 : 32–34; 3 : 10; 6 : 56; Luke 4 : 23).

One important city, of course, was visited by Jesus and that is the city of Jerusalem itself, but again we are left in doubt how often He did so. Luke records a tradition that as a child He was taken up every year in accordance with the requirements of the Law (Luke 2 : 41), and, as is well known, the Synoptic Gospels mention only one visit to Jerusalem in the course of His ministry, while St. John suggests that He was in the city on at least three previous occasions. The question is not really a geographical one, but it illustrates again the utter impossibility of any attempt to plot the ministry of Our Lord on a map.

Jerusalem (Figs. 29 and 30, also Plates I–VII), so soon to be razed to the ground, was at this time strikingly different from the Jerusalem of the Old Testament, though even then it had had the reputation of being a notable city (Ps. 48 : 2, 12–14; Lam. 2 : 15). It had grown up originally as one of the towns on the ancient water-parting route along the plateau, and had early a name for both strength and sanctity (Gen. 14 : 18; 2 Sam. 5 : 6). The two, in fact, may be said to have been in some conflict with each other. The sacred spring of Gihon, at which, it would appear, the new king was proclaimed (1 Kings 1 : 33, 38, 45) and from which the royal procession ascended the hill of the Lord (Ps. 24 : 3–10), lay outside the city walls at the foot of the hill in the Kidron valley, and the high place stood also outside the city walls, on the northern side where afterwards the Temple came to be built. The problem of the water supply, Gihon being the only spring, was always an acute one for the defenders of the city, and the stairway whereby the earlier inhabitants brought water from the spring up to the town seems also to have supplied the port of entry for David's troops (2 Sam. 5 : 8). Later rulers endeavoured to remedy this defect. Isaiah met Ahaz inspecting the water conduit at the

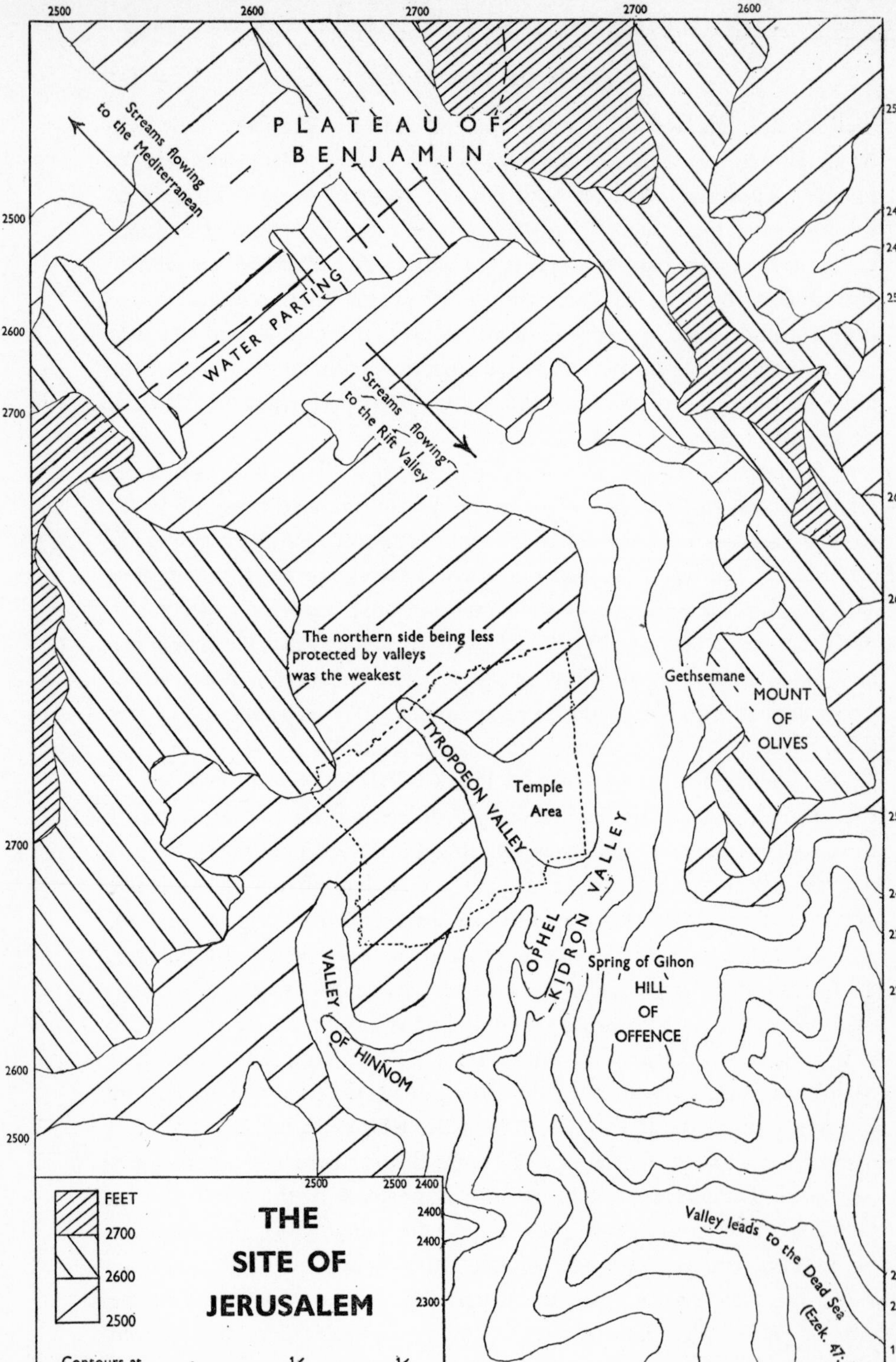

Fig. 29. The Site of Jerusalem

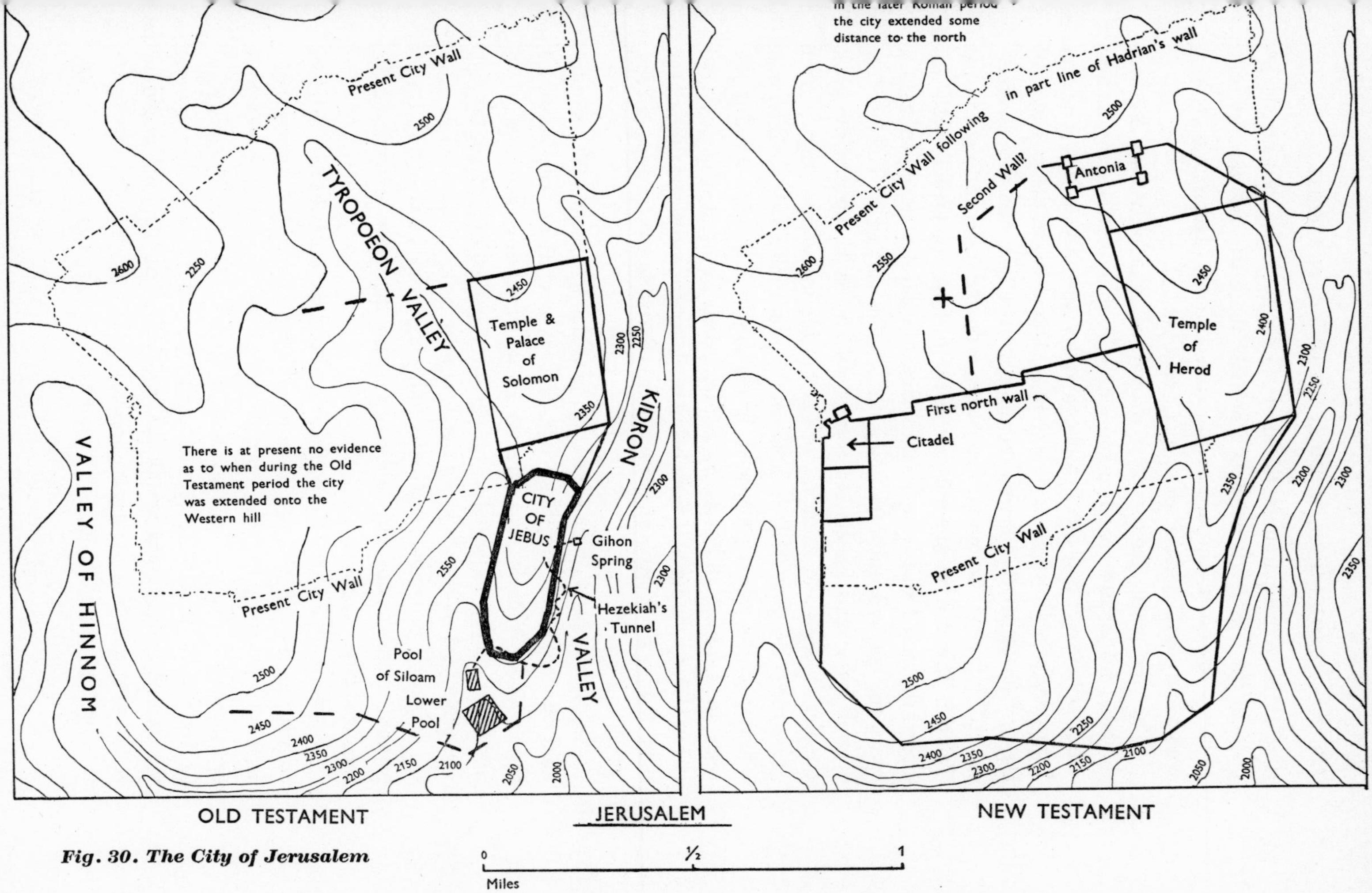

Fig. 30. The City of Jerusalem

time of the Syro-Ephraimite threat of 734 B.C. (Is. 7 : 3), and later Hezekiah cut the famous tunnel which brought the water into the city itself (2 Kings 20 : 20; 2 Chron. 32 : 30). His successor, Manasseh, is credited with having walled in the spring (2 Chron. 33 : 14).

The first town, Jebus, was a stronghold with only two or three thousand inhabitants, perched on a narrow spur between the Kidron valley on the east and the Tyropoeon valley on the west, the slopes on both sides being in those days very steep. David began the extension of the city up on to the plateau on the northern side, and this was continued by his son, Solomon. Here were built the royal fortress and the Temple. This was an integral part of the fortress, for David's walls included the sacred area, which has remained to this day an immense open space, the covered sanctuary being but a small part of it. This was the typical Syrian and Phoenician pattern which can be seen in the great temples of Jerash and Palmyra, for the worshippers stood in the open air (Ezra 10 : 9, also Plate IV), the house of the god being a little building into which only the priests penetrated. In David's time the Ark stood in the open, hidden from all but the eyes of the priests by a tent which covered it, but already suggestions were being made for the transformation of the old threshing floor into a sacred area of the Syro-Phoenician type (2 Sam. 7 : 2).

The fortification of the sacred area provided Jerusalem with a stronghold on the weaker, northern, side, and even when the city expanded round it, the Temple Area with its great defensive walls remained an important citadel. Repeatedly, in siege after siege, the agony of the city was prolonged by the ability of the Temple to hold out for months after the city itself had fallen, and even today the stout walls of the *Haram* form a notable second line of defence within the outer bulwarks of the medieval city.

By the period of the Gospels the city had long outgrown its original constricted site on the promontory of Ophel, and had spread both westwards across the Tyropoeon valley on to what is now (but wrongly) called the "Hill of Zion", and northwards on to the plateau. The westward expansion gave the city another strong defensive slope on the west, where the ground drops down steeply into the Valley of Hinnom, notorious in the period before the Exile for the human sacrifices practised there (2 Kings 23 : 10; 2 Chron. 28 : 3; 33 : 6; Jer. 7 : 31; 19 : 6; 32 : 35). The southern wall still included the hill of Ophel and the Pool of Siloam, which now lie outside the walls, but concerning the extent of the city to the north we are uncertain.

At a later date under Herod Agrippa, but before the final destruction of the city in A.D. 70, the so-called "Third Wall" had been built, either on the line of the present north wall, where was also the wall of Hadrian's Aelia Capitolina, or possibly even further to the north, where there are traces of a city wall which may belong to this period. However, during the period of the Gospels the northern section of the city was enclosed by a somewhat temporary curtain, the "Second Wall", about which we are quite in the dark. It is a great pity that this should be so, since it leaves us in the dark also about whether the traditional place of Calvary is the correct one, for it must have been outside the wall. Scholars vary in their opinions, which, it must be admitted, many of them seem to hold for theological rather than scientific reasons, Catholics tending to support the traditional site, and Protestants tending to be suspicious of it. Actually, there is really surprisingly little evidence, and certainly none that would compel us at present to reject the tradition.

After Pentecost the biblical attention moves away from Jerusalem into "all Judaea and Samaria and to the end of the earth" (Acts 1 : 8), as, largely stimulated by persecution (Acts 8 : 1; 11 : 19), the believers fanned outward into the surrounding countries (Fig. 31). Curiously enough, the Book of Acts gives no account of their spreading eastward across the Jordan into that region which has been so often the recipient of refugees, although we know that in fact many did go there, and that the Church was early established on the eastern plateau. However, the north–south movement along the Palestinian bridge is very clearly marked. Philip's journey to Gaza, when he met the Ethiopian eunuch returning from Jerusalem to the Nile valley (Acts 8 : 26–40), is an example of the one direction, and the extension of the Faith northward through Samaria and Syria to Antioch, which was to become one of its greatest centres, is an example of the other. Yet, the new orientation of Palestine as part of the vast Roman empire is demonstrated by the rapidity with which the Word spread overseas, the impression being given that it did so almost immediately, for we are told that it was converts from Cyprus and Cyrene who came to Antioch and began there the conversion of the Gentiles (Acts 11 : 20).

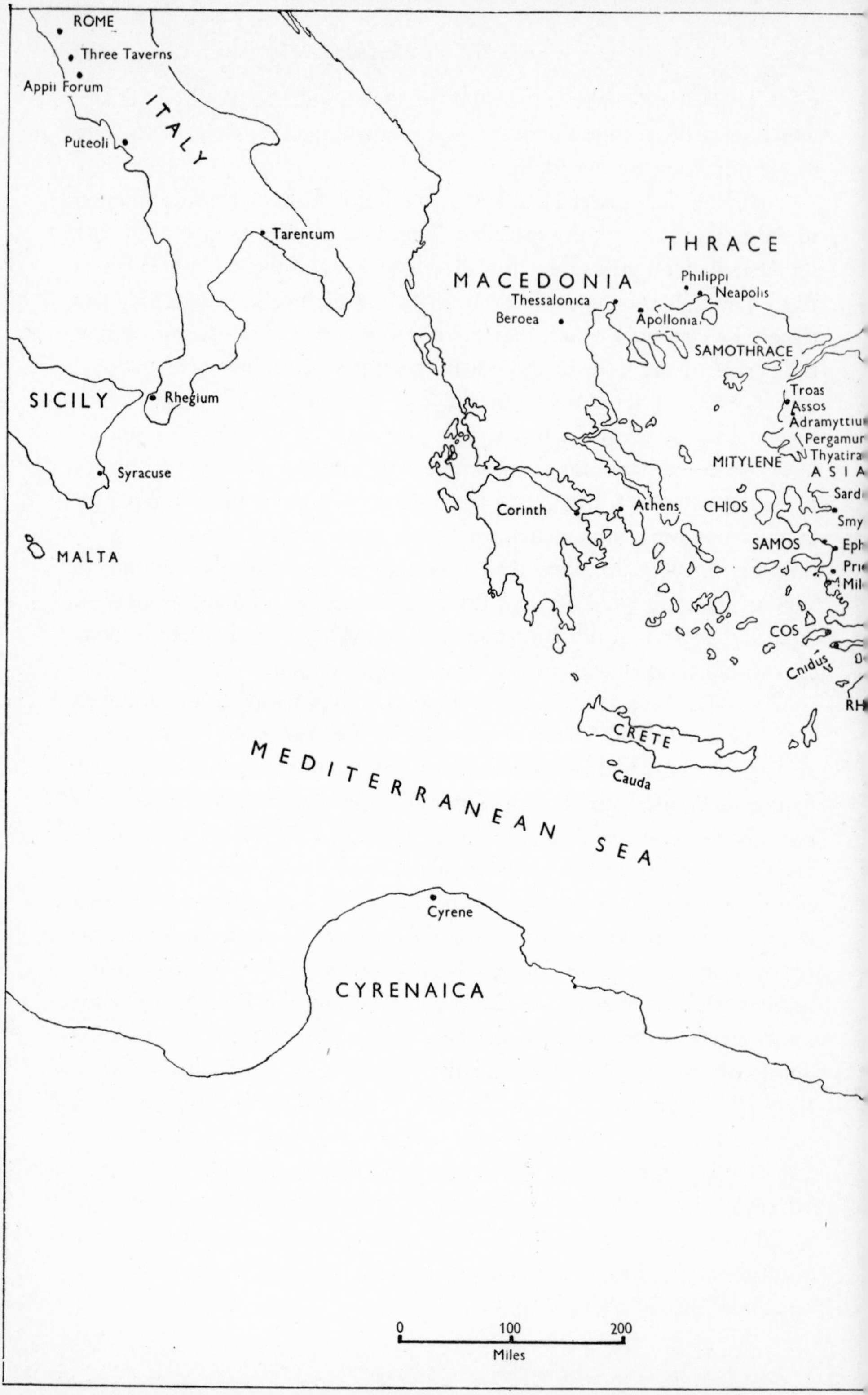

Fig. 31. The Eastern Mediterranean in the New Testament

THE EASTERN MEDITERRANEAN IN THE NEW TESTAMENT
BLACK SEA
ITHYNIA & PONTUS
CAPPADOCIA
GALATIA
adelphia
odicea
ssae
Antioch
Iconium
Lystra
Derbe
Perga
Attalia
Myra
PAMPHYLIA
CILICIA
Tarsus
Seleucia
Antioch
SYRIA
CYPRUS
Salamis
Paphos
R. Tigris
R. Euphrates
Sidon
Damascus
Tyre
Ptolemais
Caesarea
Alexandria
Gaza
Jerusalem
NABATEANS
EGYPT
Petra

The missionary journeys of St. Paul, which occupy the whole of the last sixteen chapters of the Book of Acts, have so often been traced in biblical atlases and geographies that it is not necessary to do so again. However, certain comments may perhaps be made. The first is to emphasize their coastal character. The picture has so often been drawn of St. Paul and his companions tramping along the magnificent Roman roads that the impression is left by some authors that the expansion of Christianity in some sense depended upon these great arteries of communication. It is true, of course, that he must have used them both for his own travelling and for the dispatch of his correspondence, and it would certainly not do to disparage the importance of the highly developed network of roads within the eastern Roman empire. However, with the exception of the first journey, which took Paul and Barnabas northward across the Taurus mountains from Perga close to the coast, the effective missionary work was almost exclusively in the coastal regions, and travelling was done as much by sea as by land. One might almost say that only very rarely did Paul establish a church out of sight of the typically Mediterranean olive groves.

The configuration of Asia Minor is the key to this, for it is flanked on both the north and the south by high mountain ranges, which run out to sea in the west. The interior, between the mountains, is a high plateau, with a bitter winter and a dry and dusty summer, lying in a marked rain shadow. The greatest concentration of population is therefore along the coasts, the interior being relatively uninhabited, except at the foot of the mountains where the streams provide sufficient water for agriculture: Pisidian Antioch, Iconium and Lystra, which were visited on this first journey (Acts 13 : 14, 51; 14 : 6), lie on the northern side of the Taurus mountains, which form the southern boundary of the plateau. On the two subsequent journeys Paul visited all these places again, this time travelling, it would seem, by road. To do this he would presumably strike inland from his own city of Tarsus (Acts 9 : 11, 30; 11 : 25; 21 : 39; 22 : 3) by way of the narrow defile of the Cilician Gates which lead up on to the plateau. He would then follow the northern foot of the Taurus mountains in a westerly direction. However, no activity is recorded at any other places along this route, and the suggestion is certainly that he passed through the area somewhat rapidly. It is worthy of note that Tarsus itself, although ten miles inland, was in those days a seaport, since ships could ascend the River Cnydus to a point not far below the city, or even, if they were small, to Tarsus itself. Paul would therefore have grown up as familiar with the sea as a means of transport as he was with the land.

The second point is connected with the first: it is that all the three places which became the great centres of early Christianity, Antioch, Ephesus, and Corinth, stood at the junction of vital land and sea routes. Ephesus and Corinth were ports, and Antioch lay only a few miles inland from its port of Seleucia. Antioch was an immense city, rivalled by only one or two others in the whole Empire, and it owed its importance to its position at the junction of the north–south route through the Cilician Gates into northern Syria and thence southwards through Hamath to Damascus, with the west–east route which came by sea to the port of Seleucia and then crossed the Syrian Saddle by way of Aleppo to the Euphrates. There were really several cities grouped together to form a vast urban complex and surrounded by a tremendous wall. First, there was the "Old City" on the west, which was itself enclosed by a wall, thus forming a city within a city. Second, there was the "Island City" standing on a large island in the Orontes and containing the residence of the governor. Finally, there was the new city built by the notorious Antiochus Epiphanes, a vast area on the south and east of the Old City.

Corinth, the second of these cities, was a port with two harbours, one facing west into the Gulf of Corinth, and the other facing east into the Gulf of Salamis, the western harbour being called Lechaeum and the eastern Cenchreae (Acts 18 : 18, Rom. 16 : 1). The Isthmus of Corinth, which divided the two harbours, was the only land route between northern and southern Greece. Consequently Corinth lay on a most important crossroads, of whose significance she was well aware, for she was able to exact very heavy tolls on the ships which were hauled bodily across the isthmus from one port to the other. It is clear from the letters which Paul wrote to the Corinthian church that the converts had been drawn largely from the riff-raff of the city, which held in those days the kind of unenviable moral reputation which Port Said or Marseilles came to have in much later years. Indeed, one must wonder whether it would not be correct to attribute the strength of the Christian Church in these three great entrepôt cities in large measure to the fact that they all contained so many undesirables. It would have been comparatively easy for an itinerant preacher who was able to work with his hands (Acts 20 : 34), making the sails for which in all these cities there must have been an insatiable demand, to move into a city which sheltered so much flotsam and jetsam already. Among these depressed groups, for whom society had but little use even if for economic reasons it was prepared to tolerate them, the Christian message fell on ready ears.

Naturally, this could not be the whole reason, and a part of the explanation must be sought also in the strong strategic sense which a seasoned traveller like Paul would be bound to possess. To teach and preach in Antioch, Corinth, or Ephesus would inevitably mean that sooner or later the Word would be carried far afield by the restless transient hearers both by land and sea. At Ephesus it would spread northward and southward along the coast, westward to the innumerable islands, and eastward up into the interior plateau of Anatolia by the valleys which come down to the coast at this point. There was a whole cluster of ports in this region, none of them very far from the others: Smyrna, Ephesus, Priene, and Miletus. All of them were incredibly wealthy and had truly splendid public buildings, for there was already something of the ostentation of Asia rather than the restraint of Greece in the immensity of the theatres and temples along this coast. The great sanctuary of Artemis at Ephesus is now but a heap of stones in a marsh, but to stand in the upper ranks of the gigantic theatre overlooking the silted harbour, and to imagine the excited crowd pouring along the road from the agora into the tumultuous arena is to gain a new respect for the courage of someone who could dare to challenge such assured magnificence. Only Priene, so beautifully planned, has a sense of proportion, fortunately demanded of it by its narrow site.

The city of Ephesus reappears in the Book of Revelation as one of the seven churches of Asia. These are arranged in a circle starting with Ephesus, and then curving round by way of Smyrna, Pergamum, Thyatira, Sardis, and Philadelphia to Laodicea, the last five lying inland. The exiled author on the island of Patmos must surely have known these cities personally, for he seems to have envisaged a messenger carrying his letter round to all the cities in turn, and for this reason to have addressed them in a geographical sequence. Moreover, it is probably not fanciful to see in some of the phrases he uses those touches which betoken a personal acquaintance. Thus the "throne of Satan" at Pergamum (Rev. 2 : 13) may be a reference either to the gigantic altar of Zeus which stood on the acropolis, and was one of the seven wonders of the ancient world, or possibly to the towering acropolis hill itself, or even to the strange, elongated temple of Dionysus rising in a monumental flight of steps at the far end of the theatre terrace.

Then there is the famous rebuke to the Christians of Laodicea for being lukewarm in their faith (Rev. 3 : 15, 16), a choice of words in which it is singularly tempting to see a geographical reference. Laodicea lies in the Lycus valley, near the modern town of Denizli, much of which has been built unfortunately out of its stones. Centrally placed on a low plateau, it holds a position between Hierapolis on one side (Col. 4 : 13) and Colossae on the other, and though its ruins have not been excavated, it must once have been an extensive city with two theatres and a huge stadium. But, whatever its ancient attractions, it must always have had to give place to Hierapolis for magnificence and to Colossae for charm. Hierapolis was an immense city round a group of very strong thermal springs, which have built the impressive and dazzling travertine terraces on which the city stands. Colossae, on the other hand, though there is nothing of it to be seen above ground today save a single broken pillar, had an altogether delightful position at the foot of the mountains of Caria where the plentiful streams nourish shady and luxurious orchards. Poor Laodicea, in the sun-bitten centre of the valley, had neither the medicinal hot waters of the one city nor the cool, refreshing fountains of the other, and the scathing comment was as well deserved physically as, one presumes, it was spiritually.

Another suggestion which is often made is that the "salve to anoint your eyes that you may see" (Rev. 3 : 18) is a reference to the preparation of "Phrygian eye-powder" which, it is believed, was prepared at Laodicea.[58]

This seems to have been a strange corner of early Christendom, already beyond the reach of the olive, and therefore already less Mediterranean and more Asiatic. It is not perhaps surprising that the most bizarre of the New Testament books, which otherwise are notable for their remarkable restraint, should reflect a personal knowledge of the region, or that Paul's short letter to the people of Colossae should have so much reference to the strange forms the Colossian faith had taken. The fascination with angelology which the Apostle rebukes (Col. 1 : 16; 2 : 15, 18), and the scrupulosity about holy days (2 : 16), and the exaggerated asceticism (2 : 23) indicate an exotic religious outlook from which, for all their innumerable faults, the Corinthians were commendably free.

NOTES

1 Richard Hartshorne, *Perspective on the Nature of Geography* (Rand McNally, Chicago, 1959), p. 21.

2 *op. cit.*, p. 47.

3 John Bright, *A History of Israel* (Westminster, Philadelphia, 1959), pp. 63–64.

4 Kathleen Kenyon, *Digging Up Jericho* (Ernest Benn, London, 1957), p. 74.

5 The question is discussed in detail in J. Simons, *The Geographical and Topographical Texts of the Old Testament* (Brill, Leiden, 1959), pp. 98–102.

6 See Theophile J. Meek in *The Interpreter's Bible*, Vol. V (Abingdon, New York, 1951), p. 123.

7 Gen. 12 : 10 (26 : 1 is presumably a doublet); 43 : 1; Ruth 1 : 1; 2 Sam. 21 : 1; 1 Kings 18 : 2; 2 Kings 6 : 25; 7 : 4; 25 : 3. The recent three seriously dry years in Palestine (1957–60) throw an interesting light on the three years of drought in the time of Elijah (1 Kings 17 : 1; 18 : 1–2), for in the summer of 1960 the universal comment of the Jordanian farmer was, "We have had no rain for three years," by which he meant that for three years the rain had been woefully deficient, rather than that there had been none at all. The similarity of this sentence to 1 Kings 17 : 1 will be immediately apparent.

8 M. du Bruit, O.P., *Geographie de la Terre Sainte* (La "Bible de Jerusalem", Etudes Annexes), 2 vols. (Editions du Cerf, Paris, 1958), p. 50.

9 The territory of Gad is notoriously difficult to determine. In Num. 32 : 33–38 it overlaps the territory of Reuben, which lay south of Gilead. It seems probable that the name was early confused with that of Gilead, and in any case the tribe soon vanished before the expansionist policies of Manasseh on the one hand and the Ammonites on the other.

10 For *Mishor* as a regional name see Deut. 4 : 43; Josh. 20 : 8; Jer. 48 : 21. See also the discussion in Simons, *op. cit.*, pp. 63–64.

11 The eight seasons are summarized in the *Bulletin of the American Schools of Oriental Research*, Nos. 131, pp. 6–15; 137, pp. 10–22; 138, pp. 7–29; 142, pp. 17–35; 145, pp. 11–25; 149, pp. 8–17; 152, pp. 18–38; 159, pp. 3–14, and also *The Biblical Archaeologist*, XVIII: 1, pp. 2–9; XXII: 4, pp. 82–97, as well as in his book *Rivers in the Desert* (Farrar, Straus and Cudahy, New York, 1959). See also Y. Aharoni, M. Evenari, L. Shanan and N. H. Tadmore, "The Ancient Desert Agriculture of the Negev" in *Ktavim* 8, 1958, pp. 127–30; 9, 1959, pp. 107–29; *Israel Exploration Journal* 8, 1958, pp. 231–68; *Ktavim* 9, 1959, pp. 223–40; *I.E.J.* 10, 1960, pp. 23–36, 97–111.

12 And most unfortunately so. The well-meaning artists fix for ever in the young minds Palestine as they saw it, treeless for the most part, with unwalled towns and villages, approached by narrow lanes between hedges of prickly pear. I have in front of me as I write, a Bible published by Harper and Brothers in New York which shows Ruth and Boaz apparently by the Lake of Galilee (certainly not near Bethlehem), and a mosque with its minaret in the New Testament Jericho (pp. 316 and 956). The films do even more harm. In *Ben Hur* the unfortunate traveller from Jerusalem to Caesarea was conducted all round the southern end of the Dead Sea, while the great chariot race at Jerusalem (and apparently

also the Crucifixion if the evidence of one flash of lightning were to be believed) took place in the distant city of Petra! This cult of the picturesque is quite disastrous.

13 Kathleen Kenyon, *op. cit.*, p. 184.

14 Jebus (the only hill town), Bethshan, Taanach, Ibleam, Dor, Megiddo, Gezer, Kitron, Nahalol, Accho, Sidon, Ahlab, Achzib, Helbah, Aphek, Rehob, Har-heres, Ajalon, Shaalbim.

15 Henri Frankfort, *Kingship and the Gods* (Univ. of Chicago, 1948), passim.
Sigmund Mowinckel, *He That Cometh* (Blackwell, Oxford, 1956), p. 27.

16 "It would be no exaggeration to call the place divine—a place where the rarest and loveliest things are found in such abundance. . . . This is due, I think, to the warmth of the air and the fertilizing power of the water. . . . The air too is so mild that the inhabitants dress in linen when the rest of Judaea is under snow." Josephus, *The Jewish War*, A New Translation by G. A. Williamson (Penguin Books, Harmondsworth, 1959), p. 385.

17 It is true that the regional method has been criticized by some, e.g. G. H. T. Kimble, "The Inadequacy of the Regional Concept", Chap. IX of *London Essays in Geography*, ed. L. D. Stamp and S. W. Wooldridge (Longmans, London, 1951). Nevertheless it is generally accepted by most modern geographers.

18 Although he had put forward his views as early as 1888 in an article called "Les divisions fondamentales du sol français", *Bulletin Littéraire*, vol. ii, pp. 1–7 and 49–57, the classic statement is in his great work *Tableau de la Géographie de la France*, published in 1903. The history of this type of study by French geographers may be found briefly summarized in F. J. Monkhouse, *Western Europe* (Longmans, London, 1959), pp. 1–5.

19 Is. 33 : 9; 35 : 2. See also the discussion of this subject in the writer's *Geography of the Bible* (Harpers, New York, 1957; Lutterworth, London), pp. 136–37.

20 J. Simons, *The Geographical and Topographical Texts of the Old Testament* (E. J. Brill, Leiden, 1959), pp. 34–35.

21 For a fuller discussion of this problem see Y. M. Goblet, *Political Geography and the World Map* (George Philip and Son, London, 1956), pp. 162–82; Gordon East, *The Geography Behind History* (Nelson, London, 1938), pp. 116–35; and A. E. Moodie, *Geography Behind Politics* (Hutchinson, London, 1947), pp. 72–102.

22 Not "stone" as the RSV has it; the Authorized Version is better here. "As common as stones" is understandably the Palestinian equivalent of the English phrase "as common as dirt".

23 George Adam Smith, *The Historical Geography of the Holy Land* (Hodder and Stoughton, London), twentieth edition, p. 134.

24 The concept of the sea as representing chaos is dealt with at length in Aubrey R. Johnson, *Sacral Kingship in Ancient Israel* (Univ. of Wales, Cardiff, 1955), passim, though it is possible that he sees this symbolism in rather too many instances.

25 It is necessary to insist that the map should be treated with caution. There are, of course, no ancient statistics on which such a map can be based, and the evidence therefore has to be drawn from modern usage. In general terms, however, the ancient cultivation of these products cannot have varied greatly in distribution once the hills had been brought under the plough, though we have good reason to think that the total quantities were not the same.

26 e.g. Baasha (1 Kings 15 : 27), Zimri (1 Kings 16 : 9–10), Omri (I Kings 16 : 15–18), and Jehu (2 Kings 9 : 4–10).

27 E. A. Speiser, " 'Coming' and 'Going' at the 'City' Gate", in *Bulletin of the American Schools of Oriental Research*, No. 144, Dec. 1956, pp. 20–24.

28 Indian elephants, certainly, as must have been also the famous elephants of Hannibal. Too much ink has been wasted over the problem of how Hannibal could have used the African elephant, which has never been tamed, for despite the distance, it would actually

have been easier for him to have obtained elephants by the normal trade routes from India than from across the Sahara desert.

29 A. W. Kinglake, *Eothen*, edit. R. W. Jepson (Longmans, London, 1935), p. 146. *Eothen* was first published by Ollivier of Pall Mall in 1844.

30 It is generally accepted that the Philistines already knew the use of iron, while the Israelites were still restricted to bronze, and that this is the meaning of 1 Sam. 13 : 19–21.

31 Simons questions whether it is not a misreading for "Ge", or valley, *op. cit.*, p. 363.

32 James B. Pritchard, *Ancient Near Eastern Texts Relating to the Old Testament* (Princeton University Press, 1950), p. 237.

33 W. F. Albright, *The Archaeology of Palestine* (Penguin Books, Harmondsworth, 4th Edit. 1960), p. 117.

34 Beth-haggan of 2 Kings 9 : 27 is presumably the same place.

35 See for instance R. B. Y. Scott, "The Book of Isaiah" in *The Interpreter's Bible* (Abingdon, New York, Vol. V, 1951), pp. 245–46.

36 Kathleen Kenyon, *op. cit.*, pp. 75–76.

37 See for instance E. A. Speiser, "The Biblical Idea of History in its Common Near Eastern Setting", in *Israel Exploration Journal*, Vol. 7, 1957, pp. 201–16.

38 See George Ernest Wright, *Biblical Archaeology* (Gerald Duckworth and Co., London, 1957), pp. 136–45.

39 Henri Frankfort, *The Birth of Civilization in the Near East* (Doubleday Anchor Edition, 1956), p. 9.

40 So George Ernest Wright and Floyd Vivian Filson, *The Westminster Historical Atlas to the Bible* (Westminster Press, Philadelphia), Plate V, and Luc H. Grollenberg, *Atlas of the Bible* (Nelson and Sons, London), Map 9.

41 Both M. du Buit, *op. cit.*, p. 115, and Emil G. Kraeling, *Bible Atlas* (Rand McNally, New York, 1956), pp. 107–13, wisely refuse to reach any definite decision on this matter. Kraeling gives an admirable summary of the evidence.

42 Deir ez-Zor has on an average 29 rainy days a year, with an average yearly total of 6·3 inches. The average January temperature is 45°F. but 16°F. has been recorded. Baghdad has 28 rainy days with 5·5 inches, a January temperature of 48°F. and an absolute minimum of 19°F. This should be compared with the Nile valley above Cairo, where the annual average rainfall is less than 2 inches, the January temperature 53°F. and frost is practically unknown.

43 Henri Frankfort, *op. cit.*, p. 54.

44 See A. Malamat, "The Kingdom of David and Solomon in its contact with Aram Naharaim", in *Biblical Archaeologist*, XXI, 1958, pp. 96–103.

45 Y. Yadin, Y. Aharoni, R. Amiran, T. Dothan, I. Dunayevsky, J. Perrot, *Hazor I. The First Season* (Magnes Press, The Hebrew University, Jerusalem, 1958). See also the preliminary communiqués on the excavations published in *Israel Exploration Journal*, 6, 1956, pp. 120–25; 7, 1957, pp. 118–23; 8, 1958, pp. 1–14; 9, 1959, pp. 74–88. Also Y. Yadin, "Solomon's City Wall and Gate at Gezer", in *IEJ*, 8, 1958, pp. 80–86, and Y. Yadin, "New Light on Solomon's Megiddo", in *Biblical Archaeologist*, XXIII, 1960, pp. 62–68.

46 Gus W. Van Beek, "Frankincense and Myrrh", in *Biblical Archaeologist*, XXIII, 1960, pp. 70–95. I am indebted to this article for most of the information given here on this subject.

47 Gus W. Van Beek and A. Jamme, "An Inscribed South Arabian Clay Stamp from Bethel", in *Bulletin of the American Schools of Oriental Research*, 151, October 1958, pp. 9–16.

48 V. Gordon Childe, *New Light on the Most Ancient East* (Routledge & Kegan Paul, London, 1954), p. 170.

49 Livy, 44 : 12.

50 Tacitus, *Hist.* 5 : 9.

51 Josephus, *The Jewish War*, Penguin edition, p. 41.

52 R. H. Lightfoot, *History and Interpretation of the Gospels* (Harper, New York, 1935), p. 113; Hodder and Stoughton, London.

53 R. H. Lightfoot, *St. John's Gospel* (Oxford University Press, 1956), p. 122.

54 Frederick C. Grant, "The Gospel according to St. Mark," in *The Interpreter's Bible* (Vol. VII, 1951), p. 631.

55 Harold A. Guy, *The Origin of the Gospel of Mark* (Hodder and Stoughton, London; Harper, New York, 1955), p. 27.

56 The English versions have Dalmanutha, but this place is quite unknown, and there is textual authority for reading Magdala, which is probably correct.

57 Josephus correctly notes the curious fact that some of these fish resemble those found much further south in the Nile valley. *Jewish War* (Penguin edition), p. 383.

58 See Sherman E. Johnson, "Laodicea and its Neighbors" in *Biblical Archaeologist*, XIII, 1950, pp. 1–18.

2

CARTOGRAPHY OF THE BIBLE

Comments on the Coloured Maps

pp. 141–144

I

PHYSICAL MAP OF PALESTINE

II

CLIMATIC TYPES OF THE LEVANT

III

LAND OF THE PATRIARCHS

IV

JOSHUA AND JUDGES

V

GRAIN AND WINE AND OIL

VI

THE IMPERIAL PATTERN

VII

THE ASSYRIAN MENACE

VIII

THE NORTHERN BATTLEFIELD

IX

THE SOUTHERN BATTLEFIELD

X

GALILEE OF THE GOSPELS

COMMENTS ON THE COLOURED MAPS

I. PHYSICAL MAP OF PALESTINE

The important points to notice about this map are (a) the division of the country into the four longitudinal zones, the Coast Plain, the Western Highlands, the Rift Valley and the Eastern Plateau; (b) the interruption of the Coast Plain by the headland of Mount Carmel, and of the Western Highlands by the lowland Esdraelon Corridor from Accho to Bethshan; (c) the Eastern Plateau is generally higher than the Western Highlands, but very much higher in the south; (d) the marked NE–SW trend of the hills in the south of Palestine; (e) the fact that the Rift Valley is below sea-level from the Lake of Galilee to south of the Dead Sea; (f) the four great canyons entering the Rift Valley from the east: the Yarmuq, the Jabbok, the Arnon, and the Zered.

II. CLIMATIC TYPES OF THE LEVANT

The outstanding facts about the climate of the Levant are (a) in general the summer is dry and hot, while the winters are cool and rainy; (b) both the amount of rain and the period of the year during which it falls increase as one goes north; (c) rainfall increases in amount as one goes up a mountain; (d) rainfall decreases towards the south and towards the east. It is very markedly less on the eastern side of any hill or mountain. With these facts in mind one may divide the Levant into climatic regions as follows:

(1) *The Phoenician Coast Type:* The winters are mild and very wet, the rain falling in torrential storms. Sometimes the rain is prolonged for a week or more, and the absolutely rainless months are fewer in number, decreasing to only two in the extreme north. The summers are hot and humid. This is very marked in a place like Beirut, which is shut in by the Lebanese mountains. On the other hand this region is protected from the fierce desert siroccos which afflict other parts of the country in spring and autumn.

(2) *The Sharonian Coast Type:* Here the rainless season is longer, and lasts for at least five months. The rainfall is less in amount, and the storms usually last for three days, being very heavy on the first two days, and coming in intermittent squalls on the third. In a good year rain falls with surprising regularity once a week. In the southern part of this region the rainfall is very markedly less. The winter temperatures are very mild, but the summers are hot, though they are moderated by the very regular sea-breeze which develops around 9 a.m. The south-eastward facing coasts of Turkey and Cyprus have been included in this type, though they have cooler winters, because being in a rain-shadow they have less rain than one would expect so far north.

(3) *The Libanian Mountain Type:* The chief characteristics of this type are cool summers, and the very cold winters with heavy snowfalls. The snow is thick enough in the higher parts for skiing, and the high passes are closed in winter.

(4) *The Israelian Hill Type:* This is in many ways the most attractive climate of all, for though the winters are cold, the sun is warm, and during the summer the nights are almost always cool and refreshing. The daily maxima in summer are often higher than those on the coast, but it is a dry heat and therefore much less exhausting, and there is usually a strong breeze. The wet days in winter are very chilly, however, and snow may fall occasionally after Christmas (Plate II). Heavy snow occurs about once every ten years in Jerusalem, but is more common further east, and the Jebel Druze may be snow-covered for prolonged periods.

(5) *The Hamathian Steppe Type:* This is a transitional type, characterized by the features of both the Mediterranean and the desert. The most important fact is that everywhere there is sufficient rain for agriculture, though this is much more assured in the north, the average being between 10 and 20 inches. The winters can be surprisingly cold, since this is a plateau type, and also open to the bitter winds from the interior of Arabia. Even in the extreme south, in Edom, snow falls almost every year.

(6) *The Syrian Steppe Type:* This is distinguished from the last type in that here the rain is just on the frontier of sufficiency, that is to say around 8 inches yearly. It is much more regular in the north where the division from the Hamathian type is not a sharp division but a very gradual transition zone. In the south the rainfall is most untrustworthy. The

sections of this type on the coast and in the Rift Valley have mild winters, but on the plateau the winter can be very cold.

(7) *The Arabian Desert Type:* This is a "tame" desert. That is to say that every year there is some rain, though it is very erratic, and tends to fall in one or two heavy storms at either the beginning or end of the rainy season. It is also often very limited in extent, and five or ten miles may divide a place with a heavy storm of rain from a place with almost none. The summers are very hot, and the winters are bitterly cold. Even when the sun is shining strongly the wind can be icy. In a good year the winter rains fall far out into the desert, which then for a brief period is carpeted with flowers and young grass, a truly wonderful sight.

III. LAND OF THE PATRIARCHS

There are really two regions to be noticed here, the piedmont zone in the far north of Syria, where the Euphrates leaves the mountains, and the region round Hebron and Beersheba in the south. Both are steppeland regions. The former is the land of Haran from which Abraham came, and the latter is the grazing area to which he moved. At this period the Hebrews were nomads, with herds of sheep and goats, and using donkeys for transport. They moved to and fro along the full extent of the Levant "bridge" apparently without any serious difficulty. Chapter 14 of Genesis describes an early Mesopotamian invasion along this bridge during the Patriarchal period, along the eastern side of the Rift Valley.

IV. JOSHUA AND JUDGES

Discussed in the text, pages 62 following. The Joshua stories are the earliest example of the importance of the Southern Battlefield (Map IX), since they recount stories of the penetration of the Israelites across the territory of Benjamin and down the Valley of Ajalon into the Judaean Moat and the Shephelah.

V. GRAIN AND WINE AND OIL

Discussed in the text, pages 75 following.

VI. THE IMPERIAL PATTERN

Discussed in the text, pages 106 following.

VII. THE ASSYRIAN MENACE

This map illustrates the nature of the Assyrian pressure into the Levant and southwards towards Egypt, as well as the terrifying smallness of the territory of Judah. The original purpose of the Assyrian invasion of the Levant was to get the valuable timber of the Phoenician mountains, but in the eighth century B.C. a new purpose developed, that of control of the whole Levant bridge, and then, in the seventh century, the subjugation of Egypt.

VIII. THE NORTHERN BATTLEFIELD

Discussed in the text, pages 87 following.

IX. THE SOUTHERN BATTLEFIELD

Discussed in the text, pages 91 following.

X. GALILEE OF THE GOSPELS

For reasons discussed in the text (pages 119–120) we know remarkably little about Our Lord's movements about Galilee during His ministry there. The headquarters was undoubtedly Capernaum on the north-western side of the Lake, and much of His work seems to have been in this area, extending from Magdala in the south-west to Bethsaida in the north-east. This is the section of the Lake coast with broadest extent of plain, which is nowhere large. It is widest just north of Magdala in the Plain of Gennesaret, but immediately south of Magdala the sharp bluff of "Herod's Cliff" brings it to an end. Magdala was the point where the Trunk Road left the Lake and struck inland by way of the Valley of the Robbers. At the head of the valley was Arbela where the road divided, one route going through Cana on the north side of the Asochis plain to Ptolemais, another through Sepphoris across the Turan plain, and thence to the Jokneam pass across Carmel to Dora and Caesarea, while the third was the Trunk Road. The steep cliffs with the inaccessible caves made the Valley of the Robbers a very dangerous section of the road.

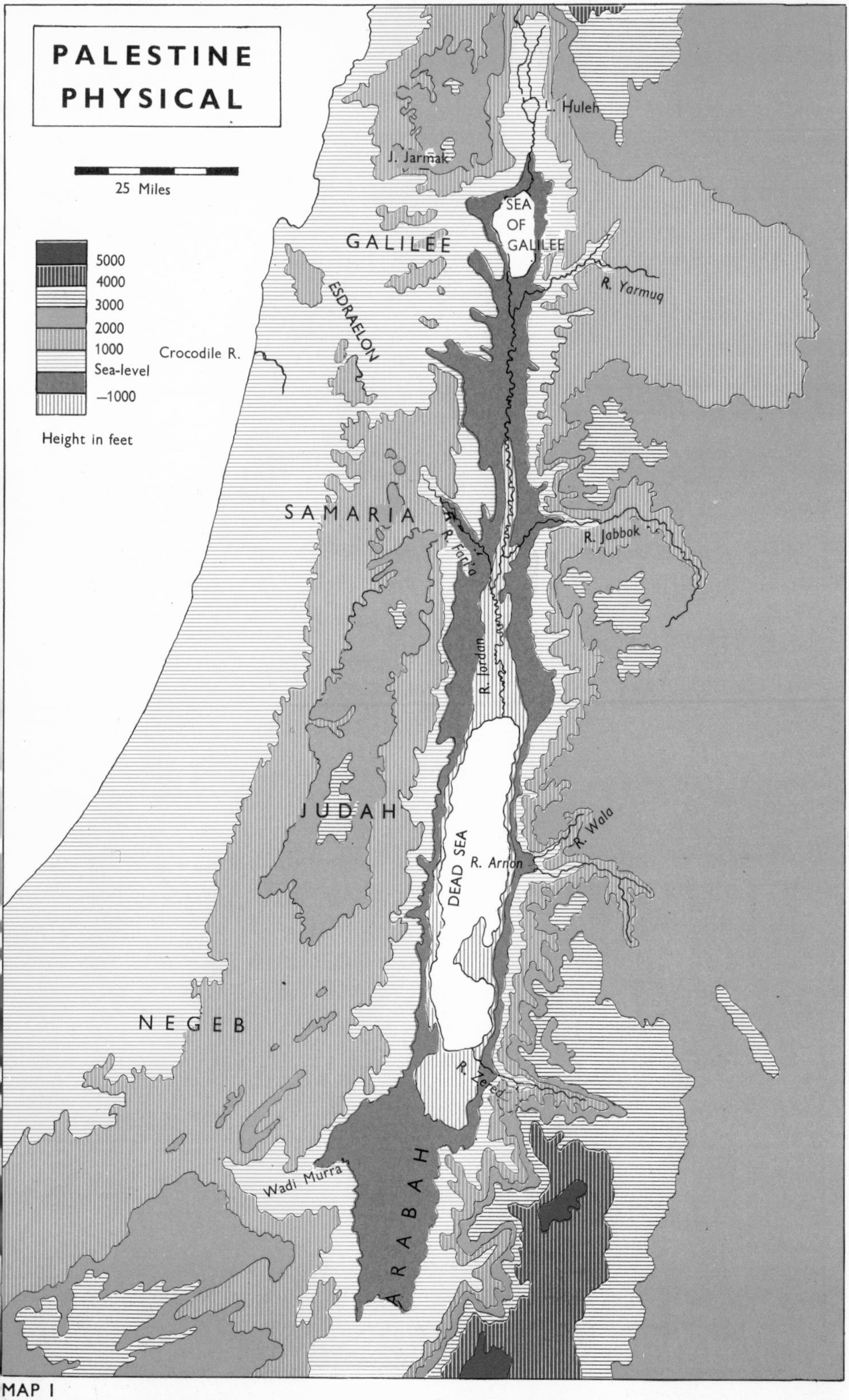
PALESTINE
PHYSICAL
25 Miles
5000
4000
3000
2000
1000
Sea-level
–1000
Height in feet
L. Huleh
J. Jarmak
SEA
OF
GALILEE
GALILEE
R. Yarmuq
ESDRAELON
Crocodile R.
SAMARIA
R. Far'a
R. Jabbok
R. Jordan
JUDAH
DEAD SEA
R. Wala
R. Arnon
NEGEB
R. Zered
ARABAH
Wadi Murra

MAP I

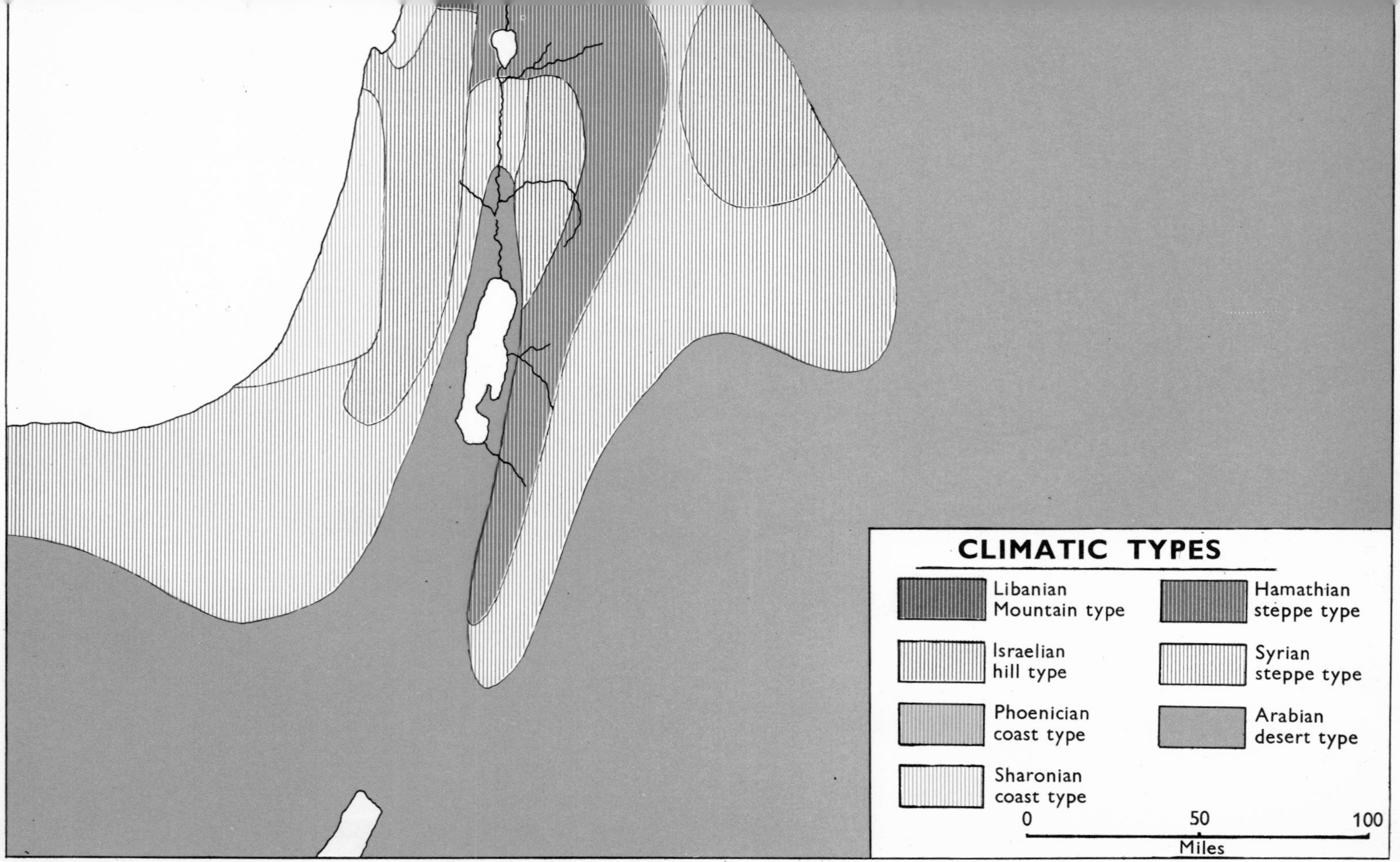
CLIMATIC TYPES
Libanian Mountain type
Hamathian steppe type
Israelian hill type
Syrian steppe type
Phoenician coast type
Arabian desert type
Sharonian coast type
0
50
100
Miles

MAP II

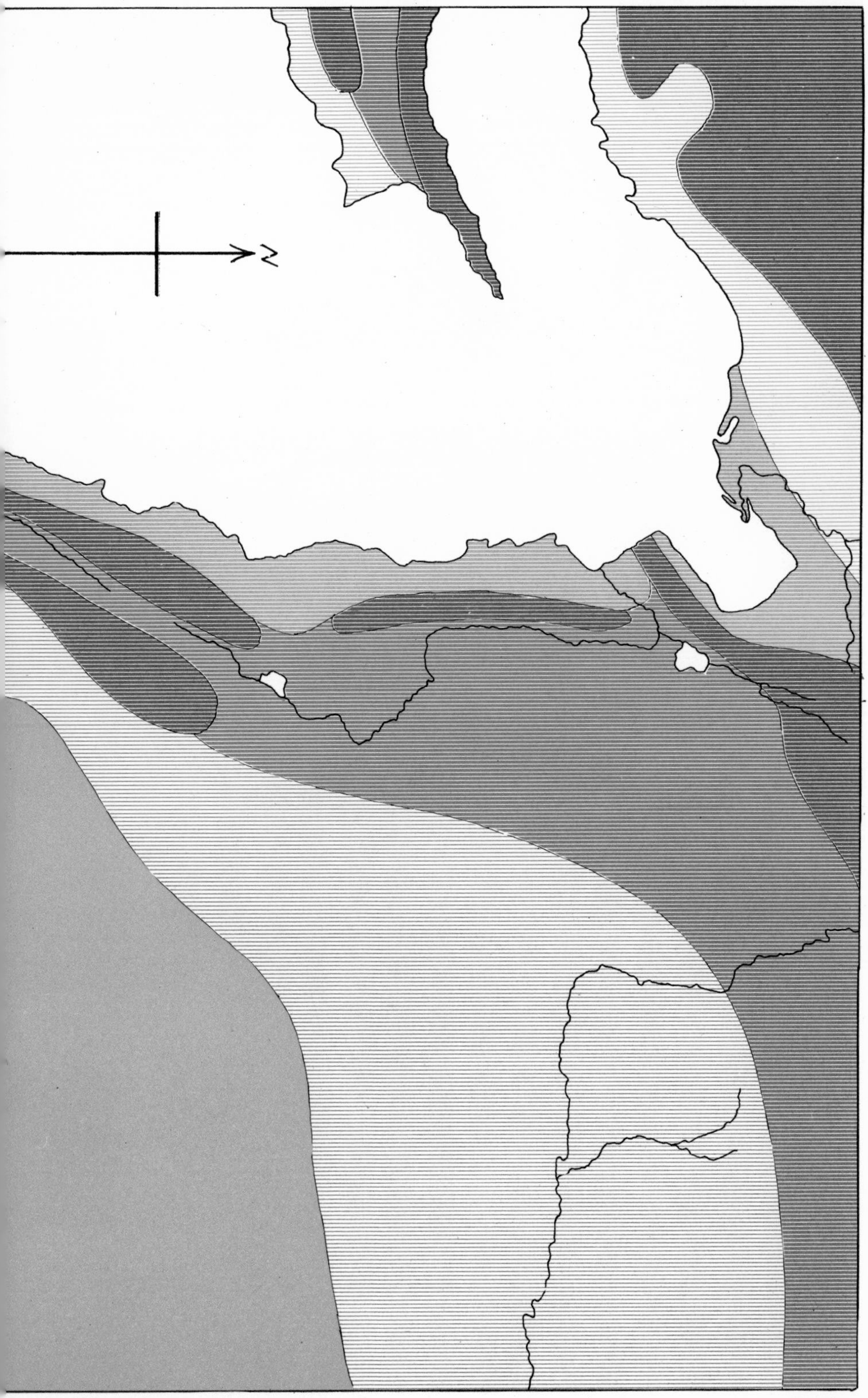
N

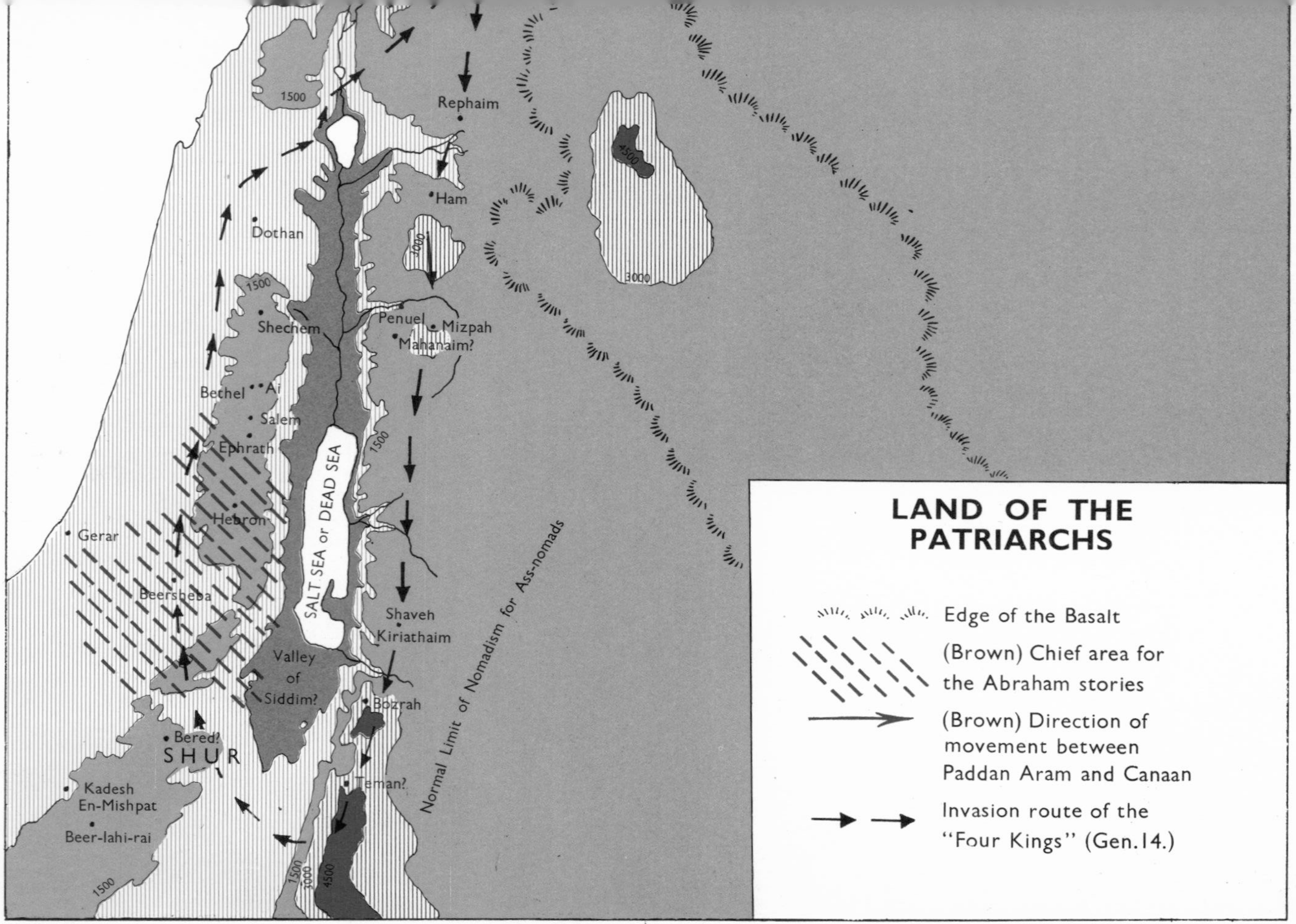
LAND OF THE PATRIARCHS
Edge of the Basalt
(Brown) Chief area for the Abraham stories
(Brown) Direction of movement between Paddan Aram and Canaan
Invasion route of the "Four Kings" (Gen.14.)
Rephaim
Ham
Dothan
Shechem
Penuel
Mizpah
Mahanaim?
Bethel
Ai
Salem
Ephrath
Hebron
Gerar
Beersheba
SALT SEA or DEAD SEA
Shaveh
Kiriathaim
Valley of Siddim?
Bozrah
Bered?
SHUR
Kadesh En-Mishpat
Beer-lahi-rai
Teman?
Normal Limit of Nomadism for Ass-nomads
1500
3000
4500

MAP III

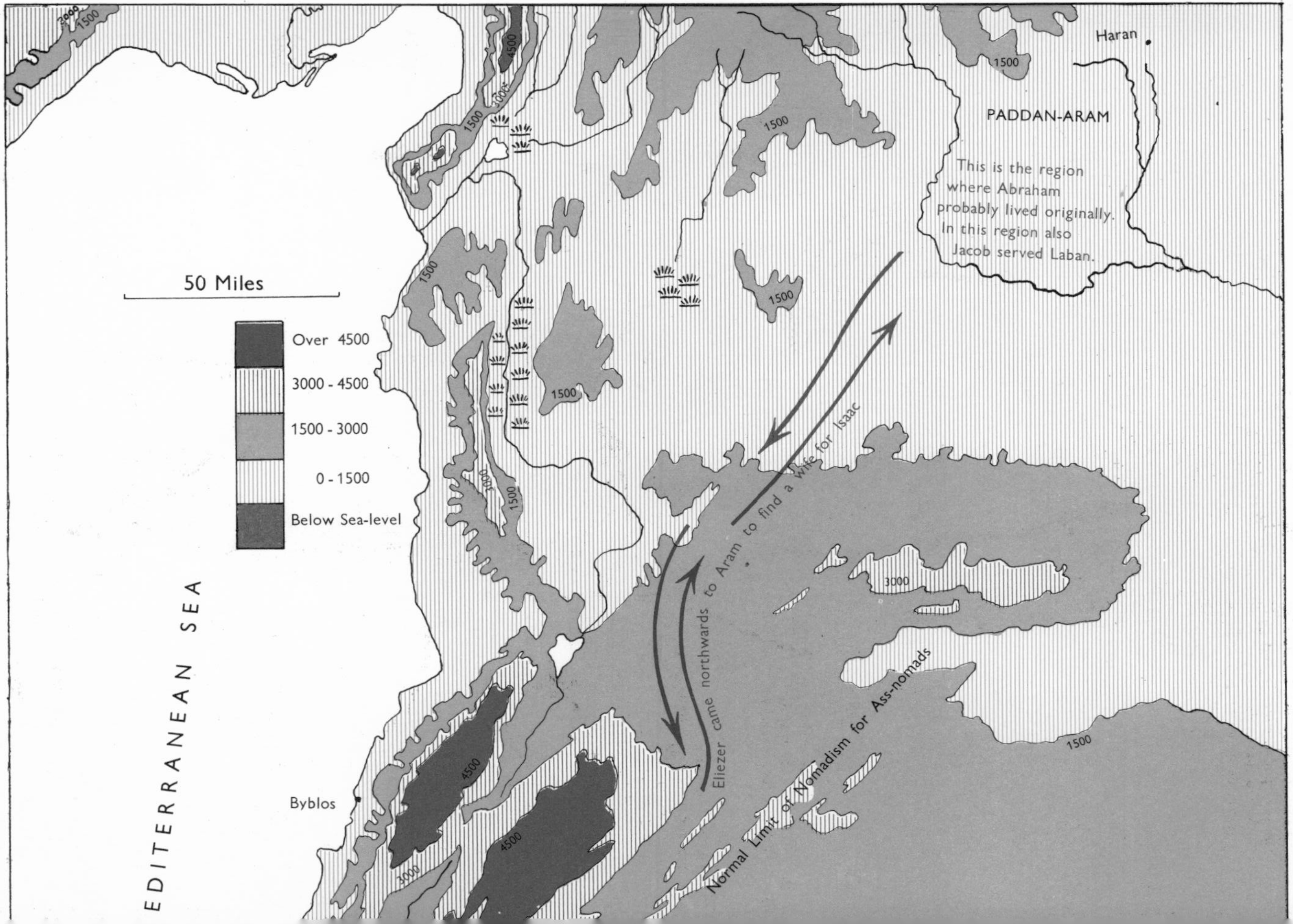

EDITERRANEAN SEA
50 Miles
Over 4500
3000 - 4500
1500 - 3000
0 - 1500
Below Sea-level
Byblos
Haran
PADDAN-ARAM
This is the region
where Abraham
probably lived originally.
In this region also
Jacob served Laban.
Eliezer came northwards to Aram to find a wife for Isaac
Normal Limit of Nomadism for Ass-nomads
1500
3000
4500

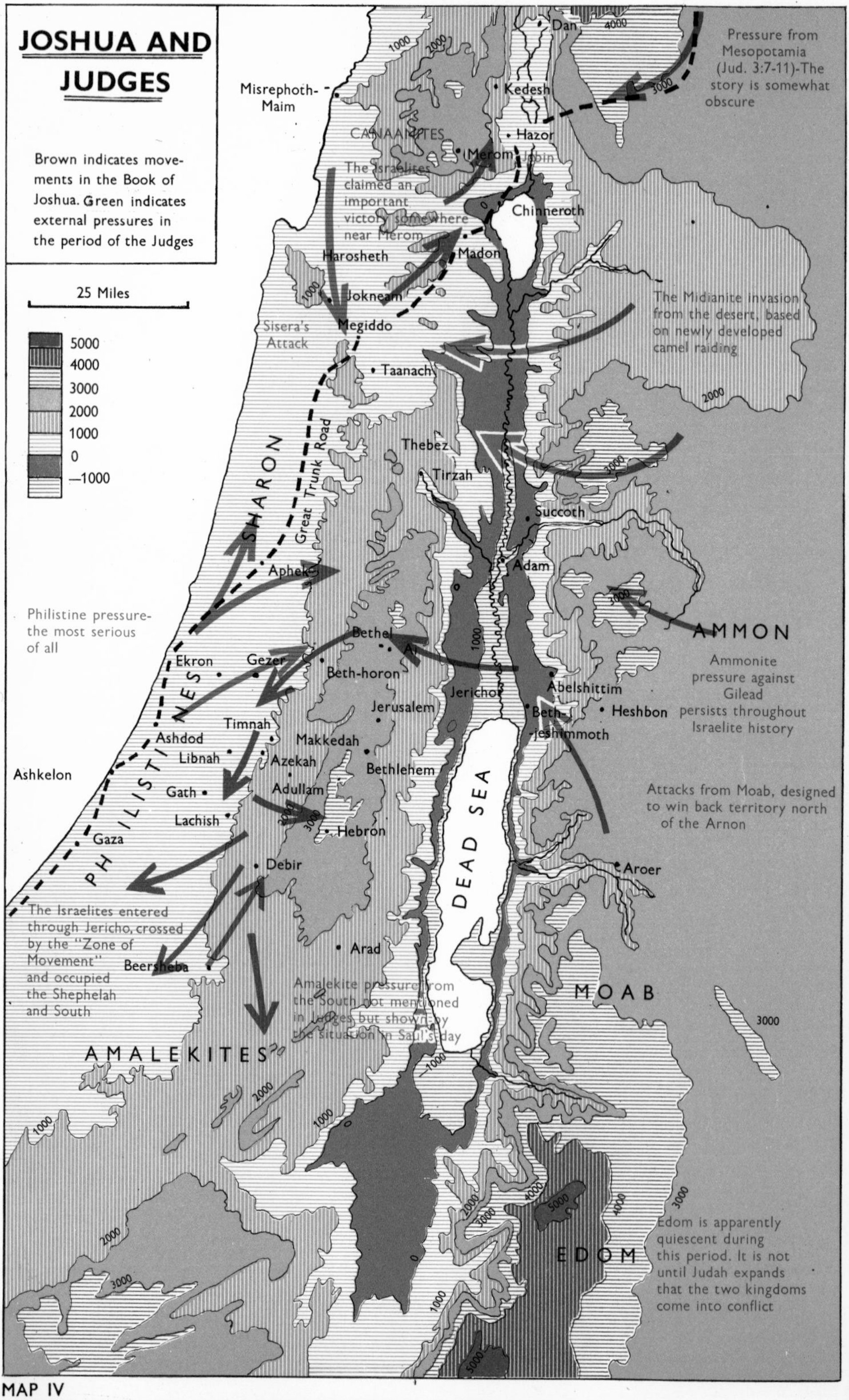
JOSHUA AND JUDGES
Brown indicates movements in the Book of Joshua. Green indicates external pressures in the period of the Judges
25 Miles
5000
4000
3000
2000
1000
0
—1000
Dan
Misrephoth-Maim
Kedesh
Pressure from Mesopotamia (Jud. 3:7-11)-The story is somewhat obscure
CANAANITES
Hazor
Merom
Jabin
The Israelites claimed an important victory somewhere near Merom
Chinneroth
Harosheth
Madon
Jokneam
Megiddo
Sisera's Attack
The Midianite invasion from the desert, based on newly developed camel raiding
Taanach
Great Trunk Road
SHARON
Thebez
Tirzah
Succoth
Aphek
Adam
Philistine pressure-the most serious of all
Bethel
Ai
AMMON
Ekron
Gezer
Beth-horon
Ammonite pressure against Gilead persists throughout Israelite history
Jericho
Abelshittim
Jerusalem
Heshbon
Beth-jeshimmoth
Timnah
Ashdod
Makkedah
Libnah
Azekah
Ashkelon
Bethlehem
DEAD SEA
Gath
Adullam
Attacks from Moab, designed to win back territory north of the Arnon
Lachish
Hebron
Gaza
PHILISTINES
Debir
Aroer
The Israelites entered through Jericho, crossed by the "Zone of Movement" and occupied the Shephelah and South
Arad
Beersheba
MOAB
Amalekite pressure from the South not mentioned in Judges but shown by the situation in Saul's day
AMALEKITES
EDOM
Edom is apparently quiescent during this period. It is not until Judah expands that the two kingdoms come into conflict

MAP IV

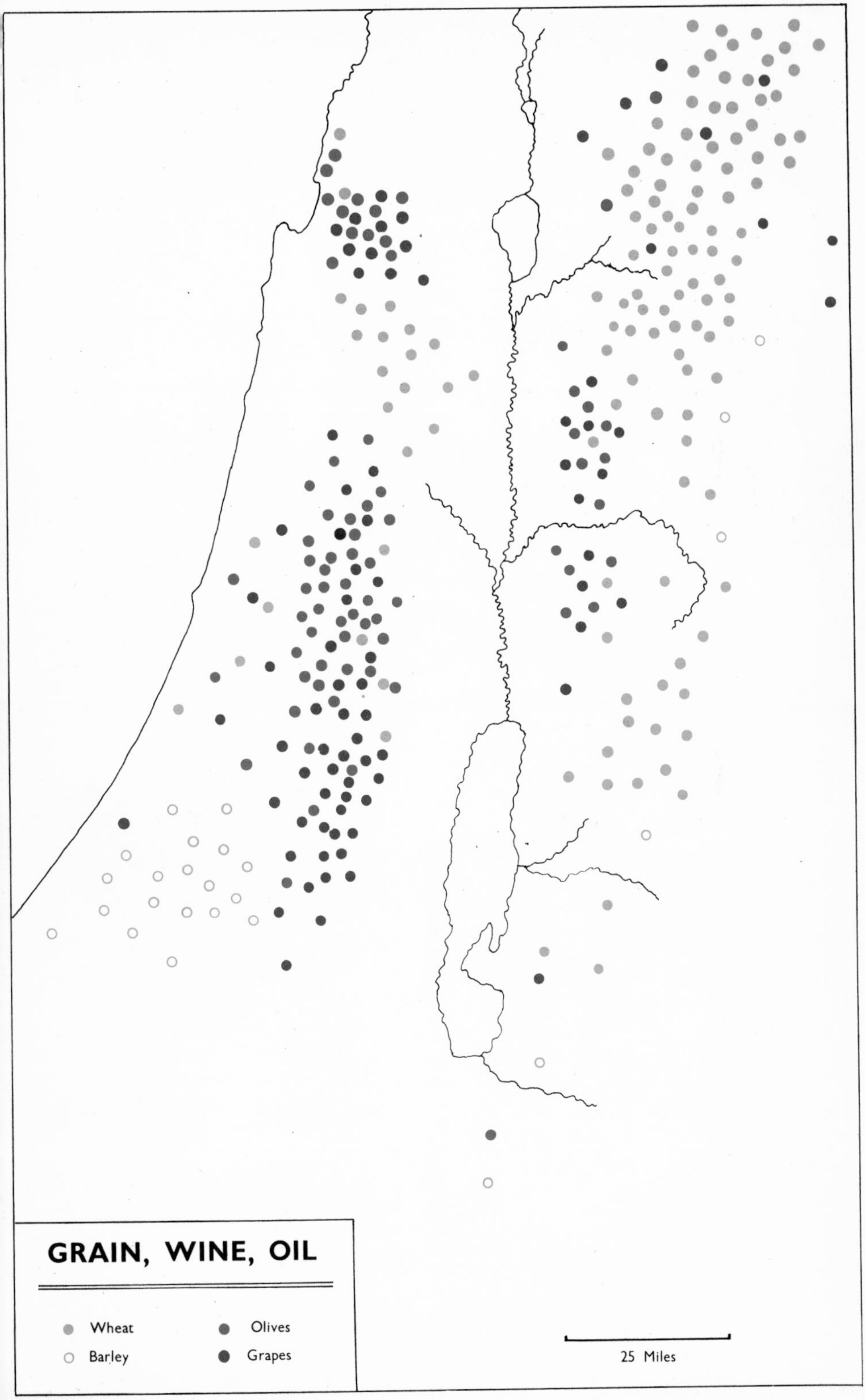

MAP V

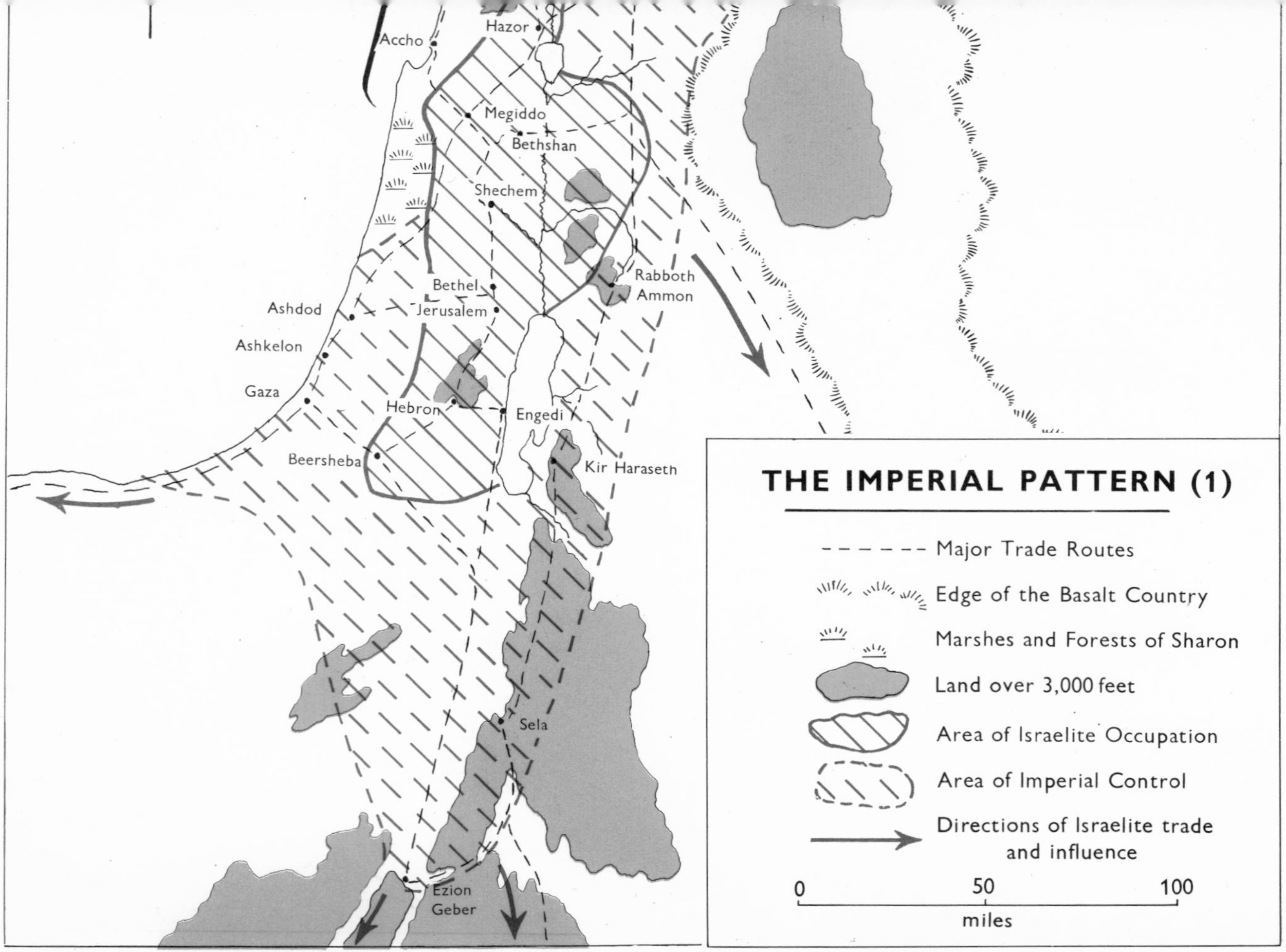
Accho
Hazor
Megiddo
Bethshan
Shechem
Bethel
Jerusalem
Ashdod
Ashkelon
Gaza
Hebron
Engedi
Beersheba
Rabboth
Ammon
Kir Haraseth
Sela
Ezion
Geber
THE IMPERIAL PATTERN (1)
Major Trade Routes
Edge of the Basalt Country
Marshes and Forests of Sharon
Land over 3,000 feet
Area of Israelite Occupation
Area of Imperial Control
Directions of Israelite trade
and influence
0
50
100
miles

MAP VI

Carchemish
Calno
Hammath
Tadmor (Palmyra)
Kedesh
Hazarenan
Sidon
N
Phoenician Coastland - the Phoenician landward expansion was
nly along this coast; their imperial interests were overseas - consequently
was usually a Phoenician - Israelite alliance against the common enemy, Syria

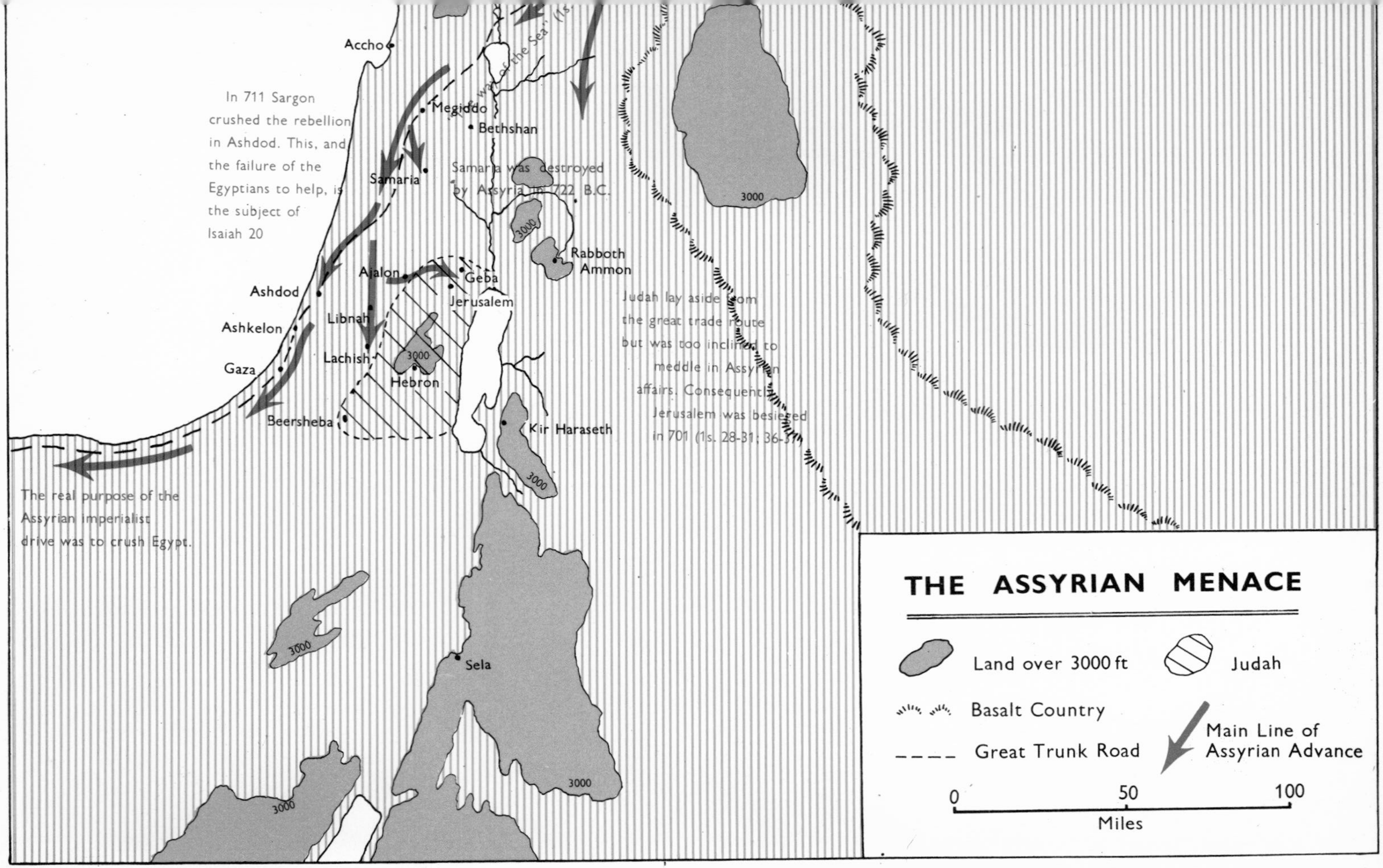
THE ASSYRIAN MENACE
Land over 3000 ft
Judah
Basalt Country
Great Trunk Road
Main Line of Assyrian Advance
0
50
100
Miles
Accho
Megiddo
Bethshan
Samaria
Ajalon
Geba
Jerusalem
Ashdod
Ashkelon
Gaza
Libnah
Lachish
Hebron
Beersheba
Rabboth Ammon
Kir Haraseth
Sela
3000
In 711 Sargon crushed the rebellion in Ashdod. This, and the failure of the Egyptians to help, is the subject of Isaiah 20
Samaria was destroyed by Assyria in 722 B.C.
Judah lay aside from the great trade route but was too inclined to meddle in Assyrian affairs. Consequently Jerusalem was besieged in 701 (Is. 28-31; 36-37)
The real purpose of the Assyrian imperialist drive was to crush Egypt.
MAP VII

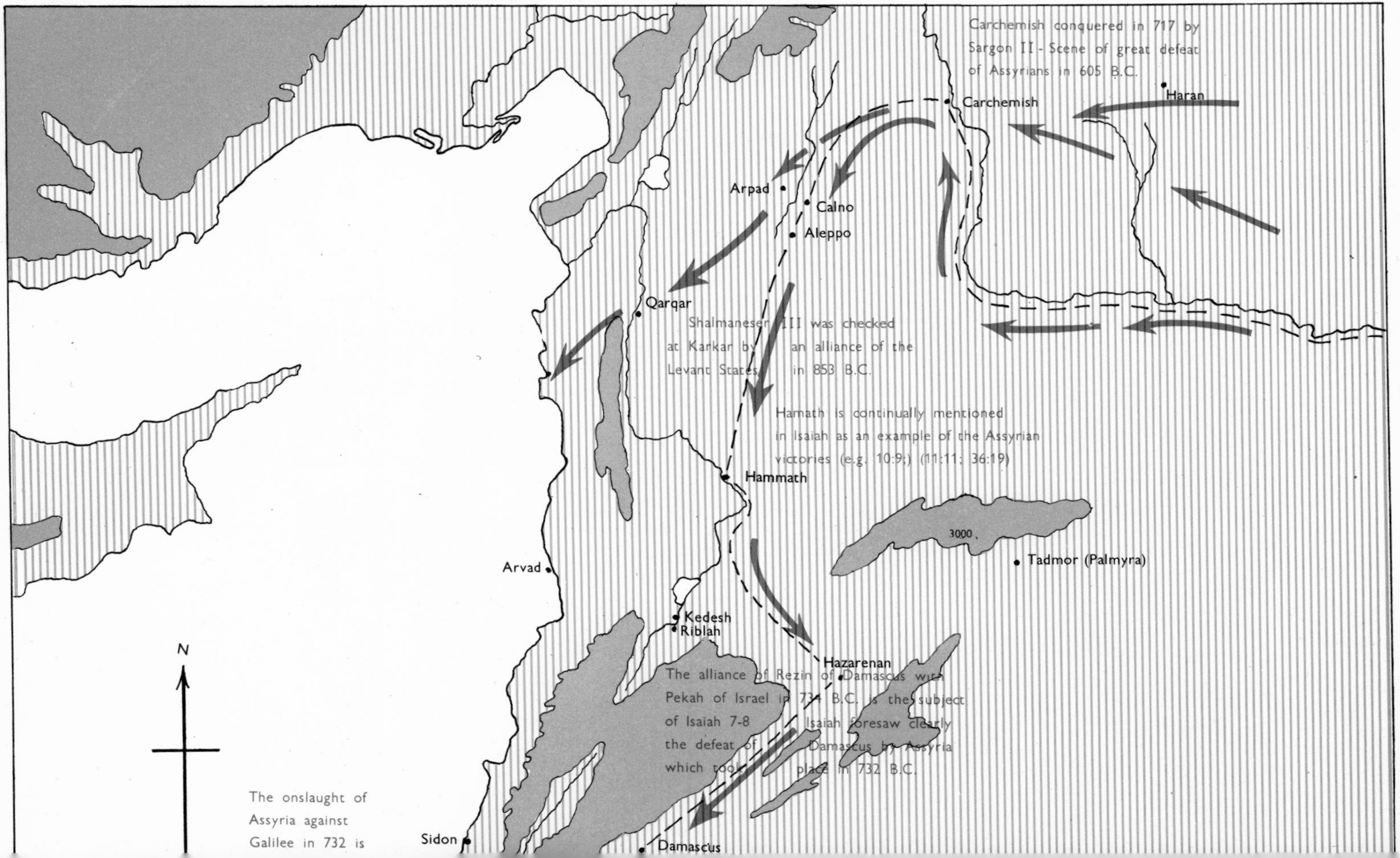
Carchemish conquered in 717 by Sargon II - Scene of great defeat of Assyrians in 605 B.C.
Haran
Carchemish
Arpad
Calno
Aleppo
Qarqar
Shalmaneser III was checked at Karkar by an alliance of the Levant States in 853 B.C.
Hamath is continually mentioned in Isaiah as an example of the Assyrian victories (e.g. 10:9;) (11:11; 36:19)
Hammath
3000
Tadmor (Palmyra)
Arvad
Kedesh
Riblah
Hazarenan
The alliance of Rezin of Damascus with Pekah of Israel in 734 B.C. is the subject of Isaiah 7-8
Isaiah foresaw clearly the defeat of Damascus by Assyria which took place in 732 B.C.
N
Sidon
Damascus

The onslaught of Assyria against Galilee in 732 is

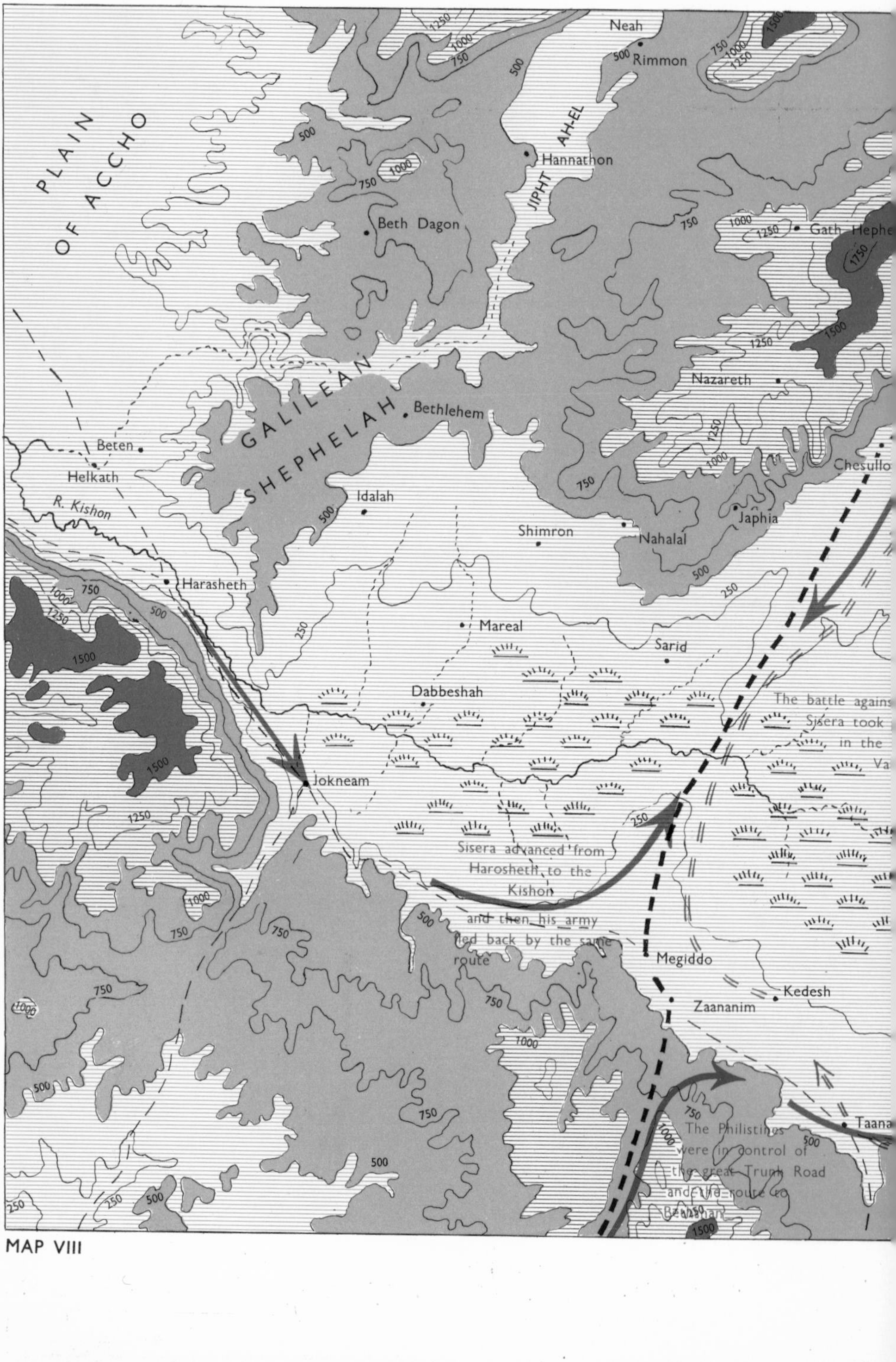

PLAIN OF ACCHO
GALILEAN SHEPHELAH
JIPHT AH-EL
Neah
Rimmon
Hannathon
Beth Dagon
Gath Hephe
Nazareth
Bethlehem
Beten
Helkath
R. Kishon
Idalah
Shimron
Nahalal
Japhia
Chesullo
Harasheth
Mareal
Sarid
Dabbeshah
Jokneam
The battle agains Sisera took in the Va
Sisera advanced from Harosheth to the Kishon and then his army fled back by the same route
Megiddo
Zaananim
Kedesh
Taana
The Philistines were in control of the great Trunk Road and the route to

MAP VIII

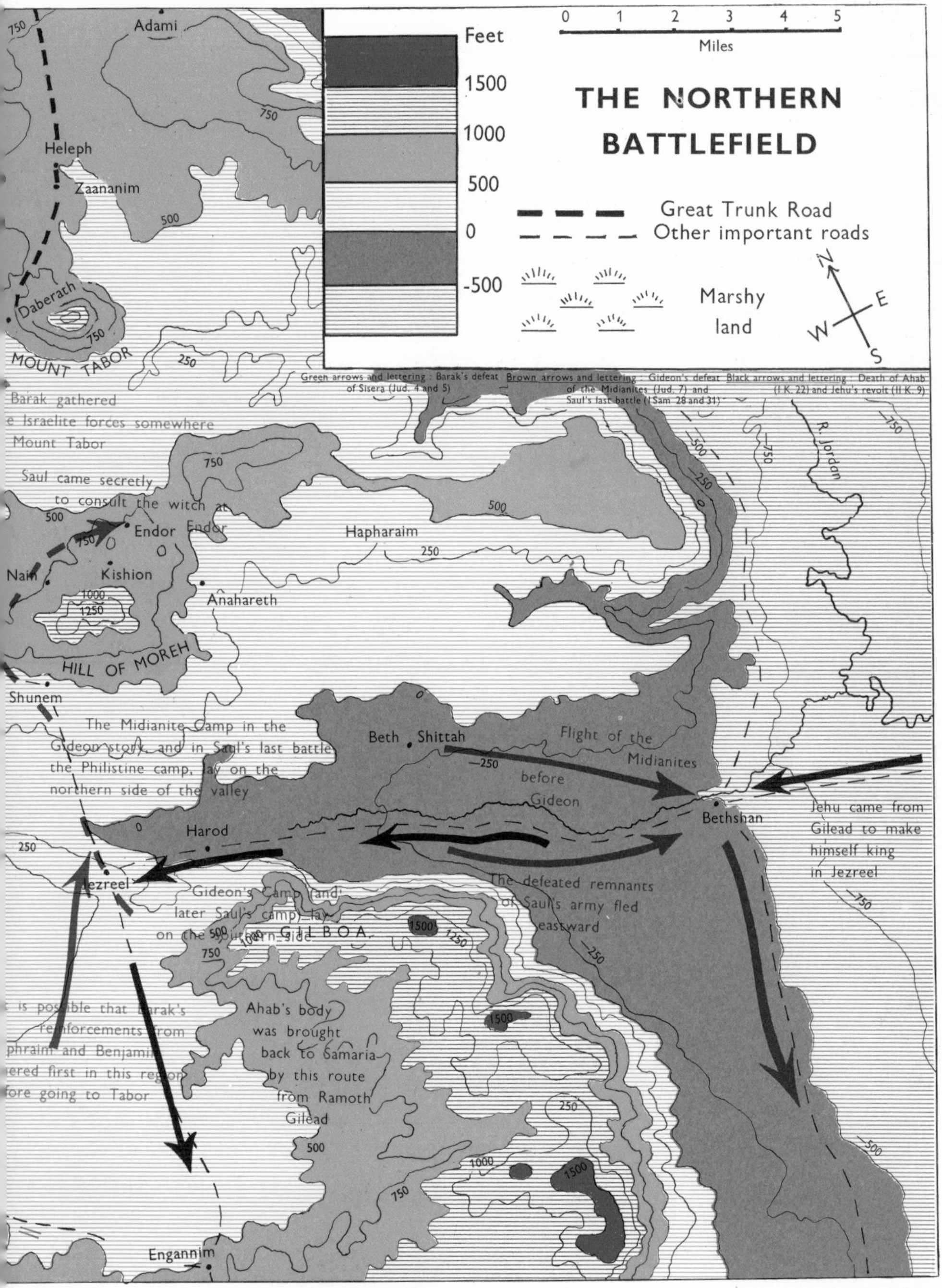

THE NORTHERN BATTLEFIELD
Feet
1500
1000
500
0
-500
0 1 2 3 4 5
Miles
Great Trunk Road
Other important roads
Marshy land
N
E
W
S
Green arrows and lettering : Barak's defeat of Sisera (Jud. 4 and 5)
Brown arrows and lettering : Gideon's defeat of the Midianites (Jud. 7) and Saul's last battle (I Sam. 28 and 31)
Black arrows and lettering : Death of Ahab (I K. 22) and Jehu's revolt (II K. 9)
Adami
Heleph
Zaananim
Daberath
MOUNT TABOR
Barak gathered
e Israelite forces somewhere
Mount Tabor
Saul came secretly
to consult the witch at Endor
Endor
Nain
Kishion
Anahareth
HILL OF MOREH
Shunem
Hapharaim
R. Jordan
The Midianite Camp in the Gideon story, and in Saul's last battle the Philistine camp, lay on the northern side of the valley
Beth Shittah
Flight of the Midianites before Gideon
Harod
Jezreel
Bethshan
Jehu came from Gilead to make himself king in Jezreel
Gideon's Camp (and later Saul's camp) lay on the southern side
GILBOA
The defeated remnants of Saul's army fled eastward
is possible that Barak's
reinforcements from
phraim and Benjamin
ered first in this region
fore going to Tabor
Ahab's body was brought back to Samaria by this route from Ramoth Gilead
Engannim

MAP IX

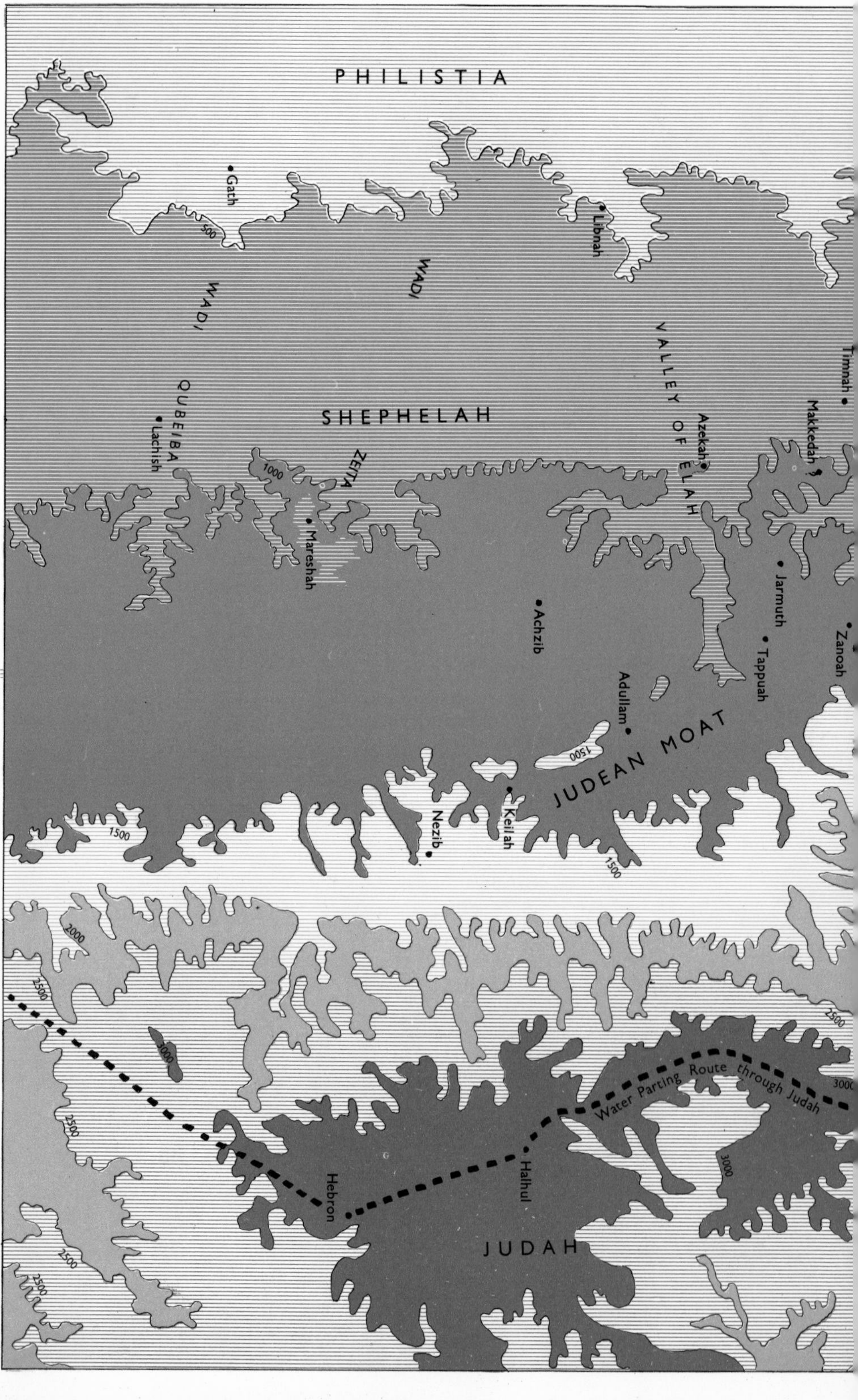
PHILISTIA
Gath
500
Libnah
WADI
WADI
QUBEIBA
SHEPHELAH
VALLEY OF ELAH
Timnah
Makkedah ?
Azekah
Lachish
1000
ZEITA
Mareshah
Jarmuth
Achzib
Zanoah
Tappuah
Adullam
1500
JUDEAN MOAT
Keil'ah
Nezib
1500
1500
2000
2500
2500
3000
3000
Water Parting Route through Judah
2500
3000
Hebron
Halhul
JUDAH
2500
2500

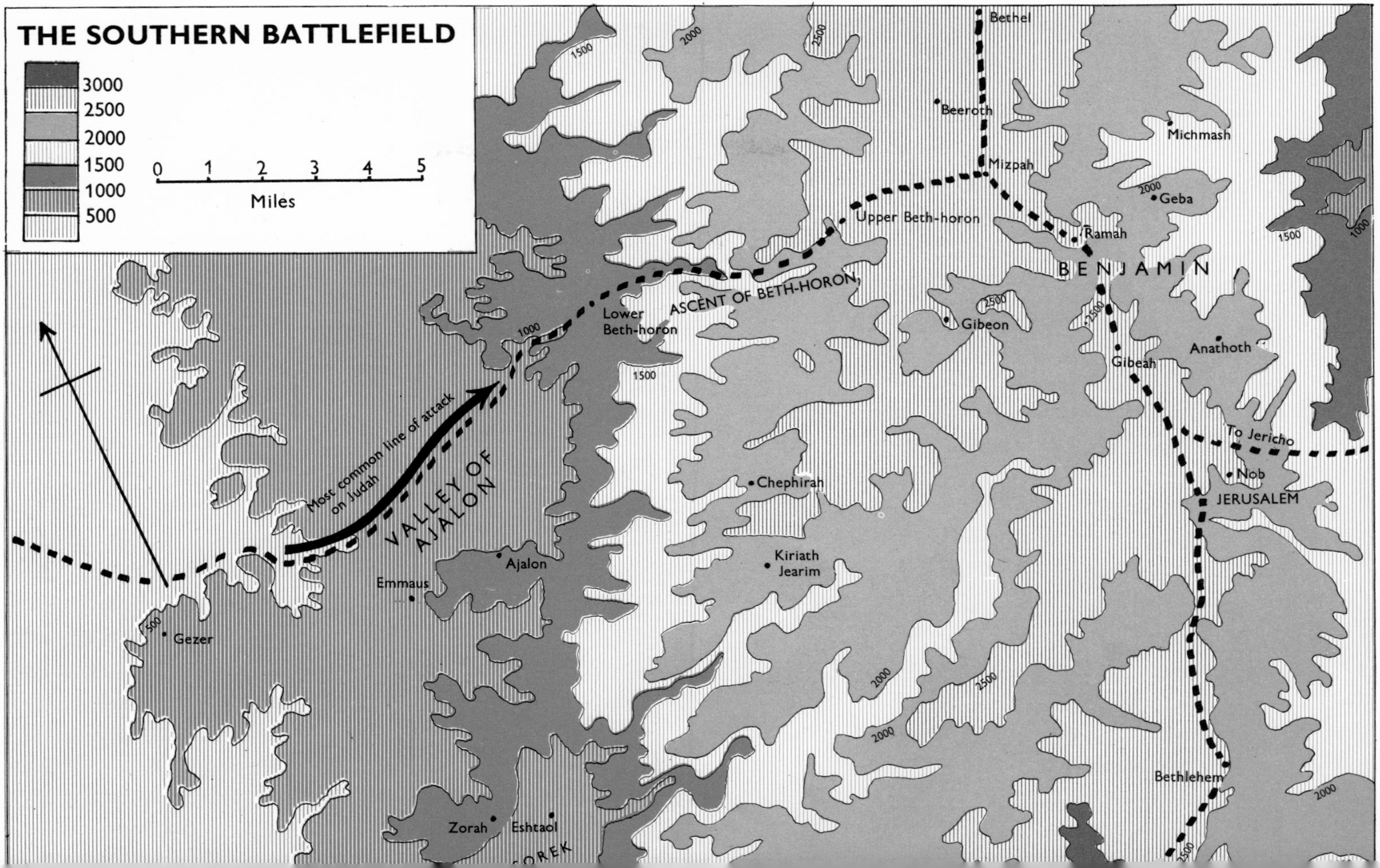
THE SOUTHERN BATTLEFIELD
3000
2500
2000
1500
1000
500
0 1 2 3 4 5
Miles
Most common line of attack on Judah
VALLEY OF AJALON
ASCENT OF BETH-HORON
Lower Beth-horon
Upper Beth-horon
Bethel
Beeroth
Mizpah
Michmash
Geba
Ramah
BENJAMIN
Gibeon
Gibeah
Anathoth
To Jericho
Nob
JERUSALEM
Chephirah
Kiriath Jearim
Ajalon
Emmaus
Gezer
Zorah
Eshtaol
Bethlehem

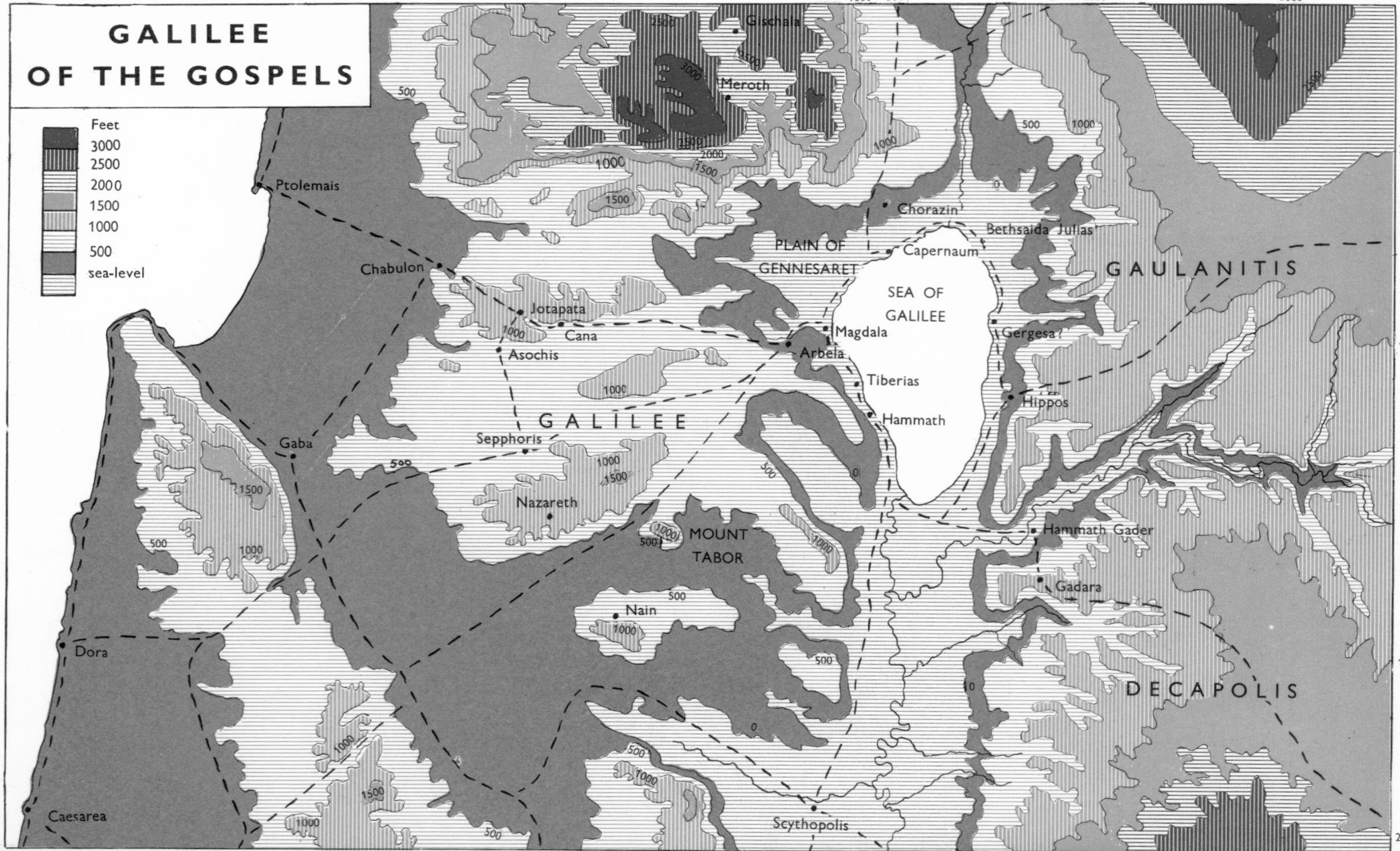
GALILEE OF THE GOSPELS
Feet
3000
2500
2000
1500
1000
500
sea-level
Ptolemais
Chabulon
Gaba
Dora
Caesarea
Gischala
Meroth
Jotapata
Cana
Asochis
Sepphoris
Nazareth
GALILEE
MOUNT TABOR
Nain
Scythopolis
Chorazin
Capernaum
PLAIN OF GENNESARET
SEA OF GALILEE
Magdala
Arbela
Tiberias
Hammath
Bethsaida Julias
Gergesa?
Hippos
Hammath Gader
Gadara
GAULANITIS
DECAPOLIS

3

CAMERA AND THE BIBLE

I

JERUSALEM, THE DOME OF THE ROCK

II

JERUSALEM, THE DAMASCUS GATE

III

JERUSALEM, THE JEWISH QUARTER

IV

JERUSALEM, THE DOME OF THE ROCK

V

JERUSALEM, A RELIGIOUS PROCESSION

VI

JERUSALEM, A ROCK-CUT TOMB

VII

JERUSALEM, THE RUSSIAN CHURCH IN GETHSEMANE

VIII

ALEPPO, THE CITADEL

IX

BEEHIVE VILLAGES IN NORTH SYRIA

X

PALMYRA, THE TEMPLE OF THE SUN

XI

PALMYRA

XII

PETRA, CLIFF DWELLINGS

I. JERUSALEM, THE DOME OF THE ROCK

The gate of the outward sanctuary which looketh toward the east. Ezek. 44 : 1

The Dome of the Rock is built over the ancient Rock of Sacrifice in the Jewish Temple. As one looks out through the smaller Dome of the Chain, the Mount of Olives is in the distance.

II. JERUSALEM, THE DAMASCUS GATE
He giveth snow like wool. Ps. 147 : 16
Heavy snow falls in Jerusalem about once every ten or fifteen years. This picture shows the north wall of Jerusalem with the Damascus Gate. The present walls were built in the sixteenth century A.D.

III. JERUSALEM, THE JEWISH QUARTER
The year of recompences for the controversy of Zion. Is. 34 : 8
The persistent lack of peace in Jerusalem throughout history is exemplified by the ruins of the Jewish Quarter in the Old City, a relic of the Arab-Jewish War of 1948–49.

IV. JERUSALEM, THE DOME OF THE ROCK
The Street of the House of God. Ezra 10 : 9
Semitic temples contained a small sanctuary in a large open space. Later colonnades were built for the convenience of the people and Herod's Temple is reported to have had a very fine one, in which, probably, Jesus taught. The present Mosque in Jerusalem preserves something of the same character.

V. JERUSALEM, A RELIGIOUS PROCESSION
Look upon Zion, the city of our solemnities. Is. 33 : 20
A religious procession to the Church of the Holy Sepulchre in Jerusalem.

VI. JERUSALEM,
A ROCK-CUT TOMB

Whom hast thou here, that thou h… hewed thee out a sepulchre? Is. 22 : 1…

A rock-cut tomb in the Kidr… valley. This is much later than t… period of Isaiah and therefore … cannot be that of Shebna. Howeve… it is one of the very few things … Jerusalem today which Jesus m… have seen.

VII. JERUSALEM, THE RUSSIAN CHURCH IN GETHSEMANE

Many nations shall come and say, Come, and let us go up to the mountain of the Lord. Micah 4 : 2

One of the characteristic features of modern Jerusalem is the mixture of architectural styles, resulting from the fact that people from widely different countries have wanted to build a church or chapel there for their pilgrims.

VIII. ALEPPO, THE CITADEL

Hath any of the gods of the nations delivered his land out of the hand of the king of Assyria? Is. 36 : 18

Built on the great *tell* of Aleppo, which marks the site of the Old Testament town, the medieval citadel has a dramatic defensive position. Aleppo held one of the most important positions at the northern extension of the Great Trunk Road (p. 84), which was followed by the Assyrian army southwards.

IX. BEEHIVE VILLAGES IN NORTH SYRIA

Where are the gods of Hamath and of Arpad? 2 Kings 18 : 34

The houses, built of mud brick, are characteristic of the Hamath and Aleppo steppes where there is no wood suitable for roofing (see p. 72).

X. PALMYRA, THE TEMPLE OF THE SUN
If I beheld the sun when it shined . . . and my heart hath been secretly enticed, or my mouth hath kissed my hand. Job 31 : 26–7

XI. PALMYRA
Tadmor in the Wilderness. 2 *Chr.* 8 : 4
The Ruins of Palmyra. In the later Roman period Palmyra replaced Petra as the major Arabian trade centre in the north, but it had always been important as an oasis on the desert route from Damascus to Assyria and Babylon. The castle on the hill is a medieval Arab building.

XII. PETRA, CLIFF DWELLINGS
Thou that dwellest in the clefts of the rock. Obad. 3
Cliff dwellings at Petra, cut in the soft Nubian sandstone of which so much of Edom is formed.

XIII. KERAK, CRUSADING CASTL
He took his eldest son . . . and offere him upon the wall. 2 *Kings* 3 : 27
Kerak is the ancient Kir-Haraseth i Moab, one of the great stronghold along the King's Highway, and dom inating an important route down t the Dead Sea.

XIV. QASR ET-TUBA
O that I had in the wilderness a lodging place of wayfaring men! Jer. 9 : 2
Caravanserais of some sort were always a necessity for desert travel. This, more grandiose than most, belongs to the early Arab period. It is interesting because it is built of brick, and thus exemplifies the Mesopotamian influence which is constantly making itself felt in the Levant.

XV. JERASH, AUTUMNAL STORM
He made darkness his secret place; his pavilion round about him were dark waters, and thick clouds of the skies. Ps. 18 : 11
The first storm of autumn over Jerash, the ancient Gerasa, one of the Decapolis. This storm was unusual in that it snowed although it was only early November.

XVI. JERASH, ENTRANCE TO THE TEMPLE OF ARTEMIS
Great multitudes of people . . . from Decapolis. Matt. 4 : 25
This is the entrance to the great Temple of Artemis at Gerasa, one of the ten Greek cities of the Decapolis east of the Lake of Galilee.

XVII. THE JORDAN VALLEY
Therefore will I remember thee from the land of Jordan. Ps. 42 : 6
This view is taken looking west in the narrow "waist" of the Rift Valley (p. 47). In the distance is the Valley of the Fari'a. In the foreground is the tomb of a Muslim holy man.

XVIII. SAMARIA, THE CRUSADERS' CHURCH

I will that thou give me by and by in a charger the head of John the Baptist. Mark 6 : 25

This Crusading Church, later converted into a mosque, is built on the traditional site of John the Baptist's tomb at Samaria. According to Josephus, however, he was imprisoned at Machaerus east of the Dead Sea.

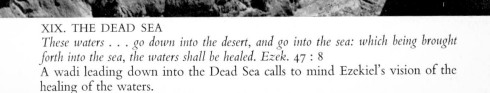

XIX. THE DEAD SEA

These waters . . . go down into the desert, and go into the sea: which being brought forth into the sea, the waters shall be healed. Ezek. 47 : 8

A wadi leading down into the Dead Sea calls to mind Ezekiel's vision of the healing of the waters.

XX. BEDOUIN TENT
The curtains of the land of Midian. Hab. 3 : 7
Open on the east, it has its back to the west from which side the rain comes. The section on the left is where guests are received. That on the right is for the women.

XXI. BEDOUIN BOY
They that watch for the morning. Ps. 130 : 6
A Bedouin boy, looking out of the open eastern side of his tent, is caught by the light of the rising sun. The Bedouin are the "Ishmaelites" or Midianites of the Bible, whose raids upon the settled land were a constant menace.

XXII. STORM OVER THE BEQA'A OF GILEAD

One piece was rained upon. Amos 4 : 7

The "trigger effect" of a slight slope is clearly visible here, since in the centre of the picture a cloud is formed as the damp air climbs the western side of the small hill, i.e. coming from the left of the picture (p. 65). The photograph was taken in the Beqa'a of Gilead (p. 51).

XXIII. "MIDIANITES, MERCHANTMEN"

There passed by Midianites, merchantmen. Gen. 37 : 28

A group of desert Arabs travelling north along the King's Highway. The picture was taken in the valley of the Zered.

XXIV. HIERAPOLIS, THE HOT SPRINGS
I know thy works, that thou art neither cold nor hot. Rev. 3 : 15
The hot springs at Hierapolis (Col. 4 : 13). It is believed by some authorities that the rebuke to Laodicea has some reference to the hot springs at Hierapolis only a few miles away (p. 133).

XXV. PERGAMUM, THE THEATRE
Even where Satan's seat is. Rev. 2 : 13
Pergamum, where the Christians are praised for resisting Satan, holds a superb position on a steep hill a little distance from the coast. The significance of the reference to Satan's seat is unknown.

XXVI. CARVING AT EPHESUS

Then the priest of Jupiter . . . brought oxen and garlands unto the gates, and would have done sacrifice with the people. Acts 14 : 13

This carving at Ephesus shows an ox, garlanded and ready for the sacrifice.

XXVII. PHILIPPI

Philippi, which is the chief city of that part of Macedonia, and a colony. Acts 16 : 12

View taken from the theatre across the ruins of ancient Philippi. The river, "where prayer was wont to be made", runs through the trees in the centre of the picture.

XXVIII. KANAWAT IN THE JEBEL DRUZE
The region of Trachonitis. Luke 3 : 1
Kanawat is the ancient Kenath of the Bible, and stands on the black, basaltic slopes of the Jebel Druze. Basalt provides the only building material and in the Roman period even the doors were made of it, as well as the pillars.

4

PLACE NAMES OF THE BIBLE

PLACE NAMES OF THE BIBLE

Small figures in this index refer to the black and white maps,
large Roman figures to the coloured maps.

This index contains all the **places** mentioned in the Bible, together with their modern equivalents, as far as these can be ascertained. Also included are places in the biblical countries which, although not named in the Bible, are often mentioned in books on the subject, and the explanation of certain geographical terms, which might not otherwise be clear.

Although possible identifications have been suggested by various people for very nearly all the biblical sites, many of these identifications are as yet only conjectural. Such sites have been described as "unknown" or "uncertain".

It has not been possible to give all the biblical references, though where places are mentioned only in the Apocrypha, references have often been given, since such names do not always occur in concordances. Nevertheless, where one name stands for more than one place, every biblical reference has been given for the alternative sites, though not for the site for which the name is most commonly used. Equally, space forbids the attempt to show every site on the maps, since this book is not a topographical atlas. However, as far as possible, an indication has been given of the approximate area, as well as the exact **tell** or **khirbeh**, if this is known.

A problem arises, as every writer on this subject knows, about the proper representation of the Arabic words. Diacritical marks are necessary if the Arabic equivalent is to be made clear, but in practice these are very irritating to the uninstructed reader. Moreover, a great many of the words are already in process of becoming anglicized. Therefore, in the text of the book diacritical marks have been kept to a minimum, but are used in this index according to one of the commonly accepted systems.

The major authorities consulted in the identification of the biblical sites were the following: Abel, **Géographie de la Palestine**; Grollenberg, **Atlas of the Bible**; Simons, **Geographical and Topographical Texts of the Bible**; and Wright and Filson, **The Westminster Historical Atlas of the Bible.** It is with gratitude that I acknowledge my indebtedness to these works.

A great many variations exist in the spelling of biblical names, far more in fact than anyone would believe who had not attempted to index them, and consistency in this matter is difficult. In general the spellings used in the Authorized Version and Revised Standard Version have provided the basis, but certain variations common in English translations and in books on Palestine have been given. Nevertheless, it must be recognized, with regret, that there has not been room for all the variant spellings and there are, inevitably, many omissions.

The following Arabic words occur frequently in the index and so their meaning is given:

Jebel. A high hill or mountain.
Khirbeh (Kh.). A ruin. When followed by a vowel it is pronounced "khirbet."
Nahr. River or stream.
Tell. A small hill. This has become a technical word in archaeology for the hill which is formed in Palestine when one town is built upon the ruins of another. However, in Arabic the word is not confined to this, and may be used also for any small hill, e.g. the little volcanic cones in Bashan.
Wādī. A valley; frequently, though not necessarily, a dry valley.

Abana, River. A river rising in the Anti-Lebanon mountains and flowing through Damascus. **Nahr Barada.**
Abarim. This appears to be a regional name for the slopes of the Eastern Plateau overlooking the Jordan Valley. The region is really the southern extension of the Gilead Dome, and should be distinguished from the Pisgah, q.v. 11, 12, 17.
Abda. One of the Byzantine cities in the southern desert of Cis-jordan. 13.
Abdon. A town in Asher, probably **Kh. 'Abdeh.**
Abel. 1. A place near Beth-shemesh 1, mentioned in I Sam. 6:18. However, the word should probably be read as "stone", as in the RSV.
2. See Abel-beth-maacah.
Abel-beth-maacah. A town in northern Cis-jordan on the scarp between the Plain of Ijon and the Huleh Basin. **Tell Abīl.** 9.
Abel-cheramim, Abel-keramim. A town near Rabboth Ammon, possibly **Na'ūr.**
Abel-maim. See Abel-beth-maacah.
Abel-mizraim. A town in Trans-jordan. Unknown.
Abel-shittim. Tell Kufrein north of the Dead Sea? IV.
Abila. See Decapolis. 10.
Abilene. A district north-east of Mount Hermon.
Abronah. A stopping place during the Exodus, possibly **'Ain ed-Defīyeh** in the Arabah north of the Red Sea.
Abydos. A city in Upper Egypt important during the XIX Dynasty. **'Arabat el-Madfūneh.**
Abu Simbel. A site in Nubia on the Nile, famous for its temples of Hatshepsut and Rameses II. 21.
Accad. The capital of Babylonia under Sargon, about 2600 B.C. **Tell ed-Deir?**
Accaron. See Ekron. 20.
Accho. A sea-port in Asher, later called Ptolemais. **Tell el-Fukhkhār,** just to the east of the modern town of Acre. VI, VII, 4, 11, 16, 27.
Accho, Plain of. The narrow coast plain immediately behind Accho. VIII.
Accho-Bethshan corridor. The important lowland gap between the Mediterranean and the Dead Sea. See also Esdraelon and Jezreel.
Aceldama, Akeldama. Traditionally the southern side of the lower Valley of Hinnom, q.v.
Achaia. A Roman province in Greece.
Achor, Valley of. Somewhere between Jericho and Bethel, though the exact site is uncertain.
Achshaph. A town in Asher, probably **Tell Keisān** near Acre.
Achzib. 1. A town in western Judah. **Tell-el-Beidā.** IX, 16.
2. A town in Asher. **er-Zīb** about two miles south of Misrephoth-maim. Josh. 19:29; Jud. 1:31.
Acrabetta. See Akrabbim.
Acre. The modern name for Accho and Ptolemais.
Adadah. Probably the same as Aroer 3.
Adam. A town about half-way between the Sea of Galilee and the Dead Sea. **Tell ed-Dāmiyeh.** IV.
Adamah. 1. See Adam.
2. A town in Naphtali, site unknown. Josh. 19:36.
Adami, Adami-nekeb. A town in Naphtali. **Kh. Dāmiyeh.** VIII.
Adar. See Hazar-addar.
Adasa. Possibly **Kh. Addāsah** north of Jerusalem. I Macc. 7:40, 45. 20.
Addan, Addon. An unknown site in Babylonia.
Addar. See Hazar-addar.
Addon. See Addan.
Adida. Probably the same as Hadid. **el-Ḥadīteh** near Lod. I Macc. 12:38; 13:13. 20.
Adithaim. A town in western Judah, possibly **Kh. el-Ḥadatha** near Ajalon.
Admah. One of the Cities of the Plain.
Ador, Adora. Probably the same as Adoraim. I Macc. 13:20. 20.
Adoraim. A hill town in Judah. **Dūrā** west of Hebron.
Adramyttium. A sea-port in north-west Asia Minor. **Edremit.** 31.
Adria, Sea of. The Mediterranean south of Italy.
Adullam. A town in the Judean Moat. **Tell esh-Sheikh Madhkār.** IV, IX, 27.
Adummin, Ascent of. The "Ascent of Blood" on the road between Jericho and Jerusalem, so called because of the deposits of red ochre. **Tala't ed-Damm.**
Aelia Capitolina. The name given to Jerusalem when it was rebuilt by the Romans after its destruction in A.D. 70.
Aenon. The place "near to Salim" where John baptized. Unknown.
Affuleh. A modern town in the Plain of Esdraelon. 14.
Ahava. A town and canal near Babylon. Unknown.
Ahlab. The same as Mahalab. 16.
Ai. 1. **et-Tell** near Bethel. The town taken by Joshua was probably Bethel, since Ai had already been in ruins for centuries. III, IV.
2. A town in Moab. Unknown. Jer. 49:3.
Aiath. Probably the same as Ai, though it may be **Kh. Ḥayyān** close by.
Aija. See Ai.
Aijalon, Ajalon. 1. A town in the original territory of Dan. VII, IX, 16.
2. A town in Zebulun, probably the same as Elon. Jud. 12:12.
Ain. 1. A town on the north-west frontier of Canaan, near Riblah. Unknown.
2. The same as Ashan. Josh. 21:16. c.f. I Chr. 6:59.
Ajalon, Valley of. The same as the Ascent of Beth-horon.
Akeldama. See Aceldama.
Akhetaton. The capital of the heretic Pharaoh, Akhnaton. **Tel el-Amarna.** 21.
Akkad. See Accad.
Akrabbim, Ascent of. "Ascent of the Scorpions", probably **Naqb es-Ṣafā.**
Alalakh. A town in northern Syria where important tablets of the seventeenth century B.C. have been found.
Alema. A town east of the Jordan. **Kh. 'Almit?** I Macc. 5:26. 20.
Aleppo. A city in northern Syria, the ancient Khalab. VII, 4, 5.
Alexandria. An important sea-port at the mouth of the Nile. 31.
Alexandrium. Fortress of Herod the Great controlling the central Rift Valley. **Qarn Ṣarṭabeh.**

Allamelech. A town in Asher. Unknown.
Allon. A town in Naphtali, probably to be read as Elon-bezaananim. Unknown.
Allon-bachuth. The place near Bethel where Deborah was buried. Unknown.
Alluvium. A geographical term for the material deposited by rivers as the result of erosion. Since it is non-porous and occurs in low-lying places, it tends to be waterlogged in the Palestinian winter. However, it is very fertile.
Almon. A town in Benjamin. **Kh. 'Almit.**
Almon-diblathaim. A stopping place during the Exodus, north of Dibon. It may be **Kh. Deleilāt esh-Sherqiyeh.**
Aloth. A region in Asher, but the text is uncertain. I Kings 4:16.
Alush. A stopping place during the Exodus. Unknown.
Amad. A border town of Asher near Helkath. Unknown.
Amalek. A tribe occupying the southern desert of Cis-jordan. IV, 18.
Amam. A place near Beersheba. Unknown.
Amana, Mount. Part of the Anti-Lebanon range. **Jebel Zebdānī.** 6.
Amanus Mountains. A range in the north of Syria on the Turkish border.
'Ammān. Present capital of the Kingdom of Jordan, the ancient Rabboth-Ammon. 14.
Ammon. The iron-age kingdom round Rabboth-Ammon. IV, 18, 20.
Amorites. A people who occupied part of Trans-jordan at the time of the Exodus. 22.
Amphipolis. A city in Thrace. **Neochori.**
Anab. A hill town in Judah. **Kh. 'Anab.**
Anahareth. A town in Issachar. **en-Na'ūrah.** VIII.
Ananiah. The Old Testament name for Bethany. **el-'Azarīyeh.** 27.
Anathoth. The home of Jeremiah north of Jerusalem. **Rās el-Kharrūbeh** near **'Anāta.** IX, 27.
Anatolia. The plateau of Asia Minor. 25.
Anem. A town in Issachar, which may be the same as En-gannim.
Aner. A town in Manasseh, possibly the same as Taanach.
Anim. A town in Judah. **Kh. Ghuwein eṭ-Ṭaḥtā?**
Anti-Lebanon Mountains. The high mountain range west of Damascus.
Antioch. 1. A city in north Syria. **Antākiyah.** 4, 31.
2. A town in Pisidia. **Yalvaç.** Acts 13:14; 14:19, 21; II Tim. 3:11. 31.
Anti-patris. The Roman name for Aphek 1. 28.
Aphek. 1. An important town at the foot of the Western Highlands. **Rās el-'Ain.** IV, 16, 18.
2. A town in the north, possibly **Afqā** east of Byblos. Josh. 13:4.
3. A town in Asher. Unknown. Josh. 19:30.
4. A town where Benhadad defeated Ahab, possibly **Fīq** east of the Sea of Galilee. I Kings 20:26, 30; II Kings 13:17.
Aphekah. Town in Judah near Hebron. Unknown.
Aphik. See Aphek 3.
Aphrah. See Beth-le-Aphrah.
Apollonia. City in Macedonia. **Pollina.** 31.
Appii Forum. Town near Rome. **Foro Appio.** 31.
'Aqabah. Modern Jordanian port on the Red Sea. 14.
Ar. Town or territory in Moab. **el-Misna'?** 10.
Arab. A town in Judah. **er-Rabīyeh?**
Arabah. Name given in the Bible to the Rift Valley, but in modern times usually kept for that part of it between the Dead Sea and the Red Sea. I, 5, 12, 17, 19.
Arabah, Brook of the. See Zered.
Arabattine. See Akrabbim. I Macc. 5:3. 20.
Arabia. The great peninsula between the Red Sea and Mesopotamia. 25.
Arabian Desert. 22.
Arad. Tel 'Arad fifteen miles south of Hebron. IV.
Arados. See Arvad. I Macc. 15:23.
Arah. May be the place meant in Josh. 13:4, if Mearah is to be read "from Arah". **Kh. 'Arā.**
Aram. The Old Testament name for Syria. Since the written word in Hebrew is very similar, it is often confused in early translations with Edom.
Aram-maacah. District round Abel-beth-Maacah.
Aram-Naharaim. The same as Padan-Aram. 5.
Aram-Rehob. The region around Rehob.
Aram-Zobah. The region around Zobah.
Ararat. A region in Armenia.
Arbata, Arbatta. Region south of Mount Carmel, which may be connected with Arubboth, q.v. I Macc. 5:23.
Arbela. 1. Kh. Irbid in Galilee. I Macc. 9:2. X, 10, 20.
2. See Riblah.
Ardh es-Suwān. The flinty desert in eastern Trans-jordan. 10, 19.
Argob. A region of Bashan, q.v. 17.
Arimathea. The same as Ramathaim-Zophim.
Armageddon. Rev. 16:16. The word is probably taken from Har-Megiddo, the Hill of Megiddo.
Arnon, River. The great canyon leading into the Dead Sea from the east. **Wādī el-Mōjib.** I, 12, 18.
Aroer. 1. Near Rabboth Ammon. Unknown. Josh. 13:25; Jud. 11:26, 33.
2. On the borders of the Arnon Canyon. **'Arā'ir.** IV, 10.
3. Town in Judah. **'Ar'arah.** I Sam. 30:28.
Arpad. **Tel Erfād.** VII.
Arruboth. Town in Solomon's third district. **Tell 'Arrabeh?**
Arumah. Town near Shechem. Unknown.
Arvad. The Island of **Ruād.** VII, 4.
Ascalon. Port in Philistia. **Ascalon.** Also spelled Ashkelon. IV, VI, VII, 14, 20, 28.
Ashan. Kh. 'Asan north-west of Beersheba.
Ashdod. Town in Philistia. **'Isdūd.** IV, VI.
Ashdoth-Pisgah. Probably to be translated "slopes of the Pisgah".
Asher. 1. Tribal district on the coast north of Carmel. May be a regional name meaning the narrow coast plain. 16, 18.
2. Town in Asher near Shechem. Unknown. Josh. 17:7.
Ashkelon. See Ascalon.
Ashnah. 1. Town near Zorah. Unknown. Josh. 15:33.
2. **Idhna** near Mareshah? Josh. 15:43.
Ashteroth. **Tell 'Ashterah** in Bashan, or **Tell Ash'ari?** 10.
Ashteroth-Karnaim. **Sheikh Ṣa'ad** in Bashan.
Ashur, Asshur. Assyria. Also town in Assyria. 24.
Asia. Used in the Bible for Asia Minor.
Asochis. **Kh. el-Lōn** in Galilee? X, 11.
Assos. A sea-port in Asia Minor. **Behramkoÿ.** 31.
Assyria. A region in northern Mesopotamia.
Atad. Town east of the Jordan. Unknown.
Ataroth. 1. Town in Trans-jordan. **Kh. 'Attarus** north of Dibon. Num. 32:3, 4.
2. Border town in Ephraim. **Tell Sheikh edh-Dhiyāb.** Josh. 16:7.
3. Southern border of Ephraim. **Tell en-Naṣbeh?** Josh. 16:2.
4. near Bethlehem. Unknown. I Chr. 2:54.
Ataroth-addar. Same as Ataroth 3.
Atharim. Unknown. May be same as Hazezon-Tamar.
Athens. 31.
Athnach. Same as Ether 2?
Atroth. Read Atroth-Shaphan. Near Jogbehah. Unknown.
Attalia. Port in Pamphilia. **Adalia.** 31.
Ava. See Ivah.
Avaris. See Raamses.
Aven. 1. Ezek. 30:17. See Beth-aven.
2. Hos. 10:8. See On.
Aven, Plain of. Somewhere north of Damascus.
Avith. Town in Edom. Unknown.
Avva. See Ivah. 4.
Avvim. May be the same as Ai, q.v.
Aza. Same as Aiath.
Azekah. Town in the Judaean Moat. **Tell ez-Zakāriyeh.** IV, IX, 27.
Azem. See Ezem.
Azmaveth. Probably **Hizmeh** north of Anathoth. 27.
Azmon. Southern border town of Judah. **Qeseimeh?**
Aznoth Tabor. Town in Naphtali. May be **Umm Jebeil** near Mount Tabor.
Azor. Town in original territory of Dan. **Yazūr.**
Azotus. New Testament name for Ashdod. 20, 28.

Azotus, Mount. Should be read "slopes".
Azraq. Oasis at northern end of the Sirhan Depression. 10.
Baal. See Baalath-beer.
Baalah. 1. See Kiriath-baal.
2. A town in Simeon. Unknown. Josh. 15:29; 19:3.
Baalah, Mount. Near Jabneel. Unknown. Josh. 15:11.
Baalath. A town in the original territory of Dan. Unknown.
Baalath-beer. A town in Simeon near Rehoboth. Unknown.
Baalbek. A town in the highest portion of the Syrian Rift Valley, famous today for its enormous temple ruins. 4.
Baale. See Kiriath-baal.
Baal-gad. A town in the Beqa'a west of Mount Hermon. Uncertain.
Baal-hamon. A town in Ephraim. Unknown.
Baal-hazor. A place in Central Palestine. **Jebel 'Asūr.**
Baal-hermon. A site on or near Mount Hermon. Unknown.
Baal-meon. Possibly **Ma'in** in Trans-jordan near Madeba. 10.
Baal-peor. See Beth-peor.
Baal-perazim. Near Jerusalem. **Ras en-Nadr** or **Sheikh Badr.**
Baal-shalisha. A town in Central Palestine, possibly **Kefr Tilt.**
Baal-tamar. A town near Gibeah. Unknown.
Baal-zephon. A stopping place during the Exodus. Unknown.
Babel. See Babylon.
Babylon. The capital of Babylonia in the Mesopotamian delta, 24, 26.
Babylon, District of. 24, 25.
Baca, Valley of. Possibly **el-Buqei'ah,** in Central Palestine.
Baghdad. The capital of modern Iraq, on the Tigris.
Bahurim. A village between Jerusalem and the Rift Valley. Possibly **Ras et-Tmīm** just east of Mount Scopus.
Bajith. Probably not a place name. The text is corrupt. Is. 15:2.
Balah. See Baalah 2.
Balikh, River. A tributary of the Euphrates in the north.
Bamoth, Bamoth-baal. These appear to be ancient holy sites in the region of Mount Nebo.
Barada, River. A river flowing through Damascus. See Abana. 6.
Basalt. A hard, volcanic rock, black in colour, which is widespread in Trans-jordan and in northern Cis-jordan.
Bascama. May be el-Jummeimeh north-east of the Sea of Galilee. I Macc. 13:23.
Bashan. The southern part of the Hauran plateau east of the Sea of Galilee. 17, 19.
Bashan-Havoth-jair. See Havoth-jair.
Basra. Modern town at the mouth of the Tigris and Euphrates.
Bayir. A small oasis in eastern Trans-jordan. 10.
Bealoth. See Baaloth-beer.
Bean. I Macc. 5:4. Probably a clan name.
Beer. 1. A well in the region east of Mattaneh. Num. 21:16.
2. Possibly **el-Bireh** not far from Hapharaim. Jud. 9:21.
Beer-elim. A place in Moab, which may be the same as Beer 1.
Beer-lahai-roi. An oasis near Kadesh Barnea. Unknown. III.
Beeroth. 1. A stopping place during the Exodus. Unknown. Deut. 10:6.
2. One of the four Hivite cities, possibly **Bireh** north of Jerusalem. IX.
Beersheba. The main southern border town of Judah. **Tell es-Saba'.** III, IV, VI, VII, 10, 12, 13, 14, 20, 22, 28.
Beersheba-Zered Depression. 5.
Be-eshterah. The same as Ashteroth.
Beirut. A modern port, the capital of Lebanon. The ancient Berytus. 5.
Bela. One of the cities of the Plain.
Bene-berak. A town in the original territory of Dan. **Ibn-Ibrāq.**
Bene-jaaken. The same as Beeroth 1.
Benjamin. A tribal territory in central Palestine between Judah and Ephraim. 16, 18, 29.
Beon. The same as Baal-meon.
Beqa'a, the. A common name for a valley between high hills. Often used especially for the Rift Valley between the Lebanon and Anti-Lebanon.
Berachah, Valley of. A valley in the Wilderness of Judah, possibly above Engedi.
Berea. 1. The same as Beeroth 1. I Macc. 9:4.
2. Beroea in northern Greece. 31.
Bered. A place near Kadesh Barnea. Exact site uncertain. III.
Beroea. The same as Berea 2.
Berothah. A town in Syria, possibly **Bereitān** in the Beqa'a.
Berytus. See Beirut. 4.
Besor, Brook. A wādī in the south, possibly the **Wādī Ghazzeh.**
Betah. See Tibhath.
Beten. A town in Asher. **Abtūn.** VIII.
Bethabara. A name given in some manuscripts in place of Bethany beyond Jordan in John 1:28.
Beth-anath. A town in Naphtali. Uncertain.
Beth-anoth. A town in Judah. Possibly **Beit 'Anūn** near Hebron.
Bethany. el-'Azarīyeh on the east slopes of the Mount of Olives. The name preserves the name of Lazarus.
Bethany beyond Jordan. Uncertain.
Beth-arabah. 'Ain Gharabeh near Jericho.
Beth-aram. See Beth-haran.
Beth-arbel. Possibly the modern **Irbid** in Trans-jordan.
Beth-asmaveth. See Azmaveth.
Beth-aven. May be either the original name of Ai or another name for Bethel.
Beth-baal-meon. Same as Baal-meon.
Beth-barah. A place in the Jordan Valley. Unknown.
Bethbasi. Kh. Beit Baṣṣah near Bethlehem. I Macc. 9:64. 20.
Beth-birei. A town in Simeon. Uncertain.
Beth-car. May be the same as Beth-horon the Lower.
Beth-dagon. 1. A town in Judah, possibly **Kh. Dajūn.** Josh. 15:41. VIII.
2. A town in Asher. Unknown. Josh. 19:27.
Beth-diblathaim. See Almon-Diblathaim.
Beth-eked. Near Jezreel. Unknown.
Bethel. 1. **Beitīn** near Ramallah. III, IV, VII, IX, 20, 27.
2. The same as Bethul. I Sam. 30:27.
Bethel, Mount. The region around Bethel 1.
Beth-emek. A town in Asher. **'Amqā** or **Tel Mimās**?
Bether. Bittīr west of Jerusalem.
Beth-ezel. Possibly **Deir el-'Asal** near Hebron.
Beth-gader. See Gedor 1.
Beth-gamul. Possibly **Kh. ej-Jumeil** near Dibon in Moab.
Beth-haccerem. 'Ain Kārim just west of Jerusalem. 27.
Beth-haggan. Probably the same as En-gannim.
Beth-haran. A town in Gad, possibly **Tell Iktanū.**
Beth-hoglah. A town in Benjamin, possibly **'Ain Hajlah** near Jericho.
Beth-horon, Ascent of. A valley leading up from Ajalon into the highlands.
Beth-horon the Lower. Beit-'ūr eṭ-Ṭahta in the Valley of Ajalon. IX.
Beth-horon the Upper. Beit-'ūr el-Fōqā. IV, IX.
Beth-jeshimmoth. A stopping place during the Exodus, probably **Tell el-'Azeimah** twelve miles from Jericho. IV.
Beth-le-aphrah. Possibly **eṭ-Ṭaiyebeh** near Hebron.
Beth-lebaoth. See Beth-birei.
Bethlehem. 1. A town in Judah, the birthplace of Jesus. **Beit Laḥm.** IV, IX, 14, 27, 28.
2. A town in Galilee. **Beit Laḥm.** Josh. 19:15; Jud. 12:8. VIII.
Beth-maacah. See Abel-beth-maacah.
Beth-meon. See Baal-meon.

Beth-marcaboth. A town near Ziklag, possibly the same as Madmennah.
Beth-nimrah. A town in Gad, possibly **Tell el-Bleibil.**
Beth-palet, Beth-pelet. A town near Beersheba, perhaps **Kh. el-Meshāsh.**
Beth-pazzez. A town in Issachar. Unknown.
Beth-peor. A place in Moab. Unknown.
Beth-phage. A village on the Mount of Olives, possibly **Kh. eṭ-Ṭūr.**
Beth-rehob. Unknown. Probably in the southern part of the Syrian Beqa'a.
Beth-saida. A town on the north-east of the Sea of Galilee. X.
Beth-san. The same as Beth-shan.
Beth-shan, Beth-shean. A fortress town guarding the eastern entrance to the Valley of Jezreel. **Tell el-Ḥuṣn** near the modern Beisan. VI, VII, VIII, 10, 11, 16.
Beth-shemesh. 1. A town in the Judaean Moat. **Tell er-Rumeileh.** IX, 16.
2. A town in Issachar. Unknown. Josh. 19:22.
3. A town in Naphtali. Unknown. Josh. 19:38.
4. The same as Heliopolis or On in Egypt.
Beth-shittah. Possibly **Shaṭṭah** east of the Spring of Harod. VIII.
Bethsur, Bethsura. See Beth-zur. 20.
Beth-tappuah. Probably **Taffūḥ** west of Hebron.
Beth-togarmah. Unknown.
Bethuel, Bethul. A town of Simeon, possibly **Kh. el-Qaryatein** near Hebron.
Beth-zechariah. Kh. Beit Zakāriyeh south-west of Jerusalem. I Macc. 6:32. 20.
Beth-zur. A town in Judah, **Kh. et-Tubeiqah** near **Burj-es-Sūr.** 27.
Betonim. A town in Gad, possibly **Kh. Batneh.**
Bezek. 1. Possibly Kh. Bezqa near Gezer, or may be the same as Bezek 2. Jud. 1:4, 5.
2. **Kh. Ibzīq** on southern slopes of Gilboa. I Sam. 11:8.
Bezer. A town in Reuben, possibly **Umm el-'Amad** north of Madeba.
Bezeth. Kh. Beit Zi'ta north of Bethlehem. I Macc. 7:19.
Bileam. See Ibleam.
Bilhah. See Baalah 2.
Bishri, Jebel. A ridge east of the Anti-Lebanon and north-east of Damascus. 24.
Bithron. A valley leading from the Jordan to Mahanaim. Unknown.
Bithynia. A region in northern Asia Minor. 31.
Bizjothah. Unknown. Probably a corrupt text.
Black Sea. 24, 31.
Bochim. See Allon-bachuth.
Bohan, Stone of. Possibly **Ḥarar el-Aṣbaḥ** in the wilderness near Jericho.
Borashan. See Ashan.
Bosor. Buṣr el-Harīri in Bashan. I Macc. 5:26. 10, 20.
Bosora. Buṣrah-eski-Shām east of Dera'a. I Macc. 5:26. 20.
Bozkath. A town near Lachish. Unknown.
Bozrah. 1. Probably **Buṣṣirah** in northern Edom. III, 10.
2. Possibly the same as Bezer in Moab. Jer. 48:24.
Bridge of Jacob's Daughters. A ford just south of the Lake of Huleh. 9.
Brook, the. I Macc. 5:37. Possibly **Nahr el-Aḥgheir** in Bashan.
Butte. A geographical term for a small, isolated hill with steep sides and a flat top, characteristic of desert scenery.
Buweida, Jebel. A ridge north-east of Damascus. 4.
Buz. A region in Arabia. Unknown.
Byblos. An important port in ancient days just north of modern Beirut. **Jebeil.** III.
Cabbon. A town in Judah, possibly **Kh. Ḥabrā** east of Lachish.
Cabul. A border town in northern Asher. **Kābūl.**
Cades. The same as Kedesh-Naphtali. 20.
Caesarea. An important Roman port south of Mount Carmel. X, 28, 31.
Caesarea-Philippi. A sacred site at one of the sources of the Jordan. **Bāniyās.** 28.
Cain. A town in south Judah. **Kh. Yaqīn.**
Cairo. The capital of modern Egypt.
Calah. A town south of Nineveh. **Nimrūd.** 24.
Callirhoe. See Zareth-shahar.
Calneh. In Gen. 10:10 probably not a place name.
Calno. An important town in northern Syria. **Kullankoÿ** north-east of Aleppo. VI, VII.
Calvary. The site of the Crucifixion, traditionally where the Holy Sepulchre stands though this is disputed by some archaeologists.
Campus Asochis. The Roman name for the modern **Sahl el-Baṭṭōf.**
Cana of Galilee. Traditionally **Kafr Kannā** near Nazareth, but more probably **Kh. Qāna** a few miles to the north of it. X.
Canaan. The name given to the country west of the Jordan.
Canatha. Qanawāt in the Jebel Druze.
Canneh. A place near Haran in northern Syria. Unknown.
Capernaum. The chief centre of Jesus' work in Galilee. **Tel Ḥūm** on the north-western shores of the Lake. X, 28.
Capharsalama. Kh. Selmā north-west of Jerusalem. I Macc. 7:31.
Caphtor. The ancient name for Crete.
Cappadocia. A region in Central Asia Minor. 31.
Carchemish. An important town on the Upper Euphrates. **Jerāblus.** VI, VII, 4, 24.
Caria Mountains. The mountain range above Colossae.
Carmel. A place in south-western Judah. **Kermel.**
Carmel, Mount. The headland interrupting the coast plain just south of Acre. 4, 11, 17.
Carnaim, Carnion. Sheikh Sa'ad in Bashan. I Macc. 5:26, 43; II Macc. 12:21. 20.
Casiphia. City in Babylonia. Unknown.
Casphor, Caspin. Possibly **Khisfīn** about nine miles east of the Sea of Galilee. I Macc. 5:26, 36; II Macc. 12:13. 20.
Cassius Mountains. Mountain range in Syria north of **Rās Shamrā.** 5.
Cauldron. A geographical term for the strange formations in the southern desert, of which the largest is the Wādī Raman. It is a huge hollow area enclosed by high, precipitous sides.
Cedron. Possibly **Qatrah** or **Mughār** on the Coast Plain. 20.
Cenchraea, Cenchreae. The port of Corinth on the Bay of Salamis.
Cenomanian Limestone. A hard limestone, characteristic of Ephraim, Judah and Mount Carmel. It forms excellent building stone, and breaks down into a fertile, dark red soil, called **terra rossa,** q.v.
Chabulon. See Cabul. X.
Chaldea. Southern Babylonia.
Characa, Charax. II Macc. 12:17. A common name for a fortified camp.
Charashim, Valley of. A valley near Lod, possibly the **Wādī esh-Shellāl.**
Chebar, River. A canal near Babylon, called the **Naru Kabari** in ancient texts.
Chephar-ammoni. See Chephar-haammoni.
Chephar-haammoni. A town in Benjamin. Unknown.
Chephirah. A town in Benjamin. **Tell Kefīreh** two miles north of Kiriath Jearim. IX, 27.
Chephirim. Neh. 6:2. Probably to be translated "one of the villages" as in RSV.
Cherith, Brook. A wādī entering the Jordan Valley from the east opposite Samaria. **Wādī Yābis**?
Cherub. A town in Babylonia. Unknown.
Chesalon. Northern border town of Judah. **Keslā** west of Jerusalem.
Chesil. See Bethul.
Chesulloth. A town in Issachar. **Iksāl.** VIII.
Chezib. The same as Achzib 1.
Chinnereth, Chinneroth. Tel el-'Oreimeh on western side of Lake of Galilee. IV.
Chinnereth, Sea of. Lake of Galilee.
Chios. An island in the Aegean Sea. 31.
Chisloth-tabor. See Chesulloth.
Chitlish. A town in Judah, possibly **Kh. el-Maghāz,** south-west of Lachish.
Chorazin. A town overlooking the Sea of Galilee from the north. **Kh. Kerāzeh.** X.

Chun. A site in the north, possibly **Rās Ba'albek.**
Cilicia. Region in the south of Asia Minor. 31.
Cilician Gates. A dramatic defile leading from Anatolia down into Syria.
Cis-jordan. Modern geographical term for the region west of the Jordan.
Cities of the Plain. Five towns (Admah, Bela, Gomorrah, Sodom, Zeboiim) which were destroyed in the time of Abraham. They may lie beneath the shallow southern end of the Dead Sea, but some archaeologists suggest that they stood at the north end.
Cnidus. On the southern shore of Asia Minor. **Cap Krio.** I Macc. 15:23; Acts 27:7. 31.
Cnydus River. A river near Tarsus.
Colossae. A town in Asia Minor near **Khonai** not far from **Denizli** in Turkey. 31.
Corinth. 31.
Corinth, Gulf of.
Corruption, Mount of. See Offence, Mount of.
Cos. An island in the Aegean Sea. 31.
Craftsmen, Valley of. See Charashim. 27.
Crete. 31.
Crocodile River. A river running into the sea just south of Mount Carmel. I, 16.
Cun. See Chun.
Cush. Ethiopia.
Cuthah. Possibly **Tell Ibrāhīm** north of Babylon.
Cyprus. 31.
Cyrenaica. The region round Cyrene. 31.
Cyrene. A town on the north coast of Libya. 31.
Dabareh. See Daberath.
Dabbeshah. Town in Zebulun. **Tell esh-Shammām** near Jokneam. VIII.
Daberath. Kh. Dabbūreh near **Dabbūrīyeh** at the foot of Mount Tabor. VIII.
Dakhla Oasis. An oasis in the Sahara desert. 21.
Dalmanutha. A site mentioned in Mark 8:10, but otherwise unknown. May be the same as Magdala.
Dalmatia. Region on the west Balkan coast.
Damascus. III, VI, VII, 4, 5, 14, 26, 27, 31.
Dan. 1. Tribal territory originally in the Ajalon region but later transferred to the northern end of the Jordan Valley. 18.
2. Chief town of the new Danite territory. **Tell el-Qādī.** VI, VII, 9.
Dan-jean. II Sam. 24:6. The text is corrupt and the place meant is probably Dan 2.
Dannah. A town of Judah. Unknown.
Daphne. Kh. Dafneh north of Lake Huleh.
Darb es-Sultan. An ancient highroad leading down the Wādī Murra, q.v.
Dathema. Tell Ḥamad in Bashan. I Macc. 5:9. 20.
Dead Sea. I, III, IV, 4, 12, 13, 16, 27, 28.
Debir. 1. Important Canaanite city west of Hebron. **Tell Beit Mirsim.** IV.
2. Town on northern border of Judah, possibly **Thoghret ed-Debr.**
3. Same as Lo-debar.
Decapolis. A loose federation of ten Hellenistic cities mainly east of the Jordan in Bashan and Gilead. They were Abila (**Tell Abīl,** south of the Yarmūq), Damascus, Dion (**Tel el-'Ashāri**), Gadara (**Umm Qeis**), Gerasa (**Jerāsh**), Hippos (**Qala'at el-Ḥuṣn**), Kanata (**Qanawāt**), Pella (**Kh. Fāhil**), Philadelphia (**'Ammān**) and Scythopolis, which was the only one west of the Jordan (**Beisān**). The number varied from time to time. X, 28.
Dedan. Possibly the oasis of **el-'Alā** in northern Arabia.
Deir ez-Zor. A modern town on the Euphrates. 24.
Delos. An island in the Aegean Sea. I Macc. 15:23.
Derbe. A town in Lycaonia near the modern **Zosta.** 31.
Diala River. A tributary of the Tigris entering south of Baghdad. 24.
Diblath. The same as Riblah.
Dibon. 1. A town on the northern edge of the Arnon canyon. **Dhibān.** 10, 22.
2. A town in the Negeb. Unknown. Neh. 11:25.
Dibon-gad. Probably the same as Dibon 1.
Diklah. A place in southern Arabia. Unknown.
Dilean. A town in western Judah, possibly **Tell en-Najileh.**
Dimnah. See Rimmon 2.
Dimon. Probably the same as Dibon 1, or possibly Madmen.
Dimonah. A town in southern Judah, possibly the same as Dibon 2.
Dinhabah. A town in Edom. Unknown.
Dion. See Decapolis. 10.
Di-zahab. A town in Moab or northern Edom. Unknown.
Docus, Dok. Jebel Qarantal, the traditional Mount of Temptation near Jericho. 20.
Dome. A geographical term for a large, rounded, uplifted area.
Dophkah. A stopping place during the Exodus. Uncertain.
Dor, Dora. el-Burj near **Ṭanṭūrah** on the coast south of Mount Carmel. X, 16, 20.
Dothan. Tell Dothān south of Jenin. III.
Downfold. A geographical term for a formation in which the rocks have been pushed downwards in a folded formation.
Druze, Jebel. Volcanic mountains in south-eastern Syria. 4.
Dumah. 1. A town in Judah. **ed-Dōmeh** south-west of Hebron.
2. A site in Arabia, possibly **Dūmet ej-Jendel.** Is. 21:11.
Eastern Plateau. The high, level area east of the Rift Valley; the beginning of the plateau of Arabia.
Ebal, Mount. One of the two mountains overlooking Shechem. **Jebel Islamīyeh.**
Ebenezer. A place near Aphek 1. **Mejdel Yābā?**
Ebez. A town in Issachar. Unknown.
Ebron. In Asher. The same as Abdon, q.v.
Ebronah. A stopping place on the Exodus. See Abronah.
Ecbatana. Hamadān in Persia. 26.
Edar, Tower of. Uncertain.
Eden, Garden of. Impossible to identify with any particular area.
Eden. A region in the middle Euphrates area. II Kings 19:12; Is. 37:12; Ezk. 27:23.
Eder. A town near Arad in southern Judah. Possibly the same as Arada.
Eder, tower of. Unknown.
Edom. The southernmost of the Trans-jordanian kingdoms. IV, 12, 18, 22.
Edrei. 1. A town on the Syrian border. **Dera'a.** 10.
2. A town in Naphtali. Unknown. Josh. 19:37.
Eglaim. A town in Moab. Unknown.
Eglon. A town in the Shephelah. **Tel el-Ḥeṣī.**
Egypt. 25, 31.
Egypt, modern state of. 14.
Egypt, River of. Probably **Wādī el-'Arīsh** in southern Palestine.
Ekron. One of the Philistine towns. **Qatra** or **'Aqīr.** IV.
Elah, Valley of. Wādī eṣ-Ṣamt which crosses the Shephelah. IX.
Elam. 1. **Kh. Beit 'Alam** west of Beth-zur. Neh. 7:34; Ezr. 2:31. 27.
2. The hill country east of Babylon. 24.
Elasa. The site of Judas' last camp, probably near **Bīr Zeit.** I Macc. 9:5.
Elath, Eloth. A town on the Gulf of 'Aqabah, possibly Ezion Geber, but more probably 'Aqabah. 10, 21, 22.
Elath, modern town of. 14.
Elealeh. A town in Moab. **el-'Al** near Heshbon.
Elephantine. Aswān in Upper Egypt.
Eleuterus, River. Nahr el-Kabīr north of Tripoli? I Macc. 11:7; 12:30.
Eleutheropolis. Beit Jibrīn in the Shephelah.
Elim. A stopping place during the Exodus, possibly **'Ain Gharandel** in the Arabah. 22.
Elkosh. Unknown.
Ellasar. Uncertain, but probably not far from Carchemish.
Elon. 1. A town in the original territory of Dan. Unknown. Josh. 19:43.
2. The same as Ajalon 1. I Kings 4:9.
Elon-beth-hanan. Probably **Beit 'Ānān** north-west of Jerusalem.
Eloth. See Elath. 10, 21, 22.
El-paran. Probably the region near the Gulf of **'Aqabah.**

Eltekeh. A town in the original territory of Dan. **Kh. el-Muqennā?**
Eltekon. A town in Judah. Unknown.
Eltolad. A town in Simeon. Unknown.
Emek-keziz. A town in Benjamin. Unknown.
Emmaus. Probably **'Imwās** near Ajalon, though other sites have been suggested. IX, 20, 28.
Enaim, Enam. A town in Judah near Adullam. Unknown.
Enan. See Hazar-enan.
Endor. Kh. es-Safsafeh, half a mile north-east of Indūr on Mount Moreh. VIII.
Eneglaim. Near Engedi on the Dead Sea. Uncertain.
En-gannim. 1. Possibly **Beit Jemāl** near Beth-shemesh 1. Josh. 15:34.
2. A town in Issachar, the modern **Jenīn**, VIII.
Engedi. Tell el-Jurn near **'Ain Jidī** on the western shore of the Dead Sea. VI.
En-Haddah. A town in Issachar, possibly **en-Ḥadetheh.**
En-hakkore. A spring in Lehi.
En-hazor. A town in Naphtali. **Kh. el-Ḥaṣīreh** or **Hazzūr.**
En-mishpat. See Kadesh Barnea.
Enoch. Unknown.
En-rimmon. A town in southern Judah. **Kh. Umm er-Ramāmīn.**
En-rogel. A spring near Jerusalem. **Bīr Ayyūb.**
En-shemesh. A town on the border of Judah. **'Ain el-Ḥōd** east of Jerusalem.
En-tappuah. Same as Tappuah 2.
Eocene limestone. A hard rock characteristic of Manasseh and the Shephelah. It is less useful for building than the Cenomanian limestone, q.v., and forms a much less fertile soil.
Ephes-dammim. Between Socoh and Azekah. Uncertain.
Ephesus. A sea-port south of Smyrna in Asia Minor. 31.
Ephraim. 1. The same as Ophrah 1?
2. Tribal district south of Manasseh. 16, 18.
Ephraim Dome. An upwarped area in central Cis-jordan. 11.
Ephraim, Forest of. Forested country in Gilead.
Ephraim, Mount. See Ephraim 2.
Ephrata(h). Bethlehem in Judah.
Ephrath. Bethlehem in Judah. III.
Ephron 1. **Eṭ-Ṭaiyebeh** in Gilead. I Macc. 5:46; II Macc. 12:27. 20.
2. The same as Ophrah 1. II Chr. 13:19.
3. Mount Ephron near Kiriath-jearim. Josh. 15:9.
Erech. The biblical name for Uruk in Babylonia. **Warkā** south of Babylon. 24.
Erg. A geographical term for a sandy desert, as opposed to **hamada,** q.v.
Eridu. One of the most ancient towns in Babylonia. **Abū Shahrein.** 24.
Esdraelon, Plain of. The Greek name for the Valley of Jezreel, q.v. I, II.
Esek. A well in southern Palestine.
Eshan. A hill town in Judah. Unknown.
Eshcol, Valley of. A valley near Hebron. Unknown.
Eshtaol. A town in the Judaean moat. **Artūf** or **Eshwa'.** IX.
Eshtemoa. A hill town in Judah. **es-Semū'** near Hebron.
Etam. 1. A hill town in Judah. **Kh. el-Khōkh** near Bethlehem.
2. A town in Simeon. Unknown. 1 Chr. 4:32.
Etam, Rock of. In northern Judah. Unknown.
Etham. A stopping place during the Exodus. In Sinai. Unknown.
Ether. 1. A town of Judah in the Shephelah. **Kh. el-'Ater** near Lachish.
2. A town in Simeon which may be the same as the above, but may be somewhat further south. Josh. 19:7.
Ethiopia. 23.
Eth-kazin. A town in Zebulun. Unknown.
Euphrates, River. 1. One of the two major rivers of Mesopotamia. 4, 23, 24, 31.
2. **Wādī Fārah** near Anathoth, the names being very similar in Hebrew. Jer. 13:4–6.
Ezek, Well of. Near Gerar. Unknown.
Ezel, Stone of. Near Gibeah of Saul. Unknown.
Ezion-geber. Tell el-Kheleifeh on the Gulf of 'Aqabah. VI.
Fair Havens. Bay in southern Crete. **Limenes Kali.**
Faiyum, the. A large and fertile depression west of the Nile.
Farafra Oasis. An oasis in the Sahara. 21.
Fari 'a River. A stream in Central Palestine flowing into the Jordan. I, 11.
Fault. A geological term for a sharp break in the rock strata, which has allowed one part to be pushed up higher than the other. There are a large number of these in Palestine, some of them of enormous size. See also **fault basin** and **rift valley.**
Fault Basin. A geological term for a depressed area which has dropped down between parallel faults.
Fertile Crescent. The name given to the sickle of inhabited land formed by Mesopotamia and the Levant Coast.
Forest. The word in biblical usage may mean any area of wild or waste land, though it may also have its more normal meaning of a wooded area.
Gaash, Mount. A hilly region by Timnath-serah.
Gaba. 1. See Geba.
2. **el-Harīthīyeh** south of Harosheth, X.
Gad. A tribal district east of the Jordan. Its extent is very uncertain, and the name may have been confused with Gilead. 16, 18.
Gad, River or Valley of. Probably the Arnon.
Gadara. See Decapolis. X, 10, 28.
Galaad. See Gilead. 20.
Galatia. A region in Asia Minor, though there is some dispute whether the region meant in the New Testament is in the north or the south. 31.
Galgala. See Galilee.
Galilee. Commonly used for the northernmost section of Cis-jordan, though probably it was kept at least in the Old Testament for Upper Galilee, q.v. I, X, 4, 17, 20, 28.
Galilee, Lower. The southern section of Galilee in which Nazareth lies.
Galilee, Sea of. The central of the three lakes on the Jordan. I, X, 11, 16.
Galilee, Upper. The northern section of Galilee. 9.
Galilee-Yarmuq Depression. 5.
Gallim. 1. A town north of Jerusalem, possibly **Kh. Ka'kūl** near Anathoth.
2. A town in Judah mentioned in Josh. 15:59 (LXX). Possibly **Beit Jālā.**
Gath. One of the five Philistine towns. **'Arāq el-Manshīyeh.** IV, IX.
Gath-hepher. A town of Zebulun. **Kh. ez-Zurrā,** near Nazareth. VIII.
Gath-rimmon. 1. A town in the original territory of Dan. Unknown.
2. A town in Manasseh, possibly **Rummāneh.** Josh. 21:25.
Gaulanitis. The plateau region east and north-east of the Sea of Galilee. X, 28.
Gaza. A sea-port in Philistia. IV, VI, VIII, 14, 20, 21, 27, 28, 31.
Gazera. See Gezer. 20.
Geba. A town in Benjamin. **Jeba'.** It is occasionally confused with Gibeah. VII, IX, 27.
Gebal. 1. See Byblos.
2. A place in northern Edom. Unknown. Ps. 83:7.
Gebim. A town of Benjamin, possibly the ruins south-west of **Shu'fāt** north of Jerusalem.
Geder. Possibly the same as Gerar.
Gederah. A town in western Judah. **Jedīreh.**
Gederoth. A town in western Judah. Unknown.
Gederothaim. A town in western Judah. Unknown.
Gedor. 1. A hill town in Judah, possibly **Kh. Jedūr** near Bethlehem. Josh. 15:58.
2. A town in western Judah. Unknown. 1 Chr. 4:18, 39.
3. A town in Benjamin. Unknown. 1 Chr. 12:7.
Gehenna. See Hinnom, Valley of.
Gennesar. See Chinnereth.
Gennesaret, Plain of. The small plain of **el-Ghuweir** on the north-west side of the Sea of Galilee.
Geon. See Gihon. Sir. 24:27.
Gerar. A town in Southern Palestine. **Tell esh-Sherī'ah or Tell ej-Jemneh.** III.
Gerasa. See Decapolis. 10, 28.

Gergesa. Possibly **el-Kursī** east of the Sea of Galilee, but it may be the same as Gerasa. X.
Gerizim, Mount. The southern of the two mountains overlooking Shechem. **Jebel eṭ-Ṭur.**
Geruth-Chimham. Jer. 41:17. To be translated "the inn of Chimham" at or near Bethlehem?
Geshur. 1. A district in Bashan.
2. A district in the Negeb or possibly Sinai. Josh. 13:2; I Sam. 27:8.
Gethsemane, Garden of. An olive orchard on the slopes of the Mount of Olives. 29.
Gezer. An important town on the border of Ephraim in the plain. **Tel Jazer.** IV, 16.
Ghab, the. The marshy valley of the Orontes north of Hamath. 5.
Giah. II Sam. 2:24. Unknown. Possibly a corrupt text.
Gibbethon. A Philistine border town. **Tell el-Melāt** near Gezer.
Gibeah. 1. A town in Judah, possibly **el-Jeba'** near Bethlehem. Josh. 15:57.
2. A town near Kiriath-jearim. Unknown. I Sam. 7:1 (the hill); II Sam. 6:3.
3. "Gibeah of Saul" in Benjamin. **Tell el-Fūl** north of Jerusalem. IX.
Gibeath. See Gibeah 3.
Gibeon. An important and apparently holy site in Benjamin. **el-Jīb.** IX, 27.
Gihon. A spring near Jerusalem. **'Ain Sittna Miriam.** 29, 30.
Gilboa, Mount. The hilly country south of the eastern portion of the Valley of Jezreel. **Jebel Fuqū'ah.** VIII, II.
Gilead. The hilly country divided by the River Jabbok. It does not extend either to the Yarmuq in the north or the Arnon in the south. 4, 5, 11, 17.
Gilgal. 1. A site near Jericho, probably a stone circle. The site is unknown, but **Kh. el-Etheleh** or **Kh. el-Mefjir** have been suggested.
2. **Jiljilyeh** north of Bethel. It is uncertain whether the Gilgal of the stories of Elijah and Elisha is this place or Gilgal 1. The same question exists for the Gilgal condemned by Amos and Hosea.
3. A place near Shechem, which may be that condemned by Amos and Hosea. Deut. 11:30.
4. On the border of Judah and Benjamin. Uncertain. Josh. 15:7; 18:17.
5. Josh. 12:23 (Hebrew). Probably Harosheth of the Gentiles.
Giloh. A hill town of Judah, possibly **Kh. Jālā** near Hebron.
Gimzo. Jimzū near Lod.
Gischala. el-Jish in Upper Galilee. X.
Gittaim. Unknown. Somewhere near Lod.
Giza. In Egypt just west of modern Cairo; the site of the Pyramids. 21.
Goath. A town near Jerusalem. Unknown.
Gob. A town near Gezer. Unknown.
Gobi Desert. The vast desert area of Central Asia.
Golan. A town in Bashan. **el-Jaulān.**
Gomorrah. One of the Cities of the Plain, q.v.
Goshen. 1. A town in Judah. Unknown, though edh-Dhaharīyeh south-west of Hebron has been suggested.
2. Josh. 15:51. This may be the same as Goshen 1.
Goshen, the Land of. The eastern part of the Nile Delta. 22.
Gozan. Probably **Tell Ḥalāf** of the River Khabur. 24.
Great Sea. The Mediterranean.
Gur, Ascent of. Probably the narrow defile south of Ibleam.
Gur-baal. A place in the Negeb. Unknown.
Hachilah, Hill of. In the south of Judah near Ziph 2. Unknown.
Hadad-Rimmon. Zech. 12:11. Once believed to be a place name, but now understood to be the name of two gods.
Hadashah. A town in western Judah near Gath. Unknown.
Hadattah. See Hazor-Hadattah.
Hadera. A modern town in the Sharon region.
Hadid. el-Ḥadīteh three miles east of Lod.
Hadrach, Land of. A region in Syria north of Hamath.
Hai. See Ai.
Haifa. A modern town at the foot of, and partly on Mount Carmel. 14.
Halah. A district in Assyria. Unknown.
Halak, Mount. A mountain in the Negeb. Uncertain, possibly **Jebel Halāq.**
Haleiqim, Jebel. A hilly region in the Negeb. 12.
Halhul. A hill town in Judah. **Ḥalḥūl** just north of Hebron. IX.
Hali. A town in Asher. Unknown.
Halicarnassus. The modern **Bodrum** in Turkey. I Macc. 15:23.
Ham. A town east of the Jordan, probably **Ḥām** south-west of Irbid. III.
Hamada. A geographical term for a "stony desert" as opposed to **erg** (q.v.) or sandy desert. Movement in the **hamada** is much easier than in the **erg.** The Palestinian and Syrian deserts are almost entirely **hamada.**
Hamath. An important town on the Orontes in Syria. **Ḥāmā.** VI, VII, 4, 5, 24.
Hamath, Entrance of. Once believed to be a name for the northern section of the **Beqa'a,** this is now generally understood to be the name of a place, Lebo-Hamath, q.v.
Hamath-Zobah. See Zobah.
Hammath (Hamath). The hot springs of **el-Ḥammām** just south of Tiberias. X.
Hammath Gader. The hot springs of **el-Ḥammeh** in the lower Yarmuq valley. X.
el-Hammeh. See Hammath Gader.
Hammon. 1. A town in Asher, possibly **Umm el-'Awānid.**
2. A town in Naphtali, possibly Hammath 1.
Hammoth-dor. See Hammath 1.
Hamonah. Unknown.
Hamon-gog, Valley of. Unknown.
Hanes. A town in Egypt, possibly Heracleopolis at the entrance to the Faiyum.
Hannathon. A town of Zebulun, possibly **Tell el-Badāwīyeh** on the western edge of the **Saḥl el-Baṭṭōf.** VIII.
Hapharaim. See Hapharaim-shion.
Hapharaim-shion. A town in Issachar, possibly **eṭ-Ṭaiyebeh** six miles east of Shunem. VIII.
Hara. I Chr. 5:26. Unknown. The text is probably corrupt.
Harada. A stopping place during the Exodus. Unknown.
Haran. A town in northern Syria. **Ḥarrān.** III, VII, 4.
Hareth, Forest of. In the south of Judah, possibly **Kharas** near Keilah.
Har-heres. The same as Beth-shemesh 1.
Harim. A town in Judah, possibly **Kh. Ḥorān** west of Bethlehem. 27.
Harod, Well or Spring of. 'Ain Jalūd in the Valley of Jezreel. VIII.
Harosheth of the Gentiles. A town in the Plain of Accho, probably **Tell el-'Amr.** IV, VIII.
Harosheth-ha-goiim. See Harosheth of the Gentiles.
Haruph. A town in southern Judah. Unknown.
Hashmonah. A stopping place on the Exodus near Kadesh Barnea. Unknown.
Hasma, Wādī. The desolate desert area beyond the southern frontier of Edom. 10.
Hathira, Jebel. One of the "cauldrons" (q.v.) in the Negeb. 12, 13, 19.
Hauran. The plateau area east of the Sea of Galilee.
Havilah. Uncertain, possibly in north-western Arabia.
Havoth-jair. A group of villages in Manasseh, though it is not clear which.
Hazar-addar. Possibly **Kh. el-Qudeirāt** in the Negeb.
Hazar-enan. Possibly **Qaryatein** between Damascus and Homs. VI, VII.
Hazar-gaddah. A place near Beersheba. Unknown.
Hazar-hatticon. A place in Bashan. Unknown.
Hazar-Ithnan. Possibly to be read separately as in the RSV.
Hazarmaveth. The huge valley of **Wādī Ḥadhramaut** in southern Arabia.
Hazar-shual. A town near Beersheba. Kh. el-Meshash?

Hazar-susah. A town in the south of Judah. **Sbalāt Abū Sūsein.**
Hazazon-Tamar, Hazezon-Tamar. 'Ain el-'Arūs south of the Dead Sea. 10.
Hazerim. Deut. 2:23. To be translated "villages".
Hazezon-Tamar. See Hazazon-Tamar.
Hazor. 1. An important town on the Trunk Road west of Lake Huleh. **Kh. Waqqās.** IV, VI, 9, 18.
2. Josh. 15:25. Unknown. Probably a corrupt text.
3. A town in Central Palestine, probably **Kh. Ḥazzūr** near Bethany. Neh. 11:33.
4. A town of Judah in the Negeb. Unknown. Josh. 15:23.
Hazor-hadattah. A town in southern Judah. Unknown.
Hebron. 1. The major town in the territory of Judah. III, IV, VI, VII, IX, 4, 12, 14, 18, 20, 22, 27, 28.
2. The same as Abdon. Josh. 19:28.
Hebron Valley. 12.
Helam. Unknown, but may be the same as Alema.
Helbah. Probably the same as Ahlab.
Helbon. May be **Ḥalbūn** about sixteen miles north of Damascus.
Heleph. A town in Naphtali, possibly **Kh. 'Arbadah.** VIII.
Heliopolis. See On. 22.
Helkath. A town in Asher, possibly **Kh. el-Herbaj.** VIII.
Helkath-Hazzurim. See Gibeon.
Hena. A place in Syria. Unknown.
Hepher. A town in Manasseh, probably **Tell Ibshār.**
Heres, Ascent of. See Beth-shemesh 1.
Hereth, Forest of. See Hareth.
Hermon, Mount. The highest part of the Anti-Lebanon. **Jebel esh-Sheikh.** 6, 9.
Herodium, the. A fortress of Herod the Great near Bethlehem. **Jebel Fureidīs.** 28.
Heshbon. A town in Moab. **Hashān** near Madeba. IV, 10, 22.
Heshmon. A town near Beersheba. Unknown.
Hethlon. A town in Syria. Unknown.
Hiddekel, River. The River Tigris.
Hierapolis. A town in the Lycus Valley in Turkey. **Pambuk Kalesi.**
Hilen. See Holon 1.
Hinge-faults. A geological term or faults (q.v.), often curving, which strike out obliquely from the main faults of a rift-valley (q.v.).
Hinnom, Valley of. Wādī er-Rehābī on the western side of Jerusalem. 29, 30.
Hippos. See Decapolis. X, 10.
Hobah. A region north of Damascus.
Holon. 1. A town of Judah, possibly **Kh. 'Alīn.**
2. A town near Madeba. Unknown. Jer. 48:21.
Homs. A modern town on the Orontes south of Hamath. 4.
Homs, Lake of. 4.
Hor, Mount. 1. A mountain on the northern frontier of Canaan. Unknown. Num. 34:7, 8.
2. A mountain in the south, possibly near Kadesh Barnea. Unknown.
Horeb, Mount. The same as Mount Sinai.
Horem. A town in Naphtali. Unknown.
Hor-hagidgad. A stopping place during the Exodus, possibly **Wādī Khadakhid.**
Hormah. A town in southern Judah. **Tell el-Mishāsh** or **Tell ash-Sherī'ah.**
Horns of Hattin. A volcanic hill above Tiberias.
Horonaim. A place in Moab. Unknown.
Hosah. A town in Asher. **Kh. el-Ḥoṣn**?
Hukkok. A town in Naphtali. **Yaqūq.**
Hukok. See Helkath.
Huleh, Lake. The first, and smallest, of the three Lakes on the Jordan. It has recently been drained. I, 9, 16.
Humtah. A place near Hebron. Unknown.
Ibleam. A town listed as belonging to Manasseh but in the territory of Asher. **Tell Bel'ameh** near Jenin. 16.
Iconium. The modern Konya in southern Asia Minor. 31.
Idalah. A town of Zebulun, possibly **Kh. el-Ḥuwwārah.** VIII.
Idumaea, Idumea. The region of southern Judaea in New Testament times. 20, 28.
Iim. 1. See Ije-abarim.
2. A town in the extreme south of Judah. Unknown, but may be Ije-abarim. Josh. 15:29.
Ije-abarim. A stopping place during the Exodus near the Brook Zered. Unknown.
Ijon. A town in Naphtali. **Tell ed-Dibbīn** in the southern Beqa'a.
Ijon, Plain of. The southern Beqa'a known today as **Merj Ayoun.** 9.
Immer. A place in Babylon. Unknown.
Indus, River. The major river of Western Pakistan. 23.
Iphtah. A town in western Judah, possibly **Tarqumīyeh** near Lachish.
Iphtahel, Valley of. See Jiphtah-el.
Irbid. A modern town in northern Trans-jordan. 14.
Ir-nahash. A town in Judah. Unknown.
Iron. A town in Naphtali. **Yarūn.**
Irpeel. A town in Benjamin, possibly **Rafāt** north-west of Jerusalem.
Ir-shemesh. See Beth-shemesh 1.
Ish-tob. See Tob.
Israel, Kingdom of. The northern territory after the division of the Kingdom.
Israel, modern state of. 14.
Issachar. A tribal district in the Valley of Jezreel. 16, 18.
Italy. 31.
Ithlah. A town in the original territory of Dan. Unknown.
Ithnan. A town in southern Judah. Unknown.
Ittah-kezin. See Eth-kezin.
Ituraea, Iturea. A territory to the north of Palestine in New Testament times.
Ivvah. Possibly **Tell Kefr- 'Ayā** near Riblah on the Orontes.
Jaar, Fields of. See Kiriath-jearim.
Jaazer. See Jazer.
Jabbok, River. A river rising at Rabboth Ammon and flowing to the Jordan. **Nahr ez-Zerqa.** I, III, 11, 18, 19.
Jabesh Gilead. A town in Trans-jordan, possibly in the Jordan valley not too far from Beth-shan. It has been variously identified, e.g. **Tell el-Maqlūb, Tell Abū Kharaz,** ruins near **Halāwā.** 10.
Jabez. A town in Judah. Unknown.
Jabneel. 1. A town in western Judah. **Yebnā.**
2. A town in Naphtali. **Kh. Jemneh**? Josh. 19:33. VIII.
Jacob's Well. A well just east of Shechem. **Bir Ya'qūb.**
Jaffa. The modern name of Joppa.
Jagur. A town in southern Judah. Unknown.
Jahaz. A town in Reuben. Uncertain.
Jair. See Havoth-jair.
Jamnia. The same as Jabneel 1. 28.
Janim. A town in Judah. **Beni Na'īm** east of Hebron?
Janoah. 1. A town in eastern Ephraim. **Kh. Yānūn.** Josh. 16:6.
2. A town in northern Palestine. Unknown. II Kings 15:29.
Janum. A town in Judah near Hebron. Unknown.
Japhia. A town in Zebulun. **Yāfā.** VIII.
Jarmak, Jebel. The highest mountain in Galilee. I.
Jarmuth. 1. A town in western Judah. **Kh. Yarmūq** near Azekah. Josh. 15:35. IX, 27.
2. A town in Issachar. Unknown. It may be the same as Ramoth in I Chr. 6:73 and Remeth in Josh. 19:21.
Jattir. A hill town of Judah. **Kh. 'Attir** south of Hebron.
Jauf. An oasis at the southern end of the Sirhan Depression. 23.
Javan. Greece.
Jazar, Jazer. A town in Trans-jordan, variously identified as **Kh. es-Sūq** south of Rabboth Ammon or **Kh. Jazzir** near Es-Salt. 20.
Jearim, Mount. Probably the same as Mount Seir.
Jebus. The early name for Jerusalem, usually said to have been confined to the southern spur between the Kidron and Tyropoeon valleys, but recent excavations have suggested that it was much more extensive. 16, 30.
Jegar-shahadutha. A town in Trans-jordan, possibly **er-Rashūni.**

Jehoshaphat, Valley of. Unknown.
Jehud. el-Yehūdīyeh near Jaffa, or else to be read as Jazur and identified with **Yazūr.**
Jekabzeel. See Kabzeel.
Jerash. A town in Trans-jordan north of Rabboth Ammon. See Decapolis.
Jericho. Tell es-Sulṭān near the modern Jericho. The New Testament ruins lie a little further south. IV, 12, 14, 18, 20, 22, 27, 28.
Jeruel, Wilderness of. The region south-east of Tekoa.
Jerusalem. IV, VI, VII, IX, 4, 10, 12, 14, 20, 21, 26, 27, 28, 29, 30, 31.
Jeshanah. Possibly **Burj el-Isāneh** north of Jerusalem.
Jeshimmon, Jeshimon. The desert region of Eastern Judah. 12, 17.
Jeshua. Possibly **es-Sa'weh** near Beersheba.
Jezreel. 1. A town in Issachar and an important town in the Northern Kingdom. **Zir'īn** in the Plain of Esdraelon. VIII.
2. A town in southern Judah. Uncertain.
Jezreel, Valley of. Usually equated with the whole lowland area between Lower Galilee and the hills of Central Palestine. However, in modern usage it is better to keep the term for the narrower valley leading down towards Beth-shan between Mount Moreh and the Hills of Gilboa. It is probable that it has this more restricted use in the Old Testament also. 11.
Jezzine. A modern town in the Beqa'a.
Jiphtah-el. A valley in Galilee, probably **Saḥl el-Baṭṭōf,** or possibly **Wādī el-Malik.**
Jogbehah. A place in Trans-jordan, probably el-Ajbeihat north-west of Rabboth Ammon.
Jokdeam. A hill town in Judah, possibly **Kh. Raqa'** south of Hebron.
Jokmeam. 1. See Kibzaim. I Chr. 6:68.
2. See Jokneam.
Jokneam. A town of Zebulun guarding a pass across Carmel. **Tell Qeimūn.** IV, VIII.
Jokneam, Pass of.
Joktheel. 1. A town in western Judah. Unknown. Josh. 15:38.
2. See Sela. II Kings 14:7.
Joppa. The chief port for Jerusalem in Old Testament times. Jaffa. 28.
Joppe. See Joppa. 20.
Jordan, modern state of. 14.
Jordan, River. The chief river of Palestine. **Naḥr el-Urdun.** I, 11, 16, 18.
Jorkeam. See Jokdeam.
Jotbah. Either the same as Jotapata or as Juttah.
Jothbath, Jothbathah. A stopping place during the Exodus, possibly **Bīr Tabā** in the southern Arabah.
Jotopata. A town in Galilee. **Kh. Shefāt.** X.
Judaea, Judea. The region around Jerusalem. 28.
Judah, Kingdom of. The southern Kingdom of Palestine after the division.
Judah, territory of. I, IX, 5, 12, 16, 18.
Judah-Gilead Dome. A geological term for the upwarped region extending from the Southern mountains of Palestine to those of Gilead. It has been cut across by the Rift Valley, q.v.
Judea. See Judaea.
Judean Moat. The narrow chalk valley lying between the Shephelah (q.v.) and the Western Highland (q.v.). IX.
Juttah. A hill town in Judah. **Yattā** near Hebron.
Kabul. A town in northern Asher. **Kābūl** (also spelled Cabul).
Kabzeel. A town near Beersheba. **Kh. Hūrā?**
Kadesh. 1. See Kadesh Barnea.
2. A town in Syria on the Orontes south of Homs. Not mentioned in the Bible. VI, VII, 4, 9.
Kadesh Barnea. The chief centre for the Israelites during the Exodus. **'Ain Qudeis.** III, 13, 22.
Kadesh Naphtali. See Kedesh Naphtali.
Kain. A hill town in Judah. **Kh. Yaqīn** near Hebron?
Kamon. Qamm south-east of the Sea of Galilee?
Kanah. A town in Asher, possibly **Qānā** seven miles south-east of Tyre.
Kanah, River. Wādī Qānah between Manasseh and Ephraim. 16.
Karem. See Beth-haccerem.
Karkaa. A town in southern Judah. Unknown.
Karkar. See Qarqar.
Karkor. Unknown. It has been identified with places as widely separated as **Qarqar** in the Wādī Sirhan and a place in the lower Jabbok valley!
Karnaim. The region east of the Sea of Galilee, and probably the same place as Ashteroth-Karnaim. 10.
Karnak. The site of the great temple of Amon-Rē near Luxor. 21.
Kartah. A town in Zebulun. Unknown.
Kartan. Probably the same as Kiriathaim.
Karun, River. The southernmost tributary of the Tigris. 24.
Kattah. A town in Zebulun. Uncertain.
Kedar. A Bedouin tribe in Arabia.
Kedemoth. A town in Reuben, possibly **ez-Za'feran.**
Kedesh. 1. See Kadesh-barnea. Josh. 15:23.
2. A town in Issachar, probably **Tell Abū Qudeis** south-east of Megiddo. Jud. 4:9–11; I Chr. 6:72. VIII.
3. See Kedesh-Naphtali.
Kedesh-Naphtali. Qadas north-west of Lake Huleh. IV, 18.
Kedron. A town south of Jamnia. **Qatrā?** I Macc. 15:39, 41; 16:9.
Kehelthah. See Makheloth.
Keilah. A town in southern Judah. **Kh. Qeilā.** IX, 27.
Kenath. A town in the Jebel Druze region. **Qanawāt.** 10.
Kerak. A modern town east of the Dead Sea, the ancient Kir-Haraseth. 12, 14.
Kerak Wādī. A steep valley leading down from Kerak to the Dead Sea. 12.
Keriot. 1. A town in eastern Judah. Unknown. Josh. 15:25.
2. A town in Moab. Unknown.
Keziz, Valley of. See Emek-keziz.
Khabur, River. A tributary of the Euphrates.
Khalasa. A Byzantine site in the Negeb. 13.
Kharaneh. A centre of desert roads in Trans-jordan. 10.
Kharga Oasis. An oasis in the Sahara desert. 21.
Khorsabad. The modern name of Dur-sharrukin, the capital of Sargon II. 24.
Khurashe, Jebel. A mountainous region in the Negeb. 13, 22.
Kibroth-hattaavah. A stopping place during the Exodus. Uncertain.
Kibzaim. A town in Ephraim. Unknown.
Kidron, Valley of. The valley between Jerusalem and the Mount of Olives. **Wādī el-Jōz,** leading into **Wādī en-Nār.** 29.
Kinah. A town near Arad. Unknown.
King's Highway, The. The highroad connecting the fortress towns on the edge of the Eastern Plateau. 22.
King's Vale. See Shaveh.
Kir. A region in eastern Mesopotamia, possibly in Elam.
Kir-Haraseth. The chief town in Moab. **el-Kerak.** VI, VIII, 10, 22.
Kir-Hareseth, Kir-Haresh, Kir-Heres. See Kir-Haraseth.
Kir of Moab. Probably the same as Kir-Haraseth.
Kiriath. See Kiriath-jearim.
Kiriathaim. 1. A town in Reuben, possibly **Kh. el-Qureiyāt,** north of Dibon. Josh. 13:19.
2. A town in Naphtali. Unknown. I Chr. 6:76 (Probably = Kartan).
Kiriathaim, Plain of. See Shaveh-Kiriathaim.
Kiriath-arba. See Hebron.
Kiriatharim. See Kiriath-jearim.
Kiriath-baal. See Kiriath-jearim.
Kiriath-huzoth. A town in Moab. Unknown.
Kiriath-jearim. A hill town in Judah. **Tell el-Azhar** near **Kiriat el-'Anab.** IX, 27.
Kiriath-sannah. See Debir 1.
Kiriath-sepher. See Debir 1.
Kirjath, Kirjath-. See Kiriath and Kiriath-.
Kishion, Kishon. A town in Issachar. **Qeisūn** near Indur. VIII.
Kishon, River. The small stream draining the Plain of Esdraelon westwards. VIII.
Kishon Gate. The western entrance to the Plain of Esdraelon.

Kithlish. See Chitlish.
Kitron. See Kattath.
Kittim. Term used in the Old Testament for Cyprus and the Cypriots.
Koulon. Josh. 15:59 (LXX). Unknown.
Kue. The ancient name of Cilicia.
Kurnub. A site in the Negeb with an important ancient dam. 10, 13.
Laban. A stopping place during the Exodus. Unknown.
Lachish. An important town in the Shephelah. **Tell ed-Duweir.** IV, VII, IX, 27.
Ladder of Tyre. Rās en-Naqūrah north of Acre.
Lahmam. A town of Judah near Lachish. Unknown.
Laish. 1. The original name of the town of Dan. **Tell el-Qādī.**
2. See Laishah. Is. 10:30.
Laishah. A town north of Jerusalem, probably **el-'Isawīyeh.**
Lakkum. A town in Naphtali. Unknown.
Lampsacus. A town in Mysia in Asia Minor.
Laodicea. 1. A town in the Lycus Valley in Turkey. **Eskihisar.** 31.
2. The modern Latakia in Syria. Not mentioned in the Bible.
Larsa. Ancient town of southern Mesopotamia. **Senkereh.**
Lasha. See Laish 1.
Lasharon. Josh. 12:18. The text is uncertain. See Sharon.
Latakia, Lattaqieh. A modern town on the Syrian coast. 4.
Lebanon, Modern state of. 14.
Lebanon Mountains. The high mountains behind Beirut.
Lebanon, Valley of. The **Beqa'a.**
Lebaoth. A town in southern Judah. Unknown.
Lebo Hamath. Lebweh in the Beqa'a. See Hamath, Entrance of. 4.
Lebonah. Lubbān north of Shiloh.
Lehabim. Libya.
Lehi. A town near Beth-shemesh 1. Unknown.
el-Leja'. A desolate basalt area south-east of Damascus. See Trachonitis. 4.
Lemmun, Wādī. A valley in Upper Galilee.
Leshem. See Laish 1.
Lessau. A place north of Jerusalem. Unknown. II Macc. 14:16.
Levant Coast. A modern name for the whole Phoenician and Palestinian coastal area.
Libnah. 1. An important town in the Shephelah region. **Tell eṣ-Ṣāfī.** IV, VII, IX.
2. A stopping place during the Exodus. Unknown.
Libya. The country and region west of Egypt.
Libyan Desert. 22.
Litani, Litany, River. A river of southern Lebanon. 4.
Lod. An important town on the coast plain. The modern Lydda. 27.
Lo-debar. A town in Trans-jordan. **Umm ed-Dabar** north of the Jabbok? 10.
Lowland. Often used in the Bible as a translation for the Shephelah, q.v.
Lubim. The people of Libya.
Lud. Lydia in Asia Minor.
Luhith, Ascent of. In Moab. Unknown.
Luxor. A town in Upper Egypt. See Karnak and Thebes.
Luz. 1. See Bethel.
2. A Hittite town. Unknown. Jud. 1:26.
Lycaonia. The southern plateau of Asia Minor in New Testament times.
Lycia. A region in Asia Minor. I Macc. 15:23; Acts 27:5. 31.
Lycus Valley. A valley leading down westwards from the central plateau of Asia Minor, in which stand the towns of Colossae, Laodicea, and Hierapolis.
Lydda. The New Testament, and also the modern western, name of Lod. 28.
Lystra. A town in Asia Minor. **Zoldera.** 31.
Maacah. The region around Abel-beth-maacah.
Ma'an. A modern town in southern Trans-jordan. 14.
Maarath. A town in Judah. **Beit Ummār** near Hebron?
Macedonia. The region at the northern end of the Aegean Sea. 31.
Machaerus. A fortress in Trans-jordan. **Mukāwer.** 10, 28.
Machir. A clan name, not a place.
Machmas. See Michmash. 20.
Machpelah, Cave of. In or near Hebron.
Madeba. A modern town in Trans-jordan on the site of the ancient Medeba.
Madmanneh. A town in southern Judah. **Umm Deimneh.**
Madmen. A town in Moab, thought by some to be identical with Dibon, but more probably **Kh. Dimneh.**
Madmenah. A town in Benjamin. Uncertain, possibly **Shu'fāt** north of Jerusalem. 27.
Madon. A Canaanite town, probably **Kh. Madjan** near the Horns of Hattin. IV.
Magadan. Matt. 15:39. Uncertain; possibly the same as Magdala.
Magbish. A town in Central Palestine. Unknown.
Magdala. A town on the Trunk Road where it leaves the Sea of Galilee. **Majdal.** X, 28.
Mahalab. Kh. el-Mahalib north of Tyre? Some scholars think that this is the correct form of Ahlab, while others think that Ahlab is the correct form of the name.
Mahanaim. A town in Trans-jordan, possibly **Kh. Mahneh** in Gilead. III, 10.
Mahaneh-dan. A town near Kiriath-jearim. Unknown.
Makaz. Possibly **Kh. el-Mukheizin** near Ekron.
Maked. A town in Gilead, possibly **Tell Miqdād.** I Macc. 5:26. 20.
Makheloth. A stopping place during the Exodus. Unknown, but it may be the same as Kehelathah.
Makkedah. A town in the Shephelah region. **Kh. Beit Maqdūm** or **Kh. el-Kheishūn**? IV, IX.
Mallus. A town in Cilicia. Unknown. II Macc. 4:30.
Malta. 31.
Mamre. Ramet el-Khalīl near Hebron.
Manahath. See Manocho.
Manasseh. A tribal district north of Ephraim and later extending across the Jordan into Gilead. 4, 16, 18.
Manocho. A hill town in Judah, possibly **Melīḥā** south-west of Jerusalem. Josh. 15:59 (LXX).
Maon. A hill town in Judah. **Tell Ma'īn** south of Hebron.
Maon, Wilderness of. The desert region east of Maon.
Maquis. A geographical term for the thick scrub characteristic of the limestone regions in Mediterranean countries after the earlier forests have been cut down.
Marah. A stopping place during the Exodus. **'Ain Hawārah**?
Maralah. A town in Zebulun. Unknown, but may be the same as Mareal.
Mareal. A town in Zebulun, possibly **Tell el-Ghaltah** north-east of Dabbeshah. VIII.
Mareshah. A town in the Shephelah region. **Tell Sandahannah.** IX.
Mari. A town on the Euphrates not far from Abu Kemal. 24.
Marib. A town in southern Arabia. 23.
Marisa. See Mareshah.
Maroth. A town in Judah, possibly the same as Maarath.
Masada. A strong fortress overlooking the Dead Sea on the west. **es-Sebbeh.** 12, 28.
Masaloth. I Macc. 9:2. This should probably be translated "slopes" or "cliffs", meaning the precipitous banks of the **Wādī Hamām** in Galilee.
Maspha. 1. See Mizpah 1. 20.
2. See Mizpah 3.
Masrekah. A town in Edom. Unknown.
Massah. A stopping place during the Exodus, near Meribah. Unknown.
Mattanah. A stopping place during the Exodus, north of Moab. **Kh. el-Medainīyeh?**
Mearah. Josh. 13:4. This should either be read "from Arah", in which case the town is probably **Kh. 'Arā,** or else it is possibly **Mogheirīyeh** near Sidon.
Mecca. A town in Western Arabia. 23.

Meconah. See Madmenah.

Medeba. A town on Trans-jordan plateau still called today **Madebā.** 10, 20, 22.

Media. The region north-east of Babylonia.

Mediterranean Sea. 21, 24.

Megiddo. The town in Issachar which controlled the most important pass across the Carmel ridge. **Tell el-Mutasellim.** IV, VI, VII, VIII, 16, 18.

Megiddo, Pass of.

Megiddo, Valley of. The Plain of Esdraelon. **Merj ibn-'Amr.**

Megiddo, Waters of. The River Kishon, which flows in the plain below Megiddo.

Meirun. A modern town in Upper Galilee.

Me-jarkon. Probably the river known in Arabic today as **Naḥr el-'Aujā** and in Hebrew as the Yarkon north of Tel Aviv.

Mekonah. See Meconah.

Melita. The New Testament name for Malta.

Memphis. One of the chief cities of ancient Egypt. **Mit Rahneh.** 21, 26.

Mephaath. A town in Moab. **Tell Jawah.**

Meribah. A stopping place during the Exodus near Kadesh-barnea. Unknown, but always coupled with Massah.

Merom. Though the identification is questioned by some scholars, it still seems best to place Merom at **Meirūn** in Upper Galilee. IV.

Merom, Waters of. The **Wādī Lemmūn** flowing down from Meirūn.

Meronoth. Perhaps **Beitūnyah** north-west of Gibeon.

Meroth. See Merom. X.

Meroz. A town in the north, possibly **Kh. Marūs** two miles north-west of Hazor.

Mesa. A geographical term for a large, flat-topped area with steep sides, characteristic of desert topography.

Mesaloth. See Masaloth.

Mesha. Unknown. Possibly the same as Massa, a north Arabian tribe.

Meshech. A region in Asia Minor.

Mesopotamia. Strictly speaking, the region between the rivers, but used generally for the whole area watered by the Tigris and Euphrates.

Meunim. Probably the people from around **Ma'an,** q.v.

Michmash. **Mukhmās** north of Jerusalem. IX, 27.

Michmethath. A border town of Manasseh, possibly **Kh. Makhneh el-Fōqā** near Shechem.

Middin. A place in the Wilderness of Judah. Unknown.

Midian, Land of. The south-eastern part of Trans-jordan.

Midian, Mountains of. A name given to the high granite mountains south of Petra.

Migdal-el. A town in Naphtali, possibly **Mejdel Islim.**

Migdal-gad. A town in western Judah, probably **Kh. el-Majdala** near Lachish.

Migdol. 1. An Egyptian border fort, possibly on **Jebel Abū Hassa.** Exod. 14:2; Num. 33:7.
2. A town east of the Nile Delta, possibly **Tell el-Heir** near Pelusium.

Migron. **Tell Miriam** south of Michmash.

Miletus. A port in south-western Asia Minor near **Söke.** 31.

Millo. "Citadel" both in Jerusalem and in Shechem, where it is also called Beth-millo.

Minni. A region in Armenia.

Minnith. A town in Trans-jordan, possibly **Kh. Hamzeh** four miles north-east of Heshbon.

Mishal. A town in Asher near Mount Carmel. Unknown.

Mishor, the. Apparently the name given to the flat plateau region of Moab. 12, 17, 19.

Misrephoth-Maim. A northern frontier town. **Kh. el-Musheirefeh** near **Rās en-Naqūrah.** IV.

Mithkah. A stopping place during the Exodus. Unknown.

Mitylene. A sea-port on the island of Lesbos in the Aegean. 31.

Mizar, Hill. Unknown.

Mizpah, Mizpeh. 1. A town and holy site in Benjamin. **Tell en-Nasbeh.** 27.
2. A town in western Judah. Unknown. Josh. 15:38.
3. A town in Gilead, possibly **Kh. Jel'ad.** Gen. 31:49; Josh. 13:26; Jud. 10:17; 11:29. III.
4. A town in Moab. Unknown. I Sam. 22:3.

Mizpah, Land of. A region in northern Palestine near Mount Hermon. Josh. 11:3, 8.

Moab. The kingdom in Trans-jordan on the plateau east of the Dead Sea. IV, 18, 22.

Moab, City of. **Kh. el-Medeinīyeh?**

Moab, Plains of. The triangular plain at the north-eastern corner of the Dead Sea. 11.

Mocha. A town in southern Arabia. 23.

Modein, Modin. A town north-west of Jerusalem. **el-'Arba'īn** near **el-Midyā.**

Modin. See Modein. I Macc. 2:1. 20.

Moeris, Lake. A large lake in the Faiyum, q.v. 21.

Moladah. A town in southern Judah. **Tell el-Milḥ** east of Beersheba.

Mongolia. The interior region of Asia.

Moreh. The plain just east of Shechem.

Moreh, Mount. The hill north of the Valley of Jezreel, sometimes wrongly called "Little Hermon". **Jebel Dāhī.** VIII.

Moresheth-gath. **Tell el-Judeideh** just east of Gath.

Moriah, Land of, and Mount. Traditionally at Jerusalem, but the exact site is unknown.

Mosera, Moseroth. A stopping place during the Exodus. Unknown.

Mozah. A town in Benjamin, possibly **Qalōniyeh.**

Mukalla. A town in southern Arabia. 23.

Murra, Wādī. An important break in the Negeb Uplands. I, 12, 13, 19.

Myndos. A town in Caria in Asia Minor. I Macc. 15:23.

Myra. A sea-port of Lycia in Asia Minor. 31.

Mysia. A region in Asia Minor.

Naamah. A town in south-western Judah, possibly **Kh. Fered** near Timnah 1.

Naarah, Naaran, Naarath. A town in Benjamin, possibly **'Ain Dūq** near Jericho.

Naasson. The same as Hazor.

Nabataea, Nabatea. A kingdom centred on Petra in southern Trans-jordan during the New Testament period. 28, 31.

Nablus. A modern town in western Cis-jordan. 14.

Nabuthea. The same as Nabataea.

Nadabatha. Possibly **Kh. Muhājit** west of Madeba, or **Kh. eṭ-Ṭeim** south of Madeba. I Macc. 9:37.

Nahalal, Nahalol. A town in Zebulun, variously identified as **Ma'lūl** or **Tell el-Beidā** or **Tell en-Naḥl,** all near the modern settlement of Nahalal.

Nahaliel, Stream. **Wādī Zerqa Ma'īn** flowing into the north end of the Dead Sea.

Nahalol. See Nahalal.

Nahor, City of. **Tell Nahīri** in Aram-naharaim.

Nain. A town on the north of Mount Moreh near Endor. **Nein.** VIII, X, 28.

Naioth. A place near Ramah 1. Unknown.

Naphath-dor, Naphoth-dor. The meaning of the term is uncertain, but it may indicate the low limestone hills just behind Dor, q.v.

Naphtali. A tribal district in eastern Galilee. 16, 18.

Nasor, Plain of. Possibly **Ardh el-Ḥeit** south-west of Lake Huleh. I Macc. 11:67.

Nazareth. A village in Lower Galilee on the same site as the present town. VIII, X, 14, 28.

Nazareth Scarp. The precipitous slope at Nazareth overlooking the Plain of Esdraelon. 11.

Neah. A town in Zebulun, possibly **Tell el-Wāwiyāt.** VIII.

Neapolis. A town in Macedonia. **Kavalla.** 31.

Neballat. **Beit Nabala** three miles north-east of Lod.

Nebo. 1. A town in Reuben, probably somewhere near **Jebel en-Nebā.**
2. A town in Judah, perhaps **Nūbā** three miles south-west of **Beit Immār.** Ezr. 2:29; Neh. 7:33. 27.

Nebo, Mount. A point on the edge of the Trans-jordan plateau near the northern end of the Dead Sea. **Jebel en-Nebā.**

Nefūd. A large area of **erg,** or sandy desert, in northern Arabia. 23.

Negeb. The southern desert in Cis-jordan. I, 17, 19.

Neiel. A town in Asher. **Kh. Ya'nīn.**

Nekeb. See Adami-nekeb.

Nephtoah. **Liftā** west of Jerusalem.
Neqb (plural: **nuqūb**). An Arabic word meaning the sharp edge of a desert plateau.
Nessana. A Byzantine town in the southern Negeb. **'Auja el-Ḥafīr.** 13.
Netophah. A town near Bethlehem. **'Ain en-Natūf** or **Kh. Bedd Falūḥ.** 27.
Nezib. A town in western Judah. **Kh. Beit Nesīb** near Lachish. IX.
Nibshan. A place in the wilderness of Judah. Unknown.
Nile, River. 21, 23.
Nimrah. See Beth-nimrah.
Nimrin, Waters of. An oasis in Moab near the Dead Sea. **Wādī en-Numeirah.**
Nineveh. The capital of Assyria. **Tell Quyunjiq** and **Tell Nebī Yūnis.** 24.
Nippur. A Sumerian city in southern Mesopotamia. **Nuffār.** 24.
No. See Thebes.
Nob. Either **eṭ-Ṭūr** on the Mount of Olives, or **Rās eṭ-Ṭala'** on Mount Scopus. IX, 27.
Nobah. 1. See Kenath.
2. A place near Jogbehah. Unknown. Jud. 8:11.
Noph. See Memphis.
Nophah. Num. 21:30. May not be a place name. The text is uncertain.
Nubian Sandstone. The dark red sandstone found in southern Trans-jordan and parts of southern Cis-jordan. Petra, q.v., is carved out of this rock.
Nuseiriyeh Mountains. Limestone mountains on the north of the Syrian coast. 5.
Nuzi. A town in Mesopotamia where important tablets have been found. **Yorghan Tepe** near Kirkuk.
Oboth. A stopping place during the Exodus. **'Ain el-Weibeh** (or **'Ain Ḥosb**) near the southern end of the Dead Sea. 10, 13.
Odollam. See Adullam.
Offence, Mount of. Traditionally on a spur of the Mount of Olives near **Silwān.** 29.
Olives, Mount of. A higher part of the plateau directly east of Jerusalem. 29.
Olivet. See Olives, Mount of.
On. **Maṭarīyeh** north-east of Cairo in Lower Egypt (also called Heliopolis). 21.
Ono. **Kefr 'Anā** near Lod.
Ophel. The citadel of Jebus on the spur south of Jerusalem. 29.
Ophir. Probably somewhere in western Arabia.
Ophni. A town in Benjamin. Unknown.
Ophrah. 1. A town in Benjamin. **eṭ-Ṭaiyebeh** north of Jerusalem.
2. A town in Manasseh, possibly **eṭ-Ṭaiyebeh** north-west of Beth-shan. Jud. 6:11, 24; 8:27, 32; 9:5.
Oreb, Rock. Somewhere in the Jordan Valley. Unknown.
Orontes, River. A river of northern Syria, flowing out near Antioch. 4.
Orthosia. A sea-port in Syria, **Ard Artūsī** north of Tripoli. I Macc. 15:37.
Padan-aram, Paddan-aram. The steppeland region at the foot of the Anatolian mountains. Also called Aram-naharaim. III.
Palestine. Often confined in modern usage to Cis-jordan (q.v.), the name was often used by earlier writers for all the area occupied by the Hebrews.
Palm Trees, City of. Used for both Jericho and Hazezon-tamar.
Palmyra. An important oasis in the Syrian desert, also called Tadmor. **Tadmūr.** VI, VII, 4. (In II Chr. 8:4 "Palmyra" should probably read "Tamar" as in I Kings 9:18.)
Pamphilia. A district in southern Asia Minor. 31.
Paneas. See Caesarea-Philippi. 9, 10.
Paphos. A town in southern Cyprus. **Baffo.** 31.
Parah. A town in Benjamin. **Tell Fārah** in the **Wādī Fārah.**
Paran, Mount. In the Wilderness of Paran, q.v.
Paran, Wilderness of. A desert region south of Kadesh Barnea.
Parthia. A region and country south of the Black Sea.
Parvaim. A region in Arabia. Unknown.
Pas-dammim. See Ephes-dammim.
Patara. A sea-port in Lycia. **Gelemish.** 31.
Patmos. An island in the eastern Aegean Sea.
Pau. A town in Edom. Unknown.
Pella. See Decapolis.
Peniel, Penuel. **Tullūl edh-Dhahab** in the Jabbok Valley. III, 10.
Peor. A town in Judah, possibly **Kh. Faghūr** near Bethlehem. Josh. 15:59 (LXX).
Peor, Mount. Near Beth-peor. Unknown.
Peraea, Perea. A Roman district on the edge of the Trans-jordan plateau.
Perez-uzzah. A place west of Jerusalem. Unknown.
Perga. A city in Pamphilia. 31.
Pergamum. A city in western Asia Minor. **Bergama** north of Smyrna. 31.
Persepolis. Cyrus' capital in Persia. **Takht-i-Jamshīd.** II Macc. 9:2. 26.
Persia. The region and country now called Iran. 25, 26.
Petah Tiqvah. A town in modern Israel north of Tel Aviv. 14.
Pethor. A town south of Carchemish. **Tell Aḥmar?**
Petra. The Nabatean capital in **Wādī Mūsā** in southern Trans-jordan. 31.
Pharathon. See Pirathon. I Macc. 9:50. 20.
Pharpar, River. One of the rivers of Damascus. **Nahr el-'Awaj.** See Abana. 6.
Phaselis. A sea-port in Lycia. **Tekirova.** I Macc. 15:23.
Philadelphia. 1. See Decapolis. 28.
2. A city near Smyrna in Asia Minor. **Alashehir.** 31
Philae. A city in Upper Egypt above Aswan. 21.
Philippi. A city of Macedonia. **Filibedjik.** 31.
Philistia. The southern portion of the Palestinian coast-plain. IX, 4, 12, 18, 19.
Phoenicia. Region and country along the coast plain of Lebanon and northern Syria, extending as far south as the Crocodile marshes.
Phoenix. A sea-port in Crete, possibly **Porto Lutro.**
Phrygia. A region of Asia Minor.
Pi-beseth. A city in the Nile Delta, later called Bubastis. **Tell Bastā.**
Pi-hahiroth. An early stopping place during the Exodus. Uncertain.
Pirathon. A town in Ephraim. **Far'atah** seven miles south-west of Nablus.
Pisgah, the. Probably a regional name for the sharp edge of the Trans-jordan plateau overlooking the Dead Sea. 17.
Pisgah, Springs of. See Ashdoth-Pisgah.
Pishon, River. Unknown.
Pisidia. A region on the southern part of the plateau of Asia Minor.
Pison. See Pishon.
Pithom. A city in the Nile Delta. **Tell er-Reṭābeh.** 21, 22.
Plain, Plains. A word often used in the Bible to describe the Jordan Valley.
Plain, Sea of the. The Dead Sea.
Pontus. A region in northern Asia Minor. 31.
Priene. A city in western Asia Minor between Ephesus and Miletus. 31.
Provincia Arabia. The Roman province in the Syrian desert in post-biblical times.
Ptolemais. The Maccabean and New Testament name for Accho. **Acre.** X, 20, 28, 31.
Punon. A stopping place during the Exodus, and probably the scene of the setting up of the brazen serpent. **Feinān** in the Arabah. 10, 12.
Puteoli. Port near Naples. **Pozzuoli.** 31.
Qarqar. A town on the Orontes north of Hamath and the scene of an important battle between Ahab and the Assyrians. Not mentioned in the Bible. VII, 4.
Qasr Hallabat. A Roman fortress in Trans-jordan north-east of 'Amman. 10.
Qasr Mahalla. A modern site on the edge of the Wādī Raman. 10, 13.
Qattara Depression. A rocky area below sea-level in the Libyan desert. 21.
Qubeibeh, Wādī. A valley leading across the Shephelah. IX.
Qumran. Site near the north-western corner of the Dead Sea where the Essene monastery stood, and near where the first Dead Sea scrolls were found.

el-Quneitrah. A road centre in Bashan. 9.
Raama, Raamah. In Arabia. Unknown.
Raamses. A city in the Nile Delta. **Ṣân el-Ḥagar.** 21, 22.
Rabbah. 1. See Rabboth Ammon.
2. A hill town in Judah. Unknown. Josh. 15:60.
Rabboth. A town in Issachar. Probably the same as Daberath.
Rabboth Ammon. The chief town of the Ammonites. **'Ammān.** VI, VII, 4, 10, 20, 27.
Rahab. A term used in the prophetic books for Egypt.
Rakkath. A town in Naphtali. **Kh. el-Quneitrah** or **Tell Eqlatīyeh.**
Rakkon. A town in the original territory of Dan. **Tell er-Reqqeit?**
Ramah. 1. A town in Benjamin. **er-Rām** five miles north of Jerusalem. IX, 27.
2. A town in Naphtali. **er-Rāmah?** Josh. 19:29.
3. A town in Asher. **er-Rāmieh,** or possibly the same as Ramah 2. Josh. 19:36.
4. The same as Ramathaim-Zophim. I Sam. 1:19; 2:11; 7:17; 8:4; 15:34; 16:13; 19:18–23; 25:1; 28:3.
5. See Ramoth-Gilead. II Chr. 22:6.
6. Ramah of the Negeb, or of the South. Unknown. Josh. 19:8; I Sam. 30:27.
Ramallah. A modern town ten miles north of Jerusalem. 14.
Raman, Jebel. The highland surrounding Wādī Raman. 12.
Raman, Wādī. An immense "cauldron" (q.v.) in the Negeb. 13, 20.
Ramath of the South. See Ramah 6.
Ramathaim. See Ramathaim-zophim.
Ramathaim-zophim. A town in western Ephraim. **Rentīs.**
Ramath-lehi. See Lehi.
Ramath-mizpeh. See Mizpah 2.
Rameses. See Raamses.
Ramoth. 1. See Ramoth-gilead.
2. See Ramah 6. I Sam. 30:27.
3. **Kōkāb el-Hāwa** overlooking the Jordan Valley, in Lower Galilee. I Chr. 6:73.
Ramoth-gilead. A town on the Israelite-Syrian border. **Tell Ramīth.** 10.
Raphana. See Raphon.
Raphon. **er-Rāfeh** in Bashan. I Macc. 5:37. 10, 20.
Rās en-Neqb. The southern edge of the Edomite territory.
Rās Shamrā. See Ugarit.
Recah. Unknown. I Chr. 4:12.
Red Sea. 10, 21.
Reed Sea. Normally translated "Red Sea", but more probably the marshes which once existed where now the Suez Canal runs. 22.
Rehob. 1. See Beth-rehob. Num. 13:21; II Sam. 10:8.
2. A town in Asher. **Tell el-Gharbi.** 16.
Rehoboth. 1. A town near Nineveh. Unknown. Gen. 10:11.
2. A well near Beersheba. **Ruheibeh.** Gen. 26:22.
3. A place in Edom. Unknown. Gen. 36:37; I Chr. 1:48.
Rehoboth-ir. See Rehoboth 1.
Rehovoth, modern town of. 14.
Rekem. A town in Benjamin. Unknown. Josh. 18:27.
Remeth. A town in Issachar. Uncertain.
Rephaim. A region east of the Jordan. III.
Rephaim, Valley of. Possibly **el-Beqa'a** south-west of Jerusalem.
Rephidim. A stopping place during the Exodus. Uncertain.
Resen. A place near Nineveh. Unknown.
Reuben. Tribal territory in the northern Moabite region. 16, 18.
Rezeph. A region east of Hamath. **Reṣṣāfeh.**
Rhegium. A town in southern Italy. **Reggio.** 31.
Rhodes. An island in the Mediterranean, and the chief town of the island. 31.
Riblah. A town on the upper Orontes. **Ribleh.** VII.
Rift Valley. A geographical term for a valley formed between two parallel faults or series of faults. The Jordan Valley, the Arabah and the Valley of Jezreel all belong to this category.
Rimmon. 1. See En-rimmon.
2. A town in Galilee. **Rummāneh** five miles north of Nazareth. VIII.
Rimmon, Rock of. Probably **Rammūn** near Bethel.
Rimmon-parez. A stopping place during the Exodus. Uncertain.
Rissah. A stopping place during the Exodus. Uncertain.
Rithmah. A stopping place during the Exodus. Uncertain.
Rogelim. A place in Trans-jordan, possibly **Bersinyā** near **Wādī er-Rujeilī.**
Rome. 31.
Ruba' el-Khālī. The "Empty Quarter". An enormous area of sandy desert in southern Arabia. 23.
Rumah. Possibly **Kh. er-Rūmeh** in Galilee.
es-Safa. A volcanic region north of the Jebel Druze. 4.
Sahara Desert. 21.
es-Sahra. A region near Damascus. 6.
Salala. A town in southern Arabia. 23.
Salamis. A sea-port in Cyprus, three miles north of Famagusta. 31.
Salamis, Gulf of. The eastern gulf at the Isthmus of Corinth.
Salecah. A town in the Jebel Druze. **Salkhād.** 10.
Salem. Usually identified with Jerusalem, though this is not certain. III.
Salim. A place in the Jordan valley. Unknown.
Salmon. A mountain in Syria. Uncertain.
Salmonah. See Zalmonah.
Salmone. **Cape Sidero** in Crete.
Salt, City of. Site in the Wilderness of Judah. Unknown.
Salt Sea. Dead Sea.
Salt, Valley of. Probably the **sebkhā** or region immediately south of the Dead Sea.
Samaria. 1. The town of Samaria at the modern **Sebāstiyeh.** VIII, 20, 28.
2. The region around the town of Samaria. I, 28.
Samos. An island in the Aegean Sea. 31.
Samothrace. An island in the north of the Aegean Sea. 31.
Sampsames. Possibly Samsun on the Black Sea. I Macc. 15:23.
Sansannah. A town in southern Judah. **Kh. esh-Shamsanīyāt?**
Sardis. A city in western Asia Minor. **Sart.** 31.
Sarepta. See Zarephath.
Sarid. A town in Zebulun. **Tell Shadūd** four miles south-west of Nazareth. VIII.
Scopus, Mount. The modern name for a high part of the plateau overlooking Jerusalem from the north-east.
Scorpions, Ascent of. See Akrabbim. **Neqb es-Safā.** 12.
Scythopolis. See Decapolis. II Macc. 12:29. X, 20, 28.
Seba. Probably the same as Sheba.
Sebam. See Sibmah.
Secacah. A place in the Wilderness of Judah. Unknown.
Sechu, Secu. A site near Ramah 1. Uncertain. May not be a place name.
Sede Boqer. A modern settlement in the Negeb. 10, 13.
Seilūn. A modern village on the site of Shiloh.
Seir. 1. Another name for Edom.
2. A hill near Chesalon. Josh. 15:10.
Seirath. A place in Ephraim. Unknown.
Sela. The chief city of Edom, probably on **Umm el-Biyārā** at Petra. VI, VII, 10.
Sela-hammahlekoth. Possibly **Wādī el-Malaqi** east of Carmel in Judah.
Seleucia. The port of Syrian Antioch. **Selūqīyeh.** 31.
Senaah. A place near Jericho. Unknown.
Seneh. The escarpment of **Wādī es-Suweinit** near Michmash.
Senir. Mount Hermon.
Sephar. In southern Arabia. Unknown.
Sepharad. Probably the same as Sardis.
Sepharvaim. A town near Riblah in Syria. Unknown.

Sepphoris. An important town in Roman Galilee. **Seffūrīyeh.** X.
Shaalabbin, Shaalbim. Probably the modern **Selbit** on the coast plain. 16.
Shaalim, Land of. A region in the territory of Ephraim.
Shaaraim. 1. A place near Azekah. Unknown.
2. See Sharuhen. I Chr. 4:31.
Shahazumah. A town in Issachar. Unknown.
Shalisha, Land of. See Baal-shalishah.
Shamir. 1. A hill town in Judah. **el-Bīreh** near **Kh. Sumārā.** Josh. 15:48.
2. Probably the same as Samaria. Judges 10:1–2.
Shapher, Mount. See Shepher.
Sharon. The coast plain south of Mount Carmel. 4, 11, 17.
esh-Sharq, Jebel. A ridge of hills east of Damascus. 4.
Sharuhen. A town in Simeon. **Tell el-Far'ah.**
Shaveh, Valley of. Uncertain. Believed to be not far from Jerusalem.
Shaveh Kiriathaim. Probably **Kh. el-Qaryatein** south of Kir Haraseth. III.
Sheba. 1. See Shema. Josh. 19:2.
2. A town or district of southern Arabia, possibly in the Yemen. 23.
Shebah. See Beersheba.
Shebam. See Sibmah.
Shebarim. A place near Ai. Unknown. Possibly it should be translated "quarries".
Shechem. An important town in Manasseh. **Tell Balāṭah** near Nablus. III, VI, 4, 18.
Shema. A town in southern Judah. Uncertain.
Shen. A place near Ebenezer. Uncertain.
Shepham. A town in Syria. Unknown.
Shephat. Possibly **Safad** in Upper Galilee.
Shephelah. The hilly region between Judah and the Coast Plain. The word means lowland, and is frequently translated as this. IX, 12, 17, 19.
Shephelah, Galilean. A modern geographical term for the Eocene limestone region of southern Galilee.
Shephelah, Israelite. Probably the Eocene limestone region of the central part of the Carmel ridge. See Josh. 11:16.
Shepher, Mount. Possibly **Jebel 'Araif en-Nafā** south of Kadesh Barnea.
Shihor. Probably a branch of the Nile near Raamses.
Shihor-libnath. This may be a town in Asher on or near Mount Carmel. Alternatively, there may be two separate sites, or it may be a river, the **Nahr ez-Zerqa.**
Shilhim. See Sharuhen.
Shiloah, Waters of. See Siloam, Pool of.
Shiloh. The site in Ephraim where the Ark was kept. **Seilūn.** 18.
Shimron. A town in Zebulun, possibly **Kh. Semūnīyeh.** VIII.
Shimron-meron. See Shimron.
Shinar, Land of. Babylonia. 24.
Shion. A town in Issachar. Unknown. May perhaps be the same as Hapharaim-Shion.
Shittim. See Abel-shittim.
Shual, Land of. A region near Ophrah 1.
Shunem. A town in Issachar. **Sulām.** VIII.
Shur. Probably part of the Sinai peninsula.
Shur, Wilderness of. 22.
Shushan. See Susa.
Sibmah. A town near Heshbon. Uncertain.
Sibraim. See Sepharvaim.
Sichem. See Shechem.
Sicily. 31.
Sicyon. A place on the Gulf of Corinth. **Vasilika.** I Macc. 15:23.
Siddim, Valley of. Possibly the shallow southern end of the Dead Sea. III.
Side. A sea-port of Pamphilia. **Eski-adalia.** I Macc. 15:23.
Sidon. An important port in Phoenicia. **Saidā** south of Beirut. VI, VII, 4, 14, 16, 27, 31.
Sihor. See Shihor.
Silla. II Kings 12:20. A corrupt text.
Siloah, Siloam. A pool inside Jerusalem which was supplied with water from the spring Gihon by means of a tunnel cut by Hezekiah. 30.
Simeon. Tribal territory in southern Palestine. 16, 18.
Sin. 1. Pelusium, the modern **Tell Farāmā**, in Egypt. Ezk. 30:15–16.
2. The city of the Sinites, possibly **Shein** north of the Lebanon.
Sin, Wilderness of. A desert region between Elim and Mount Sinai, frequently identified with **Debbet er-Ramleh** on the south-western side of the Sinai Peninsula. It should not be confused with the Wilderness of Zin, q.v.
Sinai, Mount. Traditionally Jebel Mūsā in the Sinai Peninsula, but thought by many scholars to be somewhere in north-west Arabia. 22.
Sinim. Unknown.
Sion. See Zion.
Sion, Mount. See Zion, Mount. Also, in Deut. 4:48, Sirion, Mount.
Siphmoth. A place in southern Judah near Aroer 3. Unknown.
Sippar, Sippur. An ancient town of Babylonia. **Abū Habbah** north of Babylon. 24.
Sirah, Well of. Somewhere near **Siret el-Bellā** north of Hebron.
Sirhan Depression. A long low-lying area in the Arabia Plateau on the eastern border of the modern Kingdom of Jordan. 5, 10.
Sirhan, Wādī. See Sirhan Depression.
Sirion, Mount. Another name for Mount Hermon.
Sitnah. A well between Gerar and Rehoboth 1. Unknown.
Slaughter, Valley of. See Hinnom.
Smyrna. An important port in western Asia Minor. **Izmīr.** 31.
Sochoh. **Tell er-Rās** west of Samaria.
Socoh. 1. A town in western Judah. **Kh. 'Abbād.** Josh. 15:35.
2. A hill town in Judah. **Kh. Shuweikeh.** Josh. 15:48.
3. See Sochoh. I Kings 4:10.
Sodom. See Cities of the Plain.
Sorek, Valley of. **Wādī-eṣ-Ṣurār.** A deep valley running from near Jerusalem across the Shephelah to the Coast Plain. IX.
Sparta. A city in southern Greece. **Sparte.** I Macc. 15:23.
Steppeland. A geographical term for the region found between the true desert and the cultivated land. It receives some rain and is suitable for pastoral farming rather than agriculture.
Strata. See Stratum.
Strato's Tower. See Caesarea.
Stratum (pl. strata). A layer of rock. This is level when laid down, but has often subsequently been broken or folded by great pressure.
Subeita. A Byzantine city in the Negeb. **'Sbeita.** 13.
Succoth. 1. A stopping place during the Exodus. Unknown. Exod. 12:37; 13:20; Num. 33:5–6.
2. A town in the Jordan Valley. Probably **Tell Deir Allah.** IV, 10.
Sud. A river or canal near Babylon. Unknown. Bar. 1:4.
Sumer. The very ancient kingdom in the Mesopotamian Delta.
Suph. See Zuph. Deut. 1:1.
Suphah. A place in Moab. Unknown.
Susa. Ancient capital of Elam, and later the winter capital of the Persian Empire. **Shush.** 24, 26.
Sychar. Possibly **'Askar** near Nablus.
Sychem. See Shechem.
Syene. **Aswān** in Upper Egypt.
Syracuse. A sea-port in Sicily. **Siracusa.** 31.
Syria. An important kingdom centred on Damascus, also called Aram. 4, 18, 31.
Syria, Modern State of. 14.
Syrian Desert. 23.
Syrian Saddle. A geographical term for the important break in the mountains in the extreme north of the Syrian coastal region. 5, 24.
Syrtis, the. Shallow, sandy, bay on the north coast of Tripolitania.
Taanach. A town guarding one of the passes across the Carmel ridge. **Tell Ta'nak.** IV, VIII, 16.
Taanath-Shiloh. A border town in northern Ephraim. Probably **Kh. Ta'nah el-Fōqā.**
Tabbath. A site east of the Jordan, possibly **Rās Abū Tabāt** in the **Wādī Kufrinjeh.**

Taberah. A stopping place during the Exodus. Unknown.
Tabor. I Chr. 6:77. Either Mount Tabor or Daberah.
Tabor, Mount. An isolated hill on the northern side of the Plain of Esdraelon. **Jebel eṭ-Ṭōr.** VIII, X.
Tabor, Plain of. I Sam. 10:3. Probably to be translated "Oak of Tabor". See Allon-bachuth.
Tadmor. See Palmyra. VI, VII.
Tahath. A stopping place during the Exodus. Unknown.
Tahpanes. A town in the Nile Delta, probably **Tell Defenneh.** 21.
Tamar. See Hazezon-Tamar. 10.
Tanis. See Raamses.
Taphon. See Tappuah 1. 20.
Tappuah. 1. A border town between Manasseh and Ephraim. **Sheikh Abū Zarad.**
2. A town in western Judah, perhaps **Beit Netīf.** IX, 18.
Taralah. A town in Benjamin. Unknown.
Tarentum. A sea-port in southern Italy. **Taranto.** 31.
Tarshish. The word seems to mean "metal refinery", and may have been used for a number of places from which metal was obtained, though some scholars have suggested an identification with Tartessus in Spain. A "ship of Tarshish" was a sea-going vessel such as those which brought metal to Phoenicia.
Tarsus. A city in Cilicia. 31.
Tatm. A hill town in Judah. Josh. 15:59 (LXX).
Taurus Mountains. The mountain ranges enclosing the Plateau of Anatolia on the south.
Tekoa. A town on the edge of the Wilderness of Judah. **Kh. Tequ'.** 27.
Tekoa, Wilderness of. The desert region east of Tekoa.
Tel-abib. A town in Babylonia. Unknown.
Telaim. See Telem.
Telassar. A region in Northern Mesopotamia. Unknown.
Tel Aviv–Jaffa. The modern city in the State of Israel. 14.
Telem. A town in southern Judah. **Tell Umm es-Salāfeh?**
Tel-harsa. A place in southern Mesopotamia. Unknown.
Tell Abu el-Khanzīr. A volcanic hill in Bashan. 9.
Tell Abu Nedd. A volcanic hill in Bashan. 9.
Tell Abu Yūsef. A volcanic hill in Bashan. 9.
Tellul Sha'ar. A group of volcanic hills in Bashan. 9.
Tel-melah. A place in southern Mesopotamia. Unknown.
Tema. A region in northern Arabia. Probably the oasis of **Teimā.**
Teman. A town in Edom, variously identified as **Shōbek** or a place near Petra. III, 10.
Terah. A stopping place during the Exodus. Unknown.
Terra Rossa. A geographical term for the rich, dark red soil formed from the Cenomanian limestone, q.v.
Thamnatha. See Timnah 1. 20.
Thebes. An important city in Upper Egypt, for long the capital of Egypt, near Luxor. 21, 26.
Thebez. A town in Manasseh. **Tūbās.** IV.
Thecoe. See Tekoa. 20.
Thessalonica. A city in Macedonia. **Salonike.** 31.
Thimnathah. See Timnah 1.
Thrace. A district on the northern shore of the Aegean Sea. 31.
Three Taverns. A place on the Appian Way near Rome. 31.
Thyatira. A city in western Asia Minor. **Akhisar.** 31.
Tiberias. A town on the western side of the Sea of Galilee. X, 14, 28.
Tiberias, Sea of. See Galilee, Sea of.
Tibhath. A town in Syria, probably in the Beqa'a. Unknown.
Tigris, River. One of the two great rivers of Mesopotamia. 23, 24, 31.
Timna, Timnah. 1. A town in northern Judah. **Kh. Tibneh.** IV, IX.
2. A hill town in Judah, probably **Kh. Tibneh** near Bethlehem. Josh. 15:57; Gen. 38:12.
Timnath. Judg. 14:1–5. See Timnah 1.
2. Gen. 38:12–14. See Timnah 2.
3. I Macc. 9:50. See Timnath-serah.
Timnath-heres. See Timnath-serah.
Timnath-serah. Probably **Kh. Tibneh** south of Shechem.
Tiphsah. 1. Possibly **Dibseh** on the Euphrates.
2. A town near Shechem. Unknown. II Kings 15:16.
Tirzah. An important city in Manasseh, at one time capital of the Northern Kingdom. **Tell el-Far'ah.** IV.
Tob. A town in Trans-jordan, probably **eṭ-Ṭaiyebeh** in Gilead.
Tobie. See Tob. 20.
Tochen. A place near En-rimmon. Unknown.
Togarmah. See Beth-togarmah.
Tolad. See Eltolad.
Tophel. A town in Edom, probably **Ṭafīleh.** 10.
Topheth, Tophet. See Hinnom.
Trachonitis. A lava region north of the Jebel Druze. **el-Leja'.** 4.
Trans-jordan. A geographical term for the whole area east of the Jordan Valley and the Wādī 'Arabah. See also Cis-jordan.
Tripoli. A city in Syria on the site of the modern Tripoli in Lebanon. II Macc. 14:1. 5.
Tripoli-Homs Gap. A lowland corridor striking inland from Tripoli. 5.
Troas. A city in Asia Minor. **Eskistanbul.** 31.
Trunk Road. A geographical term for the major highway leading from the Mesopotamian kingdoms through Damascus and Cis-jordan to Egypt. IV, 19.
Tubal. A region near the Black Sea, and the people of that region.
Tyre. An important sea-port in Phoenicia. **Ṣūr.** VI, VII, 4, 14, 27, 28, 31.
Tyropoeon Valley. A valley leading southwards through the city of Jerusalem. 29, 30.
Ugarit. A town on the northern Phoenician Coast at which important archaeological excavations have been made. **Rās Shamrā.** 4, 24.
Ulai. A river near Susa. Unknown.
Ummah. A town in Asher, possibly the same as Accho.
Upfold. A geological term for a formation caused by the upward folding of the rock strata, q.v.
Uphaz. Probably the same as Ophir.
Upwarp. A geological term for a large area of land which has been pushed upwards. It may include also considerable upfolds, q.v.
Ur. A very ancient site in Mesopotamia. **el-Muqaiyar.** 24.
Uruk. An ancient site in Babylonia, known in the Bible as Erech.
Usdum, Jebel. A salt mountain at the south end of the Dead Sea. 12.
Uz. A region in Arabia. Unknown.
Uzal. A region in southern Arabia. Unknown.
Uzzen-sheerah. Unknown.
Valley of the Robbers. A name given various wādīs in Palestine, of which a particularly important one was that leading down from the Horns of Hattin to Magdala on the Sea of Galilee. The Trunk Road passed through it.
Wādī. An Arabic word meaning valley, sometimes used as a geographical term for a dry valley characteristic of desert and semi-desert regions. However, in Palestine any valley is called a wādī.
Wala, River. A tributary of the Arnon. I.
Water-parting. A geographical term for the area of higher land dividing the streams which flow in one direction from those which flow in another. 29.
Water-parting Road. A geographical term for the road following the higher and relatively level land of a water-parting. The main north–south road in Central Cis-jordan is a water-parting road for much of its course.
Way of the Philistines. The road along the coast from Egypt to Philistia. 22.
Way of the Sea. Probably the Trunk Road.
Way of the Wilderness of Shur. The road leading through the Wilderness of Shur. 22.
Weibeh. An oasis in the Arabah. 10, 13.
Western Highlands. The hilly and plateau region between the Coast Plain and the Rift Valley.

Willows, Brook of the. Probably the same as the Zered.
Yarmuq, River. The river running through the southern part of Bashan to the Jordan. Not mentioned in the Bible. I, 18, 19.
Yathrib. Old name of Medina in Arabia. 23.
Yiron. A town in Naphtali. **Jarūn.**
Zaanaim, Plain of. To be read "Elon-bezaanim". Unknown.
Zaanan. See Zenan.
Zaananim. 1. A town at the entrance to the Pass of Megiddo. **Khān el-Lejjūn.** VIII.
2. A border town in Naphtali, possibly **Sūq el-Khān.** Josh. 19:33. VIII.
Zab, Great. A tributary of the Tigris. 24.
Zab, Little. A tributary of the Tigris. 24.
Zagros Mountains. The high mountain ranges overlooking Mesopotamia from the east. 24.
Zair. See Zior.
Zalmon. A mountain near Shechem, possibly to be identified with either Ebal or Gerizim.
Zalmonah. A stopping place on the Exodus. Unknown. Near Punon.
Zanoah. 1. A hill town in Judah. **Kh. Zanū'.** IX, 27.
2. **Zanūtā** near Jattir? Josh. 15:56.
Zaphon. A town in Gad, possibly **Tell el-Qos** in the Jordan Valley.
Zared. See Zered.
Zarephath. A town in Phoenicia, probably **Sarafand** north of Tyre.
Zarethan. Somewhere near Qarn Sartabeh, possibly **Tell es-Sa'idīyeh**, though the name may perhaps not stand for a town.
Zareth-shahar. See Zereth-shahar.
Zarthan. See Zarethan.
Zebdani, Jebel. 6.
Zeboiim. 1. One of the Cities of the Plain.
2. A town in Benjamin. Unknown.
Zeboim, Valley of. **Wādī Abū Dhaba'** north-east of Jerusalem.
Zebulun. A tribal district in northern Cis-jordan. 16, 18.
Zedad. A town in Syria. **Ṣadād.** 4.
Zeita, Wādī. One of the valleys leading across the Shephelah. IX.
Zelah. Possibly to be read "Zela-ha-eleph". A town in Benjamin. Unknown.
Zelzah. A town in Benjamin. Unknown.
Zemaraim. A town in Benjamin, probably at or near **Rās ez-Zeimāra.**
Zenan. A town near Lachish, perhaps **'Arāq el-Kharbā.**
Zephath. See Hormah.
Zephathah, Valley of. Possibly **Wādī eṣ-Ṣāfiyeh** near Mareshah.
Zer. A town in Naphtali. Unknown.
Zered, River. **Wādī el-Heṣā** in southern Transjordan. I, 12, 18.
Zereda, Zeredah. 1. A hill town in Ephraim. **Deir Ghassāneh.**
2. In II Chr. 4:17 it is probably an error for Zarethan.
Zererah. See Zarethan.
Zereth-shahar. Possibly the hot springs of **Zārāt** (Callirhoe) on the eastern shore of the Dead Sea.
Ziddim. A town in Naphtali. Unknown.
Zidon. See Sidon.
Ziklag. A town in southern Judah. **Tell el-Khuweilfeh.** 27.
Zin, Wilderness of. A region in the Negeb, not to be confused with the Wilderness of Sin.
Zion. See Jerusalem.
Zion, Mount. Jerusalem, often wrongly identified with the hill on the west of the city.
Zior. A hill town in Judah. **Ṣa'īr.**
Ziph. A town in southern Judah. **er-Zeifeh.** Josh. 15:24; II Chr. 11:8.
2. A hill town in Judah. **Kh. ez-Zīf.**
Ziph, Wilderness of. The region east of Ziph 2.
Ziphron. A town in Syria. Unknown.
Ziz, Ascent of. Possibly **Wādī Ḥaṣāṣeh** east of Bethlehem.
Zoan. See Raamses.
Zoar. One of the Cities of the Plain. The same as Bela.
Zobah. A town and region in Syria. Uncertain.
Zoheleth, Stone of. Near En-rogel.
Zone of Movement. A geographical term for the region between the Valley of Ajalon and the valleys leading down to Jericho, occupied by the tribe of Benjamin.
Zophim, Field of. Part of the Moabite Plateau. Unknown.
Zorah. A town between Judah and Dan. **Ṣārah.** IX, 27.
Zuph, Land of. Region near Ramathaim-Zophim.

INDEX OF BIBLICAL REFERENCES

INDEX OF BIBLICAL REFERENCES

THE OLD TESTAMENT

INDEX

TO

THE TEXT

INDEX TO THE TEXT